BALANCING THE NATIONAL INTEREST

U.S. National Security Export Controls and Global Economic Competition

Panel on the Impact of National Security Controls
on International Technology Transfer

Committee on Science, Engineering, and Public Policy

National Academy of Sciences
National Academy of Engineering
Institute of Medicine

NATIONAL ACADEMY PRESS
Washington, D.C.   1987

NATIONAL ACADEMY PRESS • 2101 Constitution Avenue, NW • Washington, DC 20418

The National Academy of Sciences (NAS) is a private, self-perpetuating society of distinguished scholars in scientific and engineering research, dedicated to the furtherance of science and technology and their use for the general welfare. Under the authority of its congressional charter of 1863, the Academy has a working mandate that calls upon it to advise the federal government on scientific and technical matters. The Academy carries out this mandate primarily through the National Research Council, which it jointly administers with the National Academy of Engineering and the Institute of Medicine. Dr. Frank Press is President of the NAS.

The National Academy of Engineering (NAE) was established in 1964, under the charter of the NAS, as a parallel organization of distinguished engineers, autonomous in its administration and in the selection of members, sharing with the NAS its responsibilities for advising the federal government. Dr. Robert M. White is President of the NAE.

The Institute of Medicine (IOM) was chartered in 1970 by the National Academy of Sciences to enlist distinguished members of appropriate professions in the examination of policy matters pertaining to the health of the public. In this, the Institute acts under both the Academy's 1863 congressional charter responsibility to be an adviser to the federal government and its own initiative in identifying issues of medical care, research, and education. Dr. Samuel O. Thier is President of the IOM.

The Committee on Science, Engineering, and Public Policy is a joint committee of the National Academy of Sciences, the National Academy of Engineering, and the Institute of Medicine. It includes members of the councils of all three bodies.

INTERNATIONAL STANDARD BOOK NUMBER 0-309-03738-7

LIBRARY OF CONGRESS CATALOG CARD NUMBER 87-60020

Printed in the United States of America

iii

Committee on Science, Engineering, and Public Policy

GILBERT S. OMENN (*Chairman*), Dean, School of Public Health and
Community Medicine, University of Washington
H. NORMAN ABRAMSON, Executive Vice President, Southwest
Research Institute
FLOYD E. BLOOM, Director and Member, Division of Pre-Clinic
Neuroscience and Endocrinology, Scripps Clinic and Research
Foundation
W. DALE COMPTON, Senior Fellow, National Academy of Engineering
EMILIO Q. DADDARIO, Esq., Wilkes, Artis, Hendrick, and Lane
GERALD P. DINNEEN, Vice President, Science and Technology,
Honeywell, Inc.
RALPH E. GOMORY, Senior Vice President and Director of Research,
Thomas J. Watson Research Center
ZVI GRILICHES, Professor, Department of Economics, Harvard
University
ARTHUR KELMAN, Wisconsin Alumni Research Foundation, Senior
Research Professor of Plant Pathology and Bacteriology, Department
of Plant Pathology, University of Wisconsin
FRANCIS E. LOW, Institute Professor, Department of Physics,
Massachusetts Institute of Technology
EDWARD A. MASON, Vice President for Research, Amoco Corporation
JOHN D. ROBERTS, Gates and Crellin Laboratories of Chemistry,
California Institute of Technology
KENNETH J. RYAN, M.D., Kate Macy Ladd Professor of Obstetrics
and Gynecology, Harvard Medical School; Chairman, Department of
Obstetrics and Gynecology, Brigham and Women's Hospital
LEON T. SILVER, Professor of Geology, Division of Geological and
Planetary Sciences, California Institute of Technology
HERBERT A. SIMON, Professor of Computer Science and Psychology,
Department of Psychology, Carnegie-Mellon University

Ex Officio

FRANK PRESS, President, National Academy of Sciences
ROBERT M. WHITE, President, National Academy of Engineering
SAMUEL O. THIER, President, Institute of Medicine
ALLAN R. HOFFMAN, Executive Director
BARBARA A. CANDLAND, Administrative Coordinator
JOANNA MASTANTUONO, Senior Secretary

v

Sponsors

This project was undertaken with both public and private sector support. The following agencies of the federal government provided support for the study: the Department of Commerce, the Department of Defense, the Department of Energy, the Department of State, the National Aeronautics and Space Administration, and the National Science Foundation. The following private organizations provided support for the study: the American Association for the Advancement of Science, the American Electronics Association, the American Geophysical Union, the American Institute of Aeronautics and Astronautics, the American Physical Society, the American Vacuum Society, the Armed Forces Communications and Electronics Association, the Computer and Business Equipment Manufacturers Association, the General Electric Company, the German Marshall Fund of the United States, the Institute of Electrical and Electronics Engineers, the National Society of Professional Engineers, the Optical Society of America, the Semiconductor Industry Association, and the U.S.-Japan Friendship Commission.

The project also received support from the National Research Council Fund, a pool of private, discretionary, nonfederal funds that is used to support a program of Academy-initiated studies of national issues in which science and technology figure significantly. The NRC Fund consists of contributions from a consortium of private foundations including the Carnegie Corporation of New York, the Charles E. Culpeper Foundation, the William and Flora Hewlett Foundation, the John D. and Catherine T. MacArthur Foundation, the Andrew W. Mellon Foundation, the Rockefeller Foundation, and the Alfred P. Sloan Foundation; the Academy Industry Program, which seeks annual contributions from companies that are concerned with the health of U.S. science and technology and with public policy issues with technological content; and the National Academy of Sciences and the National Academy of Engineering endowments.

Preface

The United States in cooperation with its allies has imposed controls since 1949 on exports to the Soviet bloc of commercial goods and information that would be of significant value to Warsaw Pact military systems. Since the late 1970s, there has been significantly increased concern in the United States about Soviet success in acquiring and applying this commercial Western technology, a concern that was translated into a vigorous effort to improve the effectiveness of national security export controls. The Department of Defense spearheaded this initiative, which has resulted in substantial strengthening of controls on dual use technology (i.e., items with both commercial and military application), primarily under the authority of the Export Administration Act of 1979, as amended. These stricter controls, however, have caused broad concern about unintended effects that may dampen the vigor of U.S. research and technology development and unnecessarily impede trade in high-technology goods.

In 1982 a panel of the National Academy complex (now known as the Corson panel after its chairman Dale Corson) examined the effect of national security export controls on the communication of basic scientific research. The results of that study led to an executive branch policy intended to minimize restraints on the vital free flow of scientific results and research findings. During the ensuing period, representatives of industry and research institutions in the United States expressed misgivings about the effect of export controls on the U.S. international competitive position, and this national controversy also required an objective examination. As a result the leadership of the National Academy complex decided in 1984 to organize a second panel to examine the effect of export controls on commercial trade in high-technology goods and information and on the vigor of U.S. high-technology industry.

The new panel recognized from the outset that Western military security depends in part on the technology advantages of the West as compared to the Soviet Union and that some restrictions on the flow of technology of military importance are indeed necessary. Furthermore, the panel was aware of the vital importance of maintaining the West's technological advantage through continued technological progress. It also took note of the fact that a 1976 study of the Defense Science Board (known as the Bucy report) had provided much of the theoretical basis from which to examine the current situation.

The panel found it appropriate to narrow and focus its efforts. Although controls for foreign policy purposes, controls on transfer of nuclear technology, and controls on arms transfer are all part of the total U.S. export control policy, in accordance with our charge we have focused on national security export controls (as specified by the Export Administration Act of 1979, as amended) imposed on dual use technology. Moreover, although certain countries other than the members of the Warsaw Pact are affected by U.S. national security export controls, we have focused primarily on issues relating to the Soviet Union and its Eastern bloc allies due to their central importance to the problem. We also have given particular attention to the role of friendly and neutral Free World nations that are not members of CoCom (the Coordinating Committee on Multilateral Export Controls), countries that may now or in the future be sources of indigenous technology and potential channels of West-East technology transfer.

The panel shares the concerns of many regarding the health of U.S. high-technology industries and the effect on national security of declining U.S. leadership in various sectors. We have, for example, taken note of other recent studies that address the loss of manufacturing capability in the semiconductor industry and the problems associated with defense procurement. Our focus in this study—and the overall effect of export controls—does not minimize the importance of other measures needed to retain and improve the vitality of high technology in the United States and its contribution to U.S. military security.

Perhaps not surprisingly the panel found the central problem of this study to be extraordinarily complex and initially difficult to grasp in its totality. Moreover, we determined that reliable quantitative data regarding the effectiveness of controls—and the impact of controls on economic development and trade—continue to be very difficult to obtain. Nevertheless, at the conclusion of its efforts the panel was convinced that it had reviewed and considered sufficient information to justify its findings and recommendations. It was unanimous in the adoption of these views.

It is clear that, for this complex problem, there are valid competing interests to be weighed in considering the course of action that will be most effective in enhancing U.S. national security. The panel hopes that this report serves to identify and explain these important issues and that our findings and recommendations will be useful to those who bear the responsibility for formulating and implementing wise policy.

The panel is grateful for the assistance provided by the liaison representatives of the various federal agencies and by the hundreds of individuals and private organizations, both in the United States and abroad, who cooperated in providing information for this study (see Appendix G). We also wish to thank the professional staff, directed by Mitchel Wallerstein, which so ably organized the panel's briefings and foreign fact-finding missions and laboriously wrote and rewrote the many preliminary drafts of this report. Finally, I personally wish to thank the members of the panel for their dedicated service in this lengthy and sometimes contentious effort.

Lew Allen, Jr.
Chairman

Contents

Executive Summary

ABSTRACT

In this study the panel was charged to examine the current system of U.S. and multilateral national security export controls and to seek strategies to regulate international technology transfer in such a manner as to achieve a desirable balance among the national objectives of military security, economic vitality, and scientific and technological advance. Three general principles underlie this analysis—namely, that it should be the policy of the United States (1) to promote the economic vitality of Free World countries, (2) to maintain and invigorate the domestic technological base, and (3) to cooperate with its allies to impede the Soviet Union and other Warsaw Pact countries in their efforts to acquire Western technology that can be used directly or indirectly to enhance their military capability.

The panel finds that national security export controls, when developed and implemented on a multilateral basis, are an appropriate policy response to two facts. One is that dual use technology—that is, technology that has both commercial and military applications—has become increasingly important to Western military security. The other is that the Soviet Union and its Warsaw Pact allies continue to pursue aggressive technology acquisition in the West. The panel further finds that efforts by the United States since the late 1970s to enhance the effectiveness of national security export controls were necessary in view of both intelligence on the nature and extent of Warsaw Pact

1

technology acquisitions and the continued diffusion of technological capability outside the United States. Nevertheless, the panel believes that U.S. control policies and procedures are in danger now of overcorrecting in that they fail to promote both military security and economic vitality, two objectives set forth in the statutes authorizing national security export controls. The panel also finds that, although appropriate statutory authority appears to exist, the U.S. policy process for national security export controls lacks proper direction and affirmative leadership at the highest level of government. The result is a complex and confusing control system that unnecessarily impedes U.S. high-technology exports to other countries of the Free World and directly affects relations with the CoCom allies.

Accordingly, the panel recommends that the United States exercise stronger leadership in building a multilateral community of common controls for dual use technologies among cooperating countries, which will involve further strengthening of the CoCom mechanism, eliminating certain controls on trade among CoCom countries, and developing effective control arrangements with other technologically advanced nations. In the domestic context the panel recommends that executive branch policy decisions on national security export controls accord greater importance than they currently do to maintaining U.S. technological strength and the economic vigor and unity of the Western alliance.

INTRODUCTION

The vigor of science and technology in the Western* democracies and the greater economic vitality of these nations in comparison to the Soviet bloc are sources of strength for the West in its continuing effort to maintain its military security. The Soviet Union lacks these advantages; it seeks to compensate for them by directing a substantial portion of its gross national product to the development and production of military equipment and by making aggressive attempts to acquire and apply Western technology to its military programs. Although the prime targets of the Soviet acquisition program are military hardware and technology related directly to military systems, dual use products and technology† available for sale in international markets also constitute major targets. The importance of dual use technology to Western economic vitality poses a policy dilemma for the West in turn: The open communication

---

* As used throughout this report, *Western* or *West* includes Japan.

†Items that have both commercial and military applications (e.g., microelectronic components or computers of certain performance parameters).

and free markets that are fundamental to the Western advantage in technology also facilitate the Soviet acquisition effort. Given what is known about the scope and extent of these Soviet activities, the West must pursue a dual strategy of continuing to maintain its technological leadership over potential adversaries while also denying—or at least impeding—their access to militarily significant Western technology.

This study had a twofold objective: (1) to examine the current system of laws, regulations, international agreements, and organizations—defined collectively as the national security export control regime*—that control the international transfer of technology through industrial channels; and (2) where appropriate, to recommend new approaches to achieve the interrelated national policy objectives of military security, scientific and technological advance, and economic vitality.

To achieve this objective the panel and its professional staff undertook a broad agenda of research and briefings.

• Pertinent public literature was analyzed as well as restricted documents from the various federal agencies involved in export control policy formulation—e.g., the Departments of Defense, Commerce, State, Treasury (U.S. Customs Service), and Justice.

• Representatives of these agencies briefed the panel, as did the Intelligence Community in classified session.

• The panel also heard the views of industry (including a broad range of sectors and firm sizes) and held a series of discussions with individuals well-versed in aspects of the national security export control regime.

• Delegations of the panel traveled to six European countries (Austria, Belgium, France, Great Britain, Sweden, and West Germany) and five Asian countries (Japan, Hong Kong, Malaysia, Singapore, and South Korea) for frank and confidential meetings with government officials, industry leaders, and other informed observers on export control matters.

• The panel commissioned a series of research reports, prepared both by outside consultants and by the panel's professional staff. Some of these studies developed and analyzed new primary data; others reexamined existing problems from new perspectives.

From these efforts has come a set of general principles and specific prescriptions for developing a more balanced and effective national

---

*The panel was not charged to consider other applications of export controls including foreign policy and short supply constraints. Thus, although foreign policy controls may occasionally become intertwined or confused with national security controls, they are examined here only to the extent that they impinge on the effective functioning of the national security export control regime.

security export control regime. The panel's findings and recommendations are set forth in the concluding sections of this summary. The three general principles that underlie the panel's analysis propose that *it should be the policy of the United States*

- to promote the economic vitality of Free World countries,
- to maintain and invigorate the domestic technological base, and
- to cooperate with its allies to impede the Soviet Union and other

Warsaw Pact countries in their efforts to acquire Western technology that can be used directly or indirectly to enhance their military capability.

As a general policy, the United States should strive to achieve clarity, simplicity, and consistency in its national security export control procedures, as well as in the multilateral CoCom* export control structure, and broader consensus on the need for national security export controls among the Free World nations that use and produce dual use technology. To achieve these ends the United States should develop policies and procedures that emphasize efficiency and effectiveness rather than total comprehensiveness.

THE TECHNOLOGY TRANSFER PROBLEM

Intelligence information reviewed by the panel—including some at high levels of classification—indicates that the Soviet technology acquisition effort is massive, well financed, and frequently effective. Militarily significant Western technology has flowed to Warsaw Pact countries in recent years through three primary channels:

- *espionage*—the theft of classified information or items of relevance to military systems;
- *diversion*—shipment of militarily significant dual use products and technology to unapproved end users, either directly through the export of controlled products without a license (i.e., smuggling), or indirectly through transshipment using a complex chain of increasingly untraceable reexports (i.e., legal transshipment of products or components by firms operating in countries that do not impose controls); and
- *legal sales*—direct trade with the Soviet bloc, usually after receipt of a license. Such trade also may include some reexports.

As in other areas of intelligence, data on Soviet acquisition of militarily sensitive technology are incomplete and fragmentary and often become

---

*CoCom, or the Coordinating Committee on Multilateral Export Controls, is an informal, nontreaty organization composed of Japan and all the member nations of the North Atlantic Treaty Organization (NATO) except Iceland.

available relatively late in the development of national security export control policy. Nevertheless, available evidence—including the so-called "Farewell" papers, which are actual Soviet documents obtained by French intelligence services in 1981 detailing the plans, organization, and financing for technology acquisition efforts in the West—indicates that, by the Soviets' own estimates, approximately 70 percent of the items they target and eventually acquire in the West are subject to some form of national security export control. There is also growing concern in the Intelligence Community about the extent to which the Soviet Union and other Warsaw Pact countries have been or may be able to obtain controlled technology in Free World countries that do not cooperate in national security export controls. This concern applies both to the industrialized neutral countries of Europe and to some of the more advanced newly industrializing countries (such as India, Singapore, and Brazil).

It is only on rare occasions—for instance, when isolated examples of specific Western components, or copies of them, appear in Soviet military equipment—that the Intelligence Community can declare without reservation that the application of Western technology has contributed substantially to Soviet military developments. As a result, assessing the impacts of technology acquired by the Soviets is subject to considerable uncertainty. In general, it appears that the loss of a few items does not raise significant risks. Although the Soviets may attempt to reverse-engineer a technology (i.e., use an item obtained in the West as a basis for producing the technology themselves for their military systems), the panel has come to believe that this process is generally unproductive for many types of items (for example, high-density semiconductor devices).

Nevertheless, certain key items of process control or manufacturing hardware (known as keystone equipment) *can* provide the Soviets with substantial leverage—even if only a few are obtained—because these items facilitate the production of quantities of other hardware. Consequently, a prevalent judgment in the United States is that the emphasis of national security export control policy properly should be on constraining the flow of manufacturing equipment (specifically, some types of turnkey plants and know-how related to that equipment) rather than on the end products of the manufacturing process.

Although there are some cases in which different conclusions can be drawn, on the basis of available information the panel has determined that for most types of dual use technology the Soviet Union is approximately 5 to 10 years behind the West and does not appear to be closing the gap. The situation is different for military technology. Although the West remains generally ahead in the most advanced systems, the Soviets' great emphasis (relative to that of the United States) on the development and production of military hardware results in fielded equipment that in specific cases is as modern as that deployed in the West. However, as indicated in the 1986 Packard commission report *A Quest for Excellence: Final Report to the President*, it is important to understand that this fact may reflect delays in the U.S. procurement process rather than a failure of export controls.

Despite years of effort, then, the Soviets continue to lag the West technologically, and this gap may actually be widening due to Soviet dependence on generally outdated Western equipment and technology (particularly in the field of computer science). Although it would be foolhardy for the United States or other CoCom nations to facilitate Soviet access to militarily critical technology, the panel considers it unlikely that an influx of Western technology will enable the Soviet bloc to reduce the current gap substantially—as long as the West continues its own rapid pace of innovation.

There are other facets of the technology transfer problem that also warrant attention. Intelligence evidence on the extent of unwanted West-East technology transfer must be juxtaposed against the fact that the United States is now confronted with a dramatically altered economic and technological environment—an environment substantially different from that existing for most of the post-World War II period. The panel reviewed in this regard the implications of the following five major developments.

1. *The character of the international marketplace is evolving in such a way that diffusion of technology is rapid and global in scope.* Factors promoting this diffusion include the tendency among multinational corporations to locate research, development, and production facilities around the world and the existence of indigenous capability in many developing countries. Massive amounts of information must be transferred by such companies as they attempt to control and coordinate their international efforts.

2. *There is a growing global market for dual use products, most of which embody advanced technology.* The high-technology sector demands heavy investment in research and development. The rapid technological advances promoted by this investment are tending to push commercial development of technology ahead of military development— a reversal of the pattern established after World War II. Acceleration of commercial development, coupled with a lengthening of the U.S. military procurement cycle, has resulted in the increased availability of dual use products embodying technology more sophisticated than that deployed by the military.

3. *Because trade is a steadily growing part of U.S. economic activity,*

policies that affect it are increasingly important to the overall U.S. economy. The United States is the single largest international trader, reporting exports of $360 billion in 1985. U.S. exports to CoCom countries represented over 60 percent of that total in 1985; in contrast, exports to Soviet bloc countries represented less than 1 percent of U.S. exports for that year. Trade policies that might diminish West-West trade thus have greater potential to damage the U.S. economy than do those that might reduce exports to the Eastern bloc. Although export controls are not a leading cause of the recent decline in U.S. high-technology performance, they may contribute to lost sales and to an environment that discourages export activities by U.S. firms.

4. *U.S. dominance over advanced technology is declining.* The United States now faces stiff competition in almost every high-technology sector from companies in both developed and developing countries with non-U.S.-source technology. The growing technical sophistication of such countries is the result of long-term efforts to develop and enhance indigenous technical capability. (In a growing number of cases, the commitment of resources by such countries now surpasses that for similar efforts made by the United States.) The newly industrializing countries currently do not possess sufficient indigenous high-technology capability to compete at the cutting edge of most industries, but many are beginning to make great strides toward this goal and are already effective competitors at somewhat lower but still technologically sophisticated levels. Thus, the United States cannot succeed in its efforts to block Soviet acquisition of militarily sensitive Western technology unless it has the full cooperation of the (increasing number of) other technologically advanced countries that may represent alternative sources of supply.

5. *Maintaining the vitality of all the Western economies has assumed greater importance for the national security of the United States.* To the extent that technological and economic leadership is now shared with the other principal CoCom countries—namely, Japan, the United Kingdom, France, and the Federal Republic of Germany—it is essential to the national security interests of the United States, for both military and trade reasons, that the economies of these countries remain strong.

THE CURRENT NATIONAL SECURITY
EXPORT CONTROL REGIME

The national security export control authority exercised by the executive branch is substantially unchanged in its basic legal structure from that originally granted by Congress in 1940 as an extraordinary war power. Two laws provide the primary statutory mandate. The Arms Export Control Act of 1976 requires government approval for the import and export of military weaponry and services. The Department of State implements the act through the International Traffic in Arms Regulations (ITAR); ITAR is based on the U.S. Munitions List, which is maintained by the Department of Defense (DoD). The Export Administration Act (EAA) of 1979, as amended, controls dual use goods and technologies that could make a significant contribution to the military capabilities of a potential adversary. EAA, which is implemented by the Department of Commerce through the Export Administration Regulations (EAR), also authorizes controls that may be necessary to serve U.S. foreign policy goals and to ensure the domestic availability of resources in short supply.

The regulations implementing the national security export control regime are extensive and complex. Many federal departments and agencies share administrative responsibility for their implementation and participate in the export control policymaking process. The roles of the executive branch agencies are assigned variously by legislation, by regulation, or by executive order. In general, the Commerce Department regulates exports of commercial equipment and technology, while the State Department controls exports of military equipment and technology. DoD advises both agencies on the strategic significance of commercial and military exports. The Department of Commerce and the U.S. Customs Service share responsibility for enforcement of national security export controls.

Multilateral agreements and procedures play an essential role in denying militarily useful technology to potential adversaries. In fact, the heart of the national security export control regime is a set of restrictions on exports to the Soviet bloc, which is maintained on a multilateral basis through the Coordinating Committee on Multilateral Export Controls (CoCom), of which the United States is a founding member. CoCom administers three lists of controlled items: munitions, nuclear energy, and dual use. Many but not all the items on the U.S. Control List parallel items found on the CoCom dual use list (known as the International List). The United States also has bilateral agreements or arrangements with a number of non-CoCom countries that provide for varying degrees of cooperation on national security export controls.

ASSESSMENT OF THE CRITICAL ISSUES

National security export control policy should be the result of a process that weighs the benefits of controls in relations with potential adversaries against their costs in terms of the domestic economy and relations with allies and friendly trading partners. The potential benefits of controls derive from two factors: (1) they make it more difficult for the Soviet Union and its allies to upgrade their military systems through information, technology, and products acquired in the West; and (2) they require the Soviet Union to commit substantial domestic resources to military research and development instead of using acquired Western technology to shortcut the technological development process.

Both the costs and benefits of controls are difficult to assess with precision. There is evidence that controls do slow Soviet acquisition efforts and increase the price of the items they acquire, a conclusion supported at the unclassified level by the Farewell papers (see p. 5), which indicate that during the Tenth Five-Year Plan (1976-1980) the Soviet acquisition program satisfied more than 3,500 specific collection requirements for hardware and documents for the 12 Soviet industrial ministries. The documents also indicate that for 1980 alone the Soviet Union allocated (in rubles) substantially more than $1 billion for the collection of Western documents, blueprints, test equipment, and other hardware.

There are also data that suggest that most of the benefits of controls are concentrated in a relatively narrow range of products and technologies. This range includes advanced equipment for manufacturing high-density semiconductors, automated process equipment for the fabrication of specialized metals and composites, very-high-speed computers, extremely precise test instruments, and aircraft components that can be readily adapted to military uses.

The potential costs of controls also are hard to measure because they derive from the web of competitive and cooperative relationships among Western countries. Nevertheless, the panel did consider it important to attempt an estimate of those costs to the U.S. economy that are associated mainly with current features peculiar to the U.S. national security export control system. Of principal concern are the present and future sales and market share (both West-West and West-East) and reduced investment in research and development that U.S. producers of goods and technologies may lose or forego—without the compensating national security benefits of denying the Soviets embargoed technology—as a result of how the U.S. control system is designed and administered and of how it compares with the control systems of other countries with competitive suppliers. For example, reduced revenue from lost sales and market share may translate into less investment, a lower growth rate, and reduced innovation, with resulting adverse effects on both the commercial and military sectors. In addition, technology controls also have created friction among the Western allies—friction that may interfere with their successful collaboration on weapons development, production, and standardization, or on other matters bearing directly on East-West relations.

In contrast to their benefits the costs of export controls are spread across an enormous volume of transactions representing a large share of

U.S. trade. Based in part on data provided by the Commerce Department, the panel estimates that 40 percent—approximately $62 billion—of all U.S. exports of nonmilitary manufactured goods in 1985 were shipped under a license requiring prior approval. In addition, U.S. controls extend to sales by U.S. foreign subsidiaries and independent foreign companies using products, components, parts, services, and technology of U.S. origin.

In an effort to assess the operation and some of the effects of export controls, the panel analyzed a sample of licenses* for goods classified by level of military sensitivity using administrative criteria developed in U.S. government deliberations and/or CoCom negotiations. The analysis showed that the broad control net is heavily weighted with transactions involving items of less than critical military importance with customers in friendly Western countries. Ninety percent of individual license applications are for exports to Free World countries. One-third of these applications are for items that may be exported to CoCom countries under a general license and even to Soviet bloc destinations without prior CoCom approval. Roughly two-thirds of license applications are for items sufficiently lacking in military importance that they may be shipped to the People's Republic of China (PRC) without prior CoCom approval. Only about 13 percent of the applications are for very sensitive items that require an individual U.S. license to all countries (i.e., they are not eligible for export under a bulk license) as well as CoCom approval for shipment to the bloc or the PRC.

The sheer volume of transactions subject to government review and approval sharply limits the ability of licensing officers to focus on more critical items. Data obtained from the Commerce Department indicate that individual license applications for exports to the Warsaw Pact and to Western countries that exercise little control—and are therefore potential points of diversion—appropriately receive more scrutiny than those for exports to CoCom destinations. But the current control regime does not apply similar discrimination to sales within the West of products having greater and lesser military significance.

The adverse competitive effects of export controls could be alleviated by the establishment of a community of common controls in dual use technology (i.e., a set of trade relationships unimpeded by national

---

*The panel requested and was granted a "national interest exception" under Section 12(c) of the Export Administration Act permitting its consultants unprecedented access to Commerce Department license files and data bases, subject to strict observance of confidentiality of business information. The subsequent analysis conducted by consultants was of a sample of 1,618 processed license applications categorized by Commerce Department license officers.

security restrictions) among cooperating Free World countries. Such an arrangement does not now exist. U.S. national security export controls encompass more products and technologies, are generally more restrictive, and entail more administrative delays and shipper uncertainties than those of the other major CoCom countries. Only the United States requires foreign resellers, even in countries that are our closest allies, to obtain the prior approval of—or to account periodically to—the U.S. government for reexports of U.S.-origin products, U.S.-origin parts and components incorporated into foreign equipment, and foreign products manufactured with U.S.-origin technology. These controls appear even more restrictive in light of the fact that many controlled products are available from or through non-CoCom countries with few or no restrictions.

There is both anecdotal and statistical evidence that the relative stringency of U.S. controls is, with increasing frequency, causing Free World customers to turn to non-U.S. suppliers or to begin to explore alternative sources including internal development. Respondents to a panel survey of U.S. companies,* reflecting on their experience during the 12 months prior to May 1986, perceived the control system as frequently having significant adverse effects on their business:

- 52 percent reported lost sales primarily as a consequence of export controls;
- 26 percent had business deals turned down (in more than 212 separate instances) by Free World customers because of controls;
- 38 percent had existing customers actually express a preference to shift to non-U.S. sources of supply to avoid entanglement in U.S. controls; and
- more than half expected the number of such occurrences to increase over the next 2 years.

In addition, the panel has documented that U.S. exporters already have lost business to suppliers in other technologically advanced nations because of unilateral controls on analytic instrument exports and on independent foreign distributors and equipment manufacturers operating under U.S. distribution licenses. In the first instance, the short-run loss attributable to export controls is about 10 percent of the value of U.S. exports; in the second instance, the loss to date is smaller. But over time, as the relative restrictiveness of U.S. controls becomes more consequen-

---

*The sample of companies surveyed was oriented toward firms in the electronics (equipment and components), aircraft (airframes, engines, and parts), instrumentation, and machine tool sectors. The 170 respondents accounted for roughly $36 billion of foreign sales in 1985 or approximately 28 percent of estimated total U.S. high-technology sales.

tial to existing and potential foreign customers, the greater the weight such restrictiveness is likely to be given in customers' choices among suppliers. (This process has been referred to by some as "de-Americanization.")

These losses are occurring at a time when U.S. producers are experiencing a decline—for reasons unrelated to export controls—in their relative competitive advantage. This decline is appearing not only in level of technology but also in price competitiveness, product quality, marketing, and service—factors that might otherwise more than compensate for the negative competitive effect of export controls. All policies that contribute to a loss of U.S. competitiveness are of concern, not solely from an economic standpoint but also due to national security considerations. By promoting the emergence and growth of alternative sources of technology to the Soviet Union, such policies make denial or delay yet more difficult to achieve.

One indicator of the *effectiveness* of the control effort is the level of corporate compliance. Although this level can never be determined precisely, there is evidence that compliance has increased in recent years as the current U.S. administration has committed substantial resources to vigorous enforcement. It is difficult, however, to determine whether the enforcement campaign has reduced the number of intentional diversions. Moreover, in terms of the enforcement of reexport controls, the overwhelming majority of applications continue to come from U.S.-headquartered companies and their foreign affiliates, suggesting that compliance by foreign-owned firms is relatively poor. A possible explanation of this phenomenon may stem from foreign attitudes toward these controls as well as from the fact that such controls often duplicate those already imposed by the exporting country. Where there are non-U.S. sources willing to supply comparable products, foreign firms that know of the attendant requirement to comply with U.S. export restrictions may have little incentive to buy U.S. products.

There are also indications that the licensing process discriminates against small- to medium-sized firms. With regard to license denials, processing delays, inaction, and conditional approvals—all factors contributing to uncertainty—there is a pronounced firm-size differential in the administration of national security export controls. Relative to those of large-volume exporters, small firm applications to Free World destinations take 25 percent longer on average.

An indicator of the *efficiency* of the administrative control effort—and a perennial concern of Congress, the business community, and the responsible agencies—is the time it takes to process export licenses. Shipping delays impose direct costs on the exporter and an indirect cost in customer confidence. Both the Commerce Department and DoD have expended substantial effort and resources to speed up the licensing process, and both have made progress in reducing *average* processing times. What averages in this instance obscure, however, is the highly skewed distribution of processing times. The distribution has an extended "tail," and it is these cases that both absorb a large proportion of the corporate resources devoted to working the system and create uncertainty in the market. The number of such cases is not insignificant; for approximately 5 percent of all applications (and there were 122,606 total applications in 1985), the processing time extends beyond 100 days.

The efficiency of U.S. export control administration is hampered to a substantial degree by the shared responsibility distributed among the relevant agencies—the Departments of Commerce, State, and Defense. It is hampered further by the fact that neither the Department of Commerce nor the Department of State has made as much progress as the Department of Defense in upgrading their human and technical resources and in automating the licensing process. The result is a lack of balance in interagency policy deliberations and inefficiency in the licensing process. Currently, there is also no effective mechanism for weeding out from the Control List those products and technologies that have ceased to be strategic or that have become so widely available that control, for all practical purposes, is impossible. The momentum is to add, not to delete, and the principal licensing agency (the Department of Commerce), with a stake in keeping its task from becoming unmanageable, has been unable to slow it down.

The Militarily Critical Technologies List (MCTL), which is maintained by DoD, serves a limited purpose within the department as a reference document for developing control proposals and informing licensing decisions. It is also useful for identifying those goods and technologies that have dual use potential. But before goods and technologies actually can be controlled, it is necessary to assess their foreign availability (and other factors affecting controllability) and then to strive to gain CoCom-wide restrictions.

One of the principal outcomes of the continuing interagency disagreement on export control policies and procedures has been the virtual breakdown of the technology decontrol process based on positive foreign availability findings, a process originally mandated by Congress in 1979. This breakdown is largely attributable to the fact that no time constraints are specified in the legislation for government completion of investigations of foreign availability. A related problem has been the substantive disagreements between the Departments of Commerce and Defense over both the criteria for determining foreign availability and the strategic importance of particular items. The resulting de facto veto authority exercised by DoD thwarts the intent of Congress, which designated the Department of Commerce as lead agency in determining foreign availability.

Through foreign policy and economic cycles, the premise that Soviet acquisitions of leading Western dual use technologies represent a serious military threat has not been seriously challenged anywhere in the Western alliance. Although there have been lapses in attention and frequent disputes over scope and means of control, this consensus continues to underlie the success of the current administration's effort to revitalize the CoCom process. The goal of U.S. policy thus should be to so improve the multilateral control system that it is possible to remove controls from West-West trade. The panel believes, however, that there are two features of current U.S. policy that impede progress toward this goal: (1) the tendency to resort to foreign policy trade sanctions to penalize Soviet political behavior without distinguishing such sanctions from national security controls and without consulting our allies before imposing them; and (2) the continuance of extraterritorial controls that signal U.S. mistrust of our CoCom partners and offend their national sovereignty.

These problems notwithstanding, the persistent efforts of the United States over the past 5 years to strengthen CoCom and improve its operational efficiency and effectiveness have produced positive results—results that have not been achieved without certain difficulties. Gaining a consensus among CoCom members has not been easy. The interests of member countries can differ significantly, and each one evaluates the value of trade restrictions against proscribed countries differently. Furthermore, additional efforts now will be required to bring about greater harmonization of national policies on the part of all participating countries to work toward a fully multilateral community of common controls.

Cooperation from countries that are not members of CoCom has become important to the success of the CoCom control efforts. It will be critical in the future as a growing number of third countries become significant markets for CoCom-controlled goods and develop indigenous products that fall within CoCom control parameters. CoCom members have formally agreed—as part of the so-called "third country initiative"—to urge non-CoCom Free World nations to establish and strengthen their controls vis-à-vis proscribed nations. In this regard the United States, with the support of its CoCom allies, has achieved some success in pursuing bilateral agreements with friendly, non-CoCom Free World countries to protect some CoCom- and U.S.-origin goods. Although such agreements have been reached with a few countries, however, none of those concluded to date comes close to meeting the comprehensive criteria proposed by the United States for protecting CoCom-proscribed technology from *all* sources including that produced indigenously.

FINDINGS AND KEY JUDGMENTS OF THE PANEL

Based on the research initiatives and deliberations undertaken in pursuit of its charge, the panel reached unanimous agreement on a series of principal findings and key judgments listed below.

I. THE PRACTICAL BASIS FOR NATIONAL SECURITY EXPORT CONTROLS

The fundamental objective of the national security export control regime maintained by CoCom is to deny—or at least to delay—the Soviet Union and its Warsaw Pact allies access to state-of-the-art Western technology that would permit them to narrow the existing gap in military systems. Yet, there are no well-defined criteria that can be used to determine whether a given technology will enhance significantly Soviet military capability. Moreover, the precise definition and implementation of such criteria will depend to a large extent on the world view of the decision maker. For an export control system to be operationally effective, however, such distinctions must be drawn. This difficulty can be surmounted in practice by establishing a definition that permits effective, practical implementation of controls with our allies, which means restricting controls to technologies that are easily identified with military uses.

II. CONSIDERATIONS INFLUENCING NATIONAL POLICY

1. **Technology lead is vital to Western security and must be maintained.**
    Western security depends on the maintenance of technology lead over potential adversaries. This lead can only be sustained through a dual policy of promoting a vigorous domestic technological base and impeding the outward flow of technologies useful to the Warsaw Pact in military systems.
2. **Export competitiveness is essential to the health of the U.S. domestic economy.**
    In some industrial sectors, especially high-technology enterprises, firms now must remain competitive in the world market to maintain a share of the U.S. domestic market, due to necessary economies of scale and the increased importance of R&D from foreign sources. The new realities of global competition are not yet fully reflected in the policies underlying current U.S. national security export controls.
3. **The scope of current U.S. national security export controls undermines their effectiveness.**
    U.S. national security export controls are not generally perceived as rational, credible, and predictable by many of the nations and

commercial interests whose active cooperation is required for an effective system. In their view the scope of current U.S. controls encompasses too many products and technologies to be administratively feasible. The panel concurs with this judgment.

4. **U.S. national security export controls impede the export sales of U.S. companies.**

There is limited but specific evidence that export sales have been lost or foregone because of uncertainty or delays in the licensing process and because of concern about future license approvals, availability of spare parts and components, and possible reexport constraints. Once changes in buying preferences occur, they may require large investments of time and effort to reverse.

5. **Pragmatic control lists must be technically sound, narrowly focused, and coordinated multilaterally.**

Although the control criteria developed in 1976 as part of the report of the Defense Science Board task force (*An Analysis of Export Control of U.S. Technology—A DoD Perspective*), also known as the Bucy report, are theoretically sound, they have not always proven useful to the implementation of national security export controls. The preparation of control lists must be a dynamic process that is both informed by advice from technical advisory groups and constrained by the need to be clear, to focus control efforts more narrowly on fewer items, and to coordinate U.S. action more closely with that of our CoCom allies.

6. **The extraterritorial aspects of U.S. controls engender mistrust and weaken allied unity.**

Several elements of U.S. national security export controls, especially the requirement for reexport authorization, are having an increasingly corrosive effect on relations with many NATO countries and on other close bilateral relationships. They signal U.S. mistrust of the will and capacity of allies to control the flow of sensitive technology to the Soviet bloc.

III.   SOVIET TECHNOLOGY ACQUISITION EFFORTS IN THE WEST

1. **Available evidence on Soviet technology acquisition efforts reinforces the need for effective multilateral export controls.**

The panel has reviewed a substantial body of evidence—both classified and unclassified—that reveals a large and aggressive Soviet effort to target and acquire Western dual use technology through espionage, diversions, and to a lesser degree legitimate trade. There is limited but specific evidence both on the means by which Soviet acquisitions are accomplished and on their important role in upgrading or modernizing Soviet military systems. Although internationally coordinated efforts are necessary to counter the use of diversions or legitimate trade for such purposes, export controls are not a means for controlling espionage, which alone accounts for a high proportion of successful Soviet acquisition activities.

2. **Despite systemic difficulties, Soviet technical capabilities have successfully supported the military objectives of the USSR.**

Because the Soviet system does not enjoy the benefits of a robust commercial sector, it is at a fundamental disadvantage in terms of the promotion of technological innovation. Nevertheless, the Soviets have demonstrated an effective technical capability to meet their military objectives.

IV.   DIFFUSION AND TRANSFER OF TECHNICAL CAPABILITY

1. **Wide global diffusion of advanced technology necessitates a fully multilateral approach to controls.**

Because advanced technology has now diffused so widely, national security export controls cannot succeed without the following: (1) an effective CoCom process by which the other major CoCom countries accept responsibility for regulating exports and reexports from their territory of CoCom-controlled technology to non-CoCom Free World countries; and (2) the adoption by the more advanced newly industrializing countries of CoCom-like standards for their own indigenous technology.

2. **Controls on the employment of foreign nationals in the U.S. R&D infrastructure must be used selectively and sparingly.**

Foreign nationals now play a significant role in U.S. domestic R&D activities as well as in the laboratories of U.S. foreign subsidiaries. Such individuals contribute significantly to U.S. technological innovation and hence promote the national interest. Sparing use should therefore be made of existing legislative authority to restrict technical exchanges or to limit full participation of foreign citizens in the U.S. R&D community. It is particularly important to distinguish, as appropriate, between citizens of nations to whom exports are proscribed and citizens of all other nations.

V.   FOREIGN AVAILABILITY AND FOREIGN CONTROL OF TECHNOLOGY

1. **The congressional mandate for decontrol of items based on foreign availability is not being fulfilled.**

The lack of action on foreign availability is inconsistent with the intent of Congress as expressed most recently in the Export Administration Amendments Act of 1985. In those cases in which there is foreign availability of U.S.-controlled items, U.S. industry is unfairly placed at a competitive disadvantage with respect to firms from other countries that are not similarly constrained. This disadvantage can lead to the erosion of competitive market advantages previously enjoyed by U.S. industry and in some cases to the permanent loss of U.S. markets.

2. **Control of "technological commodities" is impractical.**

   The control of goods for which the volume of manufacture is so large and the scope of marketing and usage so wide that they have become "technological commodities" (e.g., some classes of personal computers or memory chips) is not practical. Decontrol of such goods to all Free World destinations is, in some cases, the only appropriate solution.

3. **Bilateral agreements with Free World non-CoCom countries must protect all CoCom-origin technology and must control similar indigenously produced goods.**

   Over the short term, bilateral agreements that restrict only the reexport of U.S.-origin technology unfairly disadvantage U.S. companies in international trade. Over the long term, these agreements with non-CoCom countries will not promote the effectiveness of the CoCom export control system unless they restrict the reexport of technology from all CoCom sources as well as technology produced indigenously.

4. **Other CoCom countries must be more vigilant in preventing diversions of both CoCom-origin and indigenously produced technology.**

   Some members of CoCom could substantially improve their efforts to prevent diversions of CoCom-origin products and technology being exported to third countries. Since compliance with U.S. reexport controls is not likely to become politically acceptable in most CoCom countries, some compromise solution must be reached.

5. **The extraterritorial reach of U.S. controls damages allied relations and disadvantages U.S. exporters.**

   The extraterritorial reach of U.S. reexport controls is anathema to most U.S. trading partners. Moreover, many foreign governments do not agree that the United States has jurisdiction over the actions of their citizens outside U.S. territory. The extraterritorial extension of U.S. controls is viewed by these governments as a direct challenge to national sovereignty and a clear violation of international law. It is seen as additional evidence of mistrust by the United States of the capacity of these governments to further the West's common interest in preventing the diversion of militarily important goods and technologies.

VI. EFFECTIVENESS OF THE MULTILATERAL PROCESS

1. The United States must clearly distinguish foreign policy export controls from national security export controls.

There is much less consensus among the CoCom allies on the use of trade restrictions for foreign policy reasons than on controls in the interests of national security. Thus, to the extent that the United States fails to distinguish clearly between the two, allied cooperation in support of consensual national security objectives is undermined.

2. The impact of controls on advantageous scientific communication and transfer within the Western alliance must be minimized.

Because open scientific communication and trade within the West are as important to maintaining Western technology lead as is controlling the flow of technology to the Soviet bloc, U.S. policy should lend equal emphasis to both objectives.

3. The CoCom countries should take specific steps to bolster the efficiency and effectiveness of multilateral controls.

Among the most important issues now facing CoCom are: (a) reduction in the overall scope of the list, (b) modification of the procedures for decontrolling items from the International List of dual use items, and (c) provision of greater transparency in CoCom decision making.

4. The CoCom process would benefit if all country delegations had balanced economic and defense representation.

The U.S. delegation to CoCom, unlike those of other member nations, includes a significant contingent of defense officials. A balance of economic and defense representation on all CoCom delegations would enhance CoCom unity and the usefulness of the CoCom process, in part by helping to resolve conflicts between competing economic and military objectives.

5. Foreign perceptions of U.S. commercial advantage derived from export controls impede multilateral cooperation.

There is a widely held view in Europe and the Far East that the United States uses its national security export controls to afford commercial advantage to U.S. companies. Although the panel found no substantive evidence to support this view, the existence of these perceptions makes it difficult to gain effective multilateral cooperation.

6. Unilateral controls are of limited efficacy and may undermine allied cooperation.

The imposition by the United States of unilateral national security export controls for dual use items can be justified only as a stopgap measure pending negotiations for the imposition of multilateral controls or in rare cases in which critical national security concerns are at stake requiring unilateral restrictions. It must be recognized that, except when used as a temporary measure, the application of unilateral controls undermines the incentive of the allies to develop a sound basis for multilateral restriction.

VII.   ADMINISTRATION OF U.S. NATIONAL SECURITY EXPORT CONTROL POLICIES AND PROCEDURES

1. **The lack of high-level oversight and direction degrades the effectiveness of U.S. controls.**

   The administrative structures established by the executive branch have not proven effective in resolving the frequent policy differences among the three principal line agencies (the Departments of State, Defense, and Commerce). The White House has intervened only intermittently and then primarily to contain interagency conflict rather than to provide adequate policy direction. The lack of higher-level oversight and direction results in duplication of effort, uncertain lines of authority, serious delays in decision making, and underutilization of information-sharing capacity.

2. **Unequal effort by and resources of the three principal line agencies have led to conflict, confusion, and unbalanced policy.**

   DoD's determined efforts to reinvigorate the national security export control regime have been useful in raising the general level of awareness in the United States and in other CoCom countries. But this increasingly active DoD role also has led to an imbalance in the distribution of government effort and resources. Although DoD has created a new dedicated agency for technology security, neither the Department of Commerce nor the Department of State has been able to implement equally effective measures. The result is a lack of balance in the interagency policy formulation process and an inefficient licensing process.

3. **Shifts in responsibility within the line agencies may preclude broadly informed and balanced policy judgments.**

   Reorganization initiatives in a number of the principal line agencies tasked with managing export controls have resulted in a shift of responsibility away from organizations with expertise in technology development and international trade and toward those whose principal and often only concern is technology control. Although there have been positive effects of this shift in responsibility, there has been a loss of sustained technical input into the policy process for national security export controls.

4. **Current licensing requirements, classification procedures, and proprietary controls for technical data are both appropriate and adequate.**

   Although technical data that are not publicly available require a validated license for export to the Soviet bloc, data exports to other destinations for the most part are eligible for a general license. The need for the unhindered exchange of large volumes of data in international commerce and research indicates that a strict system of control is neither feasible nor desirable. Existing licensing requirements, classification procedures, and proprietary controls offer sufficient protection.

5. **Controls on unclassified DoD technical data have a chilling effect on the U.S. R&D community and should be imposed sparingly.**

   The Department of Defense Authorization Act (DAA) of 1984 permits DoD to impose restrictions on domestic dissemination or export of DoD-funded or DoD-generated technical data whose export would otherwise require a validated license under EAR or ITAR. Such restrictions have the effect of creating de facto a new category of unclassified but restricted information. These new, more comprehensive technical data restrictions have had a chilling effect on some professional scientific and engineering societies that have elected voluntarily to close certain sessions. It is the panel's judgment that imposing controls on technical data that are broader than those now in effect is not warranted by the demonstrable national security benefits.

6. **The congressional mandate for integrating the Militarily Critical Technologies List (MCTL) into the Commerce Department Control List practically cannot be accomplished.**

   The MCTL has been used inappropriately as a control list, and its annual revision has resulted in a voluminous itemization of many important technologies without apparent prioritization. Because the Departments of Defense and Commerce maintain fundamentally different objectives in their list development exercises, the congressionally mandated task of integrating the MCTL into the Commerce Department's control list practically cannot be accomplished.

7. **The complexity of U.S. export controls discourages compliance.**

   The complexity of U.S. controls discourages compliance, especially by foreign firms and small- to medium-sized U.S. companies. For example, the Export Administration Regulations constitute nearly 600 pages of rules and procedures. These could be reduced and simplified substantially—and made more "user friendly."

8. **There is a need for high-level industry input in the formulation of national security export control policy.**

   There is a need for an effective mechanism within the government to provide meaningful input from the private sector on the formulation of a coordinated national security export control policy. Such a group must be constituted at sufficiently high corporate levels to reflect major industry concerns, and it must be able to have an impact on the actual policy process.

9. **Voluntary cooperation from industry is important to the enforcement of export controls.**

Voluntary cooperation by U.S. industry—particularly companies with overseas subsidiaries—is important to export control enforcement, especially in the identification of violations. Companies frequently have knowledge otherwise unavailable to the government of possible violations by other firms.

10. **Adequate information to evaluate the impact of national security export controls is not maintained by the U.S. government.**

This study has revealed serious shortcomings in both the quality and quantity of information maintained and analyzed by the U.S. government on the coverage, operation, and domestic and global impacts of national security export controls. In the absence of better information, it will continue to be difficult for policymakers to arrive at more informed and balanced judgments as to the advisability of controls.

11. **A comprehensive cost/benefit analysis of controls currently is infeasible.**

Despite some preliminary efforts to assess the competitive effects of national security export controls, a *comprehensive* empirical analysis of the costs and benefits is precluded by the lack of data, by the complexity of the system, and by a variety of qualitative judgments that must enter into any evaluation.

There is little doubt that, without the heightened attention to these issues initiated in the early years of the current administration by DoD, the problem of Western technology diversion to the Soviet Union would by now be considerably worse. But the panel is concerned that this policy "correction"—useful and necessary as it was—should not now overshoot the mark. The panel wishes to reiterate therefore its concern about the continuing lack of balance within the policy process for national security export controls regarding the representation of technical, national security, economic, and domestic and international political interests. This balance should be developed and maintained within each agency, among agencies of the U.S. government, and among countries participating in CoCom.

RECOMMENDATIONS OF THE PANEL

The panel makes two basic recommendations, together with a series of corollary prescriptions.

I. STRENGTHEN THE COCOM MECHANISM

The panel recommends that the United States take the lead in further strengthening the CoCom mechanism so that it can function as the linchpin of a fully multilateral national security export control regime for dual use technologies. Under current and prospective global circumstances, such a multinational system is essential to achieve maximum export control effectiveness without impairing Western economic vitality. To strengthen the current multilateral control regime will require greater harmonization of the current U.S. approach and those of our technologically advanced allies through closer consultation and the adoption of policies that promote cooperation. The two most immediate objectives are: (1) to limit the coverage of the U.S. Control List and the CoCom International List to those items whose acquisition would significantly enhance Soviet bloc military capabilities and that are feasible to control, and (2) to obtain agreement on a common approach to reexports of CoCom-origin items.

The United States should strive to create a community of common controls in dual use technology—that is, a set of trade relationships unimpeded by national security restrictions—among those Free World nations that share an expressed willingness to adhere to common or equivalent export control restraints on the transfer of strategic and controllable goods and technologies to the Soviet Union and its Warsaw Pact allies. Accordingly, the panel recommends the following changes in U.S. policy.

1. Control Only CoCom-Proscribed Items

As a general policy, the United States should seek to control only the export of CoCom-proscribed items and then only when they are destined for a proscribed country or for a non-CoCom Free World country that has not entered into an agreement* to protect CoCom-proscribed technology.

2. Within CoCom, Seek Control on Exports to Third Countries

With respect to CoCom, the United States should negotiate agreements with member countries regarding control of exports and reexports from their territories to third (i.e., Free World non-

---

*Such an agreement might be implemented either through a formal memorandum of understanding or an informal arrangement that achieves the same result.

CoCom) countries, thereby obviating the need for U.S. reexport authorizations. For those CoCom countries with which agreement on the control of exports to third countries can be achieved, the requirement to obtain validated licenses should be eliminated— *except* for the export of extremely sensitive high-level technology (e.g., supercomputers). For those CoCom countries unwilling to agree to or unable to implement such controls, the present system of validated licenses should be retained.

3. Negotiate Comprehensive Understandings with Third Countries

With respect to non-CoCom Free World countries, the United States should, in coordination with other members of CoCom, negotiate *comprehensive* understandings—or equally effective informal arrangements considered acceptable by the Department of State—that specify controls on the export of all CoCom-proscribed goods and technology (including those produced indigenously) to the Warsaw Pact countries or to other noncooperating third countries. A graduated scheme of incentives should be developed for non-CoCom Free World countries that agree to less than comprehensive controls. Those third countries that have agreed to comprehensive arrangements should be accorded full "CoCom-like" treatment; that is, they should not be subject to U.S.- validated license or reexport authorizations as soon as they can demonstrate their ability and willingness to enforce the control agreement.

4. Remove Items Whose Control Is No Longer Feasible

Regardless of the rate of progress on CoCom and third country negotiations, the United States should actively seek to remove from both the U.S. Control List and the CoCom International List items whose control is no longer feasible because of their widespread production, distribution, and sale throughout the world. (See also Item II.4 on p. 27.)

5. Maintain Unilateral Controls Only on a Temporary Basis or for Limited, Unique National Security Circumstances

Regardless of the rate of progress on CoCom and third country negotiations, the United States should eliminate the use of unilateral national security export controls *except* in those circumstances in which active efforts are under way to negotiate multilateral controls within and outside of CoCom—in which case unilateral controls could be maintained on a temporary basis—*or* in those situations in which unique national security circumstances warrant the imposition of such controls for limited periods of time. The panel wishes to emphasize, however, that the phrase "unique national security circumstances" does not justify retaining the present U.S. unilateral Control List. Rather, the panel recommends that controls be established on a multilateral basis. In the *rare* case in which a CoCom country may believe that critical national security concerns are at stake, it may wish to reserve the right to establish a unilateral restriction on its domestic industry. This exception should be used sparingly.

6. **Eliminate Reexport Authorization Requirements in Countries Participating in a Community of Common Export Controls on Dual Use Technology**

   To further the objective of developing a community of common controls on dual use technology among cooperating countries of the Free World and to encourage international cooperation and trust, the United States should eliminate any requirement that a buyer must seek authorization for a reexport that is subject to CoCom or "CoCom-like" controls by the country initially exporting the product or technology. For effective enforcement, reliance should be placed instead on the cooperating governments.

7. **Maintain Current Control Procedures on the Transfer Within CoCom of Sensitive Information, Technical Data, and Know-how**

   The United States should continue to rely on current security classification procedures and the protection afforded by general license GTDR (technical data restricted) or by proprietary interests to control the transfer within CoCom of information, technical data, and know-how that are considered militarily important.

8. **Reduce the Scope of the CoCom List and Modify CoCom Decision-Making Policies and Procedures**

   There are a number of steps that the United States—together with its CoCom allies—should take to improve the efficiency and effectiveness of the multilateral process. The most important of these are to reduce the overall scope of the CoCom International List to improve credibility and enforcement and to add a 4-year "sunset provision" that would cause the automatic removal (unless they were periodically rejustified) of lower-level CoCom items.

9. **Maintain a Clear Separation Between National Security and Foreign Policy Export Controls**

   Existing statutory authority describes separate systems and procedures for the control of exports for foreign policy versus national security reasons. Therefore, because many of our CoCom allies continue to disagree profoundly with some unilateral U.S. foreign policy trade sanctions, the U.S. government should maintain the clearest possible distinction between the administration of national security and foreign policy controls.

II. ACCORD GREATER IMPORTANCE IN U.S. NATIONAL SE-CURITY EXPORT CONTROL DECISIONS TO MAINTAINING U.S. TECHNOLOGICAL STRENGTH, ECONOMIC VITALITY, AND ALLIED UNITY

The panel recommends that executive branch decisions concerning national security export controls accord greater importance than they currently do to maintaining U.S. technological strength, economic vigor, and allied unity. Ultimately, an effective multilateral national security export control regime can be established only through the commitment and support of the President and Congress. Nevertheless, the decision-making and advisory mechanisms of government also must be constituted and tasked appropriately to facilitate the effective implementation of the policy approach proposed above. To this end, the panel recommends the following specific changes in U.S. policy and procedures.

1. Balance the Protection of Military Security with the Promotion of National Economic Vitality Through Affirmative Policy Direction

The President should require that the National Security Council (NSC) implement the *existing* policy mandate (as set forth in the Export Administration Act of 1979, as amended), which calls for both the protection of military security and the promotion of national economic interests. NSC should provide *regular*, affirmative policy direction to the responsible line agencies, a recommendation that can be accomplished by staffing the NSC properly to deal with these matters and by assigning a senior NSC staff member specific responsibility for bringing agency representatives together to resolve policy differences. The panel further recommends that the secretaries of commerce and treasury participate in NSC meetings at which export control matters are to be addressed.

2. Provide Sufficient Resources and Authority to the Departments of Commerce and State to Allow Them to Fulfill Their Roles in the Export Control Process

To establish a more balanced policymaking process within the federal government, the Departments of Commerce and State should be allocated sufficient resources dedicated to the implementation of national security export controls. In particular the Commerce Department should upgrade significantly the capacity and sophistication of its automated systems and the quality of its in-house technical and analytic expertise. It is also essential that the State Department vigorously exercise its traditional role of ensuring that the U.S. government speaks with a single, coherent voice when dealing with foreign governments and foreign firms on these matters.

3. **Restore Technical Judgment and Overall Balance to the National Security Export Licensing Process**

The locus of responsibility and decision making within DoD has shifted from the office responsible for research and engineering to the office responsible for policy. As a result, there has been a significant reduction in the weight accorded to technical factors and a resultant imbalance in the policy process. It should now be the goal therefore to reestablish a major role for the technical side of DoD and to reduce the DoD role in detailed license review as parallel steps are taken within the Commerce Department to further strengthen its licensing procedures.

4. **Implement the Decontrol Procedures Required by Law When Foreign Availability is Found to Exist**

The lack of action by the federal government on foreign availability determinations is contrary to the mandate of the Export Administration Act of 1979, as amended. This is due in part to the fact that no specific time lines for the completion of foreign availability determinations have been specified in legislation. At the very least the Export Administration Act should impose reasonable time lines on *all* responsible agencies. Because the process for determining foreign availability is not now functioning effectively, there is a need for effective remedial action by both the executive and legislative branches.

5. **Withdraw the Statutory Requirement to Integrate the MCTL into the Commerce Department's Control List**

Congress should withdraw the statutory requirement for the integration of the Militarily Critical Technologies List into the U.S. Control List. The fundamentally different nature and functions of the two lists—the former an exhaustive list of all technologies with military utility and the latter a specific list of items requiring an export license—make this goal unattainable.

6. **Provide Effective, Two-Way Communication at the Highest Levels Between Government and the Private Sector**

A mechanism should be established (or upgraded) to provide effective, two-way communication between the highest levels of government and of the private sector on the formulation and implementation of coordinated national policies that balance military security and economic vitality. To this end the panel recommends that senior policy staff of the Executive Office of the President meet periodically with the President's Export Council and/or other respected representatives of the private sector and inform the President of the concerns of this sector regarding the domestic and international commercial impacts of national security export controls. It may be necessary for Congress to establish a mechanism to ensure appropriate consideration of industrial concerns in the formulation of national security export control policy.

1

Introduction

THE NATURE OF THE PROBLEM

The vigor of science and technology in the Western* democracies and the greater economic vitality of these nations in comparison to the Soviet bloc are sources of strength for the West in its continuing effort to maintain its military security. The West benefits from open societies with free and rapid exchange of scientific information and from competitive industrial bases, both of which drive the development of new technologies. Many of these items are dual use in character—that is, products or data with both commercial and military applications. The Soviet Union lacks the open communication and commercial advantages of the West and seeks to compensate for them, not only by directing a greater percentage† of its gross national product (GNP) to the development and production of military equipment but also by aggressive attempts to acquire and apply Western technology to its military programs.

These Soviet initiatives, in turn, pose a policy dilemma for the West because the open communication and free markets that are fundamental to the Western advantage in technology also facilitate the Soviet acquisition effort. Government controls over technology transfers collide with the character and principles of a free society, which are a source of so

---

*As used throughout this report, *Western* or *West* includes Japan.
†Nearly three times that devoted by the United States.

28

much of our strength in competition with the Soviet Union. There is a point at which interference with the free exchange of technology and information in the West could be more damaging to Western societies than the loss of technology under less-stringent controls.* The question is: Where does that point lie? And is the damage from such interference incremental and not evident until long after irreparable harm has been done? Answers to these questions may not be conclusive, but they directly affect our stakes in the long-term competition with the Soviet Union.

Given what is known about Soviet technology acquisition activities, an effective strategy for preserving the Western lead in military technology logically must include two elements. First, it is essential to maintain the vitality of the Western technological enterprise—that is, to continue to maintain technological leadership over potential adversaries. Second, it is necessary to deny—or at least impede—access by potential adversaries to militarily significant Western technology.† For a number of (primarily military) technologies, such as stealth or antisubmarine warfare (ASW) technologies, a clear and legitimate need exists for safeguards. Thus, when undertaken in tandem with efforts to invigorate the technological base, the denial strategy:

• makes it more difficult for the Soviet Union and its allies to upgrade their military systems through information, technology, and products acquired in the West; and

• requires the Soviet Union to commit substantial domestic resources to military research and development (R&D) rather than applying technology acquired in the West or simply using the results of Western R&D to avoid the costly "dead ends" that are an inevitable part of the technological development process.

In recent years the United States has pursued its policy with respect to national security export controls‡ during a period in which there have been dramatic alterations in the economic and technological environment

---

*The private sector, which is a vital source of military technology, sees some controls as essential and others as burdens. Government, on the other hand, does not incur directly the costs imposed on industry and therefore is less inclined to consider them.

†There is no standard, agreed-upon term for technology with military significance that is subject to control. Thus, a number of modifiers are used interchangeably throughout this report.

‡The term *national security export controls* is used here and throughout this report in the same sense as that employed in the Export Administration Act of 1979, as amended. The act authorizes such controls "to restrict the export of goods and technology which would make a significant contribution to the military potential of any other country or combination of countries which would prove detrimental to the national security of the United States." National security export controls that relate primarily to military matters are distinguished

that existed in the first few decades following the end of World War II. These changed circumstances have created a need for a broader definition of national security, a definition that recognizes explicitly the importance of maintaining the economic vitality and innovative capability of the United States and indeed of all Free World nations. Because the world economic and technological environment has changed, the panel believes that U.S. national security can be ensured only through the adoption and implementation of policies that simultaneously promote economic vitality, strengthen alliance relationships, and continue the maintenance of military preparedness.

Such a broadened definition of national security also must take account of several important new factors in the international environment:

• Greater scientific and technological parity now exists among the most advanced industrialized countries. In many important areas, the United States—once preeminent in most major fields—now shares technical leadership with other countries and therefore depends and must build on ideas and innovations developed abroad.

• Significant changes in the overall patterns of world trade are evidenced by the rapid emergence of major exporters among the newly industrializing countries (NICs), particularly along the Pacific rim. The result is that U.S. companies now face severe competition—at home, from import penetration, and abroad, from an ever-widening circle of firms in both industrialized and industrializing countries that are vying for global markets.

• Although in the United States the domestic market continues to absorb the majority of goods and services, foreign trade has become essential to maintaining continued economic vitality. U.S. companies—especially those operating in high-technology sectors—are turning increasingly to export markets. Transnational business organizations headquartered in many industrialized countries have become commonplace to achieve economies of scale, maintain levels of technological innovation, facilitate access to markets, and sustain profitable operations by dispersing production in a manner that lowers factor costs (e.g., labor, raw materials, etc.).

• A variety of domestic and international factors have promoted a huge increase in U.S. imports, which has in turn contributed to the foreign trade deficit. Meanwhile, increasing competition for export markets among the Western industrialized countries has created an atmosphere that makes cooperation on export controls among those countries more difficult to achieve.

---

from controls imposed for purposes of foreign policy or for protecting the domestic economy from the short supply of specific items.

Juxtaposed against these new global circumstances are the continuing realities of the East-West political struggle and its inherent military competition. In Europe, the North Atlantic Treaty Organization (NATO) alliance continues to be the centerpiece of efforts to deter aggression by the Soviet Union and the other Warsaw Pact countries. In Asia, the United States maintains close diplomatic and military relations with Japan and South Korea and is promoting closer ties with the People's Republic of China and the Southeast Asian free market countries, in part to discourage possible Soviet initiatives in that region.

In these circumstances the United States faces a policy dilemma of considerable proportions. The Western alliances depend on technological advantage to deter the Soviet Union and its allies. Moreover, Western military technology derives increasingly from technical advances in the commercial sector, advances that are the foundation for important dual use technology advantageous to the West. Because the Soviet Union now has attained numerical superiority over NATO in many important military categories, the potential loss of dual use technology has assumed greater strategic significance. Export controls are needed to help prevent the rapid erosion of this advantage, an advantage stemming in large measure from a vigorous, commercial high-technology sector that depends on innovation, competition, and trade for its strength. The rapid diffusion of technology, the importance of Western alliances, and the international character of high-technology industry all mean that: (1) export control can be neither perfect nor permanent, and (2) control policies must not interfere unnecessarily with Western commercial development and trade.

The Technology-Security Nexus

The Allied victory in World War II was made possible in large part by the mobilization of the enormous manufacturing capability of the United States. But outproducing the adversary as a military strategy presupposes an extended conflict. Since World War II, the existence of nuclear weapons has brought about an evolution of military thought. Much current thinking is that the outcome of a future global war, whether or not it involves the use of nuclear weapons, will depend more on the quality and quantity of the weapons and other war materiel on hand (or readily available for rapid mobilization and deployment) at the outbreak of hostilities than on the industrial capacity, of either side, that can be turned to military production.

At the same time the social and political structure of the Soviet Union has permitted it to place continuing emphasis on its military posture. Total uniformed personnel and the numbers of many types of military equipment in the Warsaw Pact greatly exceed the numbers of comparable personnel and equipment in NATO in the European theater. For example, NATO placed its total rapidly deployable troop strength in 1984 at 2.6 million; the estimated Warsaw Pact rapidly deployable troop strength stood at 4 million. NATO forces had 13,470 rapidly deployable main battle tanks in 1984, as compared to an estimated 26,900 for the Warsaw Pact; the total of rapidly deployable artillery and mortar pieces was 11,000 for NATO as against an estimated 19,900 pieces for the Warsaw Pact.[1] By all measures, therefore, the Western nations have been and are likely to continue to be substantially outnumbered in conventional military forces.

Therefore, the NATO countries have affirmed the importance of maintaining a technological advantage to offset the numerical advantage of the Warsaw Pact. But maintaining technological superiority in military forces is not an easy task, due largely to competing demands for economic resources that make it difficult for Western societies to sustain the investment of sufficient resources in military R&D and procurement. In recent years, spurred in part by burgeoning commercial markets for high-technology goods, the West has been able to counter partially the numerical advantage of the Warsaw Pact countries through rapid progress in science and technology.

A primary example is the explosion in electronic technology, including computers, that has occurred in commercial markets where many of the products also have important military applications. The United States has led but no longer dominates this revolution. Other Western indus-trialized nations have participated in and, particularly in the case of Japan, have taken the lead in selected areas. In addition, many newly industrializing countries (for example, the free market countries of the Pacific rim) are rapidly increasing their competence and are already competing effectively, albeit primarily at the lower end of the technology spectrum.

The Soviet Union and its Warsaw Pact allies, on the other hand, with their controlled and sluggish civilian economies, have benefited much less from technological progress in the commercial sector. The Soviet Union has offset this disadvantage, however, by giving its military first priority in the allocation of resources. The Soviets have developed and fielded in large quantity some equipment in the European theater that rivals comparable NATO systems in technical sophistication (although typically such equipment is introduced later than in the West).

The Western technology lead in military equipment, then, is critical to the maintenance of Western security. This lead is still significant and does not appear to be decreasing, but it is vulnerable to policies that dampen the continued development of the civilian market for high-technology products in the United States and abroad and to procedures that inadequately control the flow of militarily significant technology to the Soviet Union and its allies.

The Current Challenge

With increased awareness of Soviet efforts to acquire militarily significant Western technology has come a renewed emphasis on promoting and protecting the West's technology lead. This emphasis extends to military technologies and also to dual use technologies. The need to protect dual use technologies has created a new set of problems, precipitated by the perceived incompatibility between the execution of national security export controls and the realities of the global trading system. Among the new challenges confronting the United States are:

• the growing lag over the past decade between the development and application of new technologies in commercial products and the incorporation of the same or related technologies into military systems;

• the attitudes of some European countries that, unlike the United States, see the political and economic advantages of certain types of trade with the Eastern bloc (e.g., "Ostpolitik") outweighing potential damage to military security;

• extension throughout the world of technology development and manufacturing capacity, both by U.S. and foreign multinational companies, which has been driven by competitive pressures and has contributed to the growth of technology-intensive industries outside the United States; and

• greatly intensified competition for domestic and world markets, which has created an environment in which the negative effects of national security export controls can be detrimental to the health of elements of the U.S. economy.

The net result of these challenges has been a growing debate over how to reconcile the conflicting values and objectives that are the basis for U.S. national security export controls. On the one hand the United States, as the leading free market democracy, is determined to protect fundamental Western security interests by denying the Soviet Union and its allies access to advanced technology that could substantially advance Eastern bloc military capabilities. On the other hand the United States is faced with expanding technological capabilities outside the CoCom* countries and with the imperatives of the global economy—factors that

---

*Japan and all of the NATO countries except Iceland are members of the informal, nontreaty organization known as the Coordinating Committee on Multilateral Export Controls (CoCom). (See further details in Chapter 4.)

make technology more broadly available and thus make it increasingly difficult to maintain controls on any but the most critical high-technology items. It was with a view to analyzing this conflict and its implications for national security export control policy that this study was undertaken.

ORIGINS AND MANDATE OF THE STUDY

The current study had its origins in 1984 when the 98th Congress failed to reach agreement on major new amendments to the expired Export Administration Act of 1979. At the time, government and industry leaders expressed mounting concern about the apparent polarization of attitudes toward the national security export control issue and the seeming conflict between the national interests in maintaining military security and promoting international trade. Within the federal government the development of policy for national security export controls continued to be contentious and highly divisive along lines of agency jurisdiction—despite the existence of a senior interagency group charged with resolving such differences. Within the private sector the trade associations representing the industries most affected by the controls (e.g., electronics, computers, and scientific apparatus) were concerned enough to form the Industry Coalition on Technology Transfer to press the case for reform. There was in sum a clear need to move beyond the existing impasse toward a national policy that recognized fully the fundamental interests at stake.

Given the central role of science and technology in the national security export control problem and the need for an independent assessment, the National Academy complex* represented an appropriate institution to undertake a comprehensive and objective assessment, especially in view of several major studies it had completed on related topics. For example, in 1982 the Academy complex's Committee on Science, Engineering, and Public Policy (COSEPUP) convened a special panel to determine whether U.S. security interests were being compromised by the open communication of the results of basic research. The report of the resulting study, *Scientific Communication and National Security*[2] (known as the Corson report after its chairman, Dale R. Corson), which appeared in September 1982, laid the basis for the development and release in 1985 of National Security Decision Directive (NSDD) 189. This directive restated the importance to the national interest of maintaining the open communication of "fundamental" research within the constraints imposed by classification or other existing law. At the time of its report, however, the

---

*The National Academy complex includes the National Academy of Sciences, the National Academy of Engineering, and the Institute of Medicine.

Corson panel indicated that there was another major dimension to the problem that it did not have the opportunity to examine in depth: namely, that of technology transferred as part of or in association with commercial activities.

In other related activities, the Academy complex released a report in 1983 entitled *International Competition in Advanced Technology: Decisions for America*,[3] and in 1985 the National Academy of Sciences published the proceedings of a special 2-day symposium, sponsored jointly with the Council on Foreign Relations, entitled *Technological Frontiers and Foreign Relations*.[4] The leadership of the Academy complex decided to maintain its commitment to the issue by considering the national security implications of technology transfer *beyond* the stage of basic research.

There have of course been other studies of various aspects of the national security export control problem undertaken outside the Academy complex. Among the earliest and most influential of these was the 1976 report of the Defense Science Board Task Force on Export of U.S. Technology, *An Analysis of Export Control of U.S. Technology—A DoD Perspective*,[5] known as the Bucy report after its chairman J. Fred Bucy (the major recommendations of that study are considered in Chapter 5). More recently the Center for Strategic and International Studies (CSIS) issued a report in 1985 entitled *Securing Technological Advantage: Balancing Export Controls and Innovation;*[6] and the Business-Higher Education Forum published *Export Controls: The Need to Balance National Objectives*[7] in 1986. The current study builds on the intellectual foundations of these past efforts, but it departs from or goes beyond them in several respects.

To undertake the study, COSEPUP established the Panel on the Impact of National Security Controls on International Technology Transfer. The specific mix of individuals invited to serve on the panel was the result of a search process by the presidents of the National Academy of Sciences and the National Academy of Engineering with the object of ensuring balance, depth of expertise, and objectivity. The panel includes many individuals who have had substantial experience in government at the most senior levels pertaining to national security affairs; a number of others who have held senior posts in or contributed advice to the Intelligence Community; and still others who possess substantial legal expertise from relevant work both within and outside the government. Many hold (or have held) leadership positions in high-technology industries. Four members of the current panel also served on the Corson panel mentioned above.

COSEPUP charged the panel to "seek strategies to regulate the international transfer of technology through industrial channels in such a manner as to balance the national objectives of national security, economic vitality, scientific and technological advance, and commercial, educational, and personal freedom.''* The charge also stipulated the following panel tasks: (1) examination of the global technological environment, including the problem of controlling dual use technologies; (2) assessment of the control problem for the CoCom countries in terms of what was being lost through commercial channels, how it was being lost, and to whom; (3) evaluation of the effectiveness of CoCom; (4) consideration of the impacts on U.S. industry of current export control policies; and (5) examination of the current export control policies and procedures maintained by the U.S. government and by other CoCom and non-CoCom countries. The panel responded to the COSEPUP charge by mapping out and then pursuing an ambitious scope of work to fulfill its mandate.

SCOPE OF THE PANEL'S WORK

To carry out its specified tasks the panel and its professional staff undertook a broad agenda of research and briefings. The staff collected and analyzed available public literature and a large volume of restricted documents made available by the General Accounting Office and other government agencies (see the annotated bibliography in Appendix H). The panel invited representatives of all the federal agencies involved directly in the formulation or implementation of national security export control policy—namely, the Departments of Defense, Commerce, State, Treasury (U.S. Customs Service), and Justice—to appear before it. In addition the panel heard three classified briefings from the Intelligence Community, including one requiring high levels of clearance, and a briefing from the National Aeronautics and Space Administration (NASA) on technology transfer issues associated with the proposed space station. The panel's agenda also included a day of hearings devoted to the views of industry, with testimony offered by officials of both large and small companies representing a range of manufacturing sectors, and a series of discussions with individuals who have had substantial experience with various aspects of national security export controls. (Appendix G includes a list of briefers and contributors and their affiliations.)

Two panel foreign fact-finding missions constituted a second element of the study. In January 1986 delegations of the panel traveled to six European countries: Austria, Belgium, France, Great Britain, Sweden, and West Germany. In March 1986 other delegations visited five Asian

---

*Appendix A is the complete text of the COSEPUP charge.

countries: Japan, Hong Kong, Malaysia, Singapore, and South Korea. In each country, panel members held frank and confidential meetings with government officials, industry leaders, academics, and other informed observers on export control matters. (Summary reports describing the panel's foreign fact-finding missions are Appendix B of this volume.)

A third element of the study involved the commissioning of a series of research reports prepared both by outside consultants and by the panel's professional staff. Some of these reports developed and analyzed new primary data; others reexamined existing problems from new perspectives. These reports are included here (see Appendixes C and D) and in a companion volume.

FOCUS OF THE STUDY

This study examines the current system of laws, policies, procedures, regulations, international agreements, and organizations—referred to collectively as the national security export control regime—that control the international transfer of technology through industrial channels. Where appropriate, it also recommends new approaches to balancing the national policy objectives of national security, scientific and technological advance, and economic vitality. In the course of its deliberations, the panel found it both useful and appropriate to limit the focus of its effort in the following respects:

• *Concentration on impacts of controls on the Free World*   There is widespread agreement in the West that the sale of sophisticated Western technology to the Soviet bloc should be controlled. There is also widespread agreement that trade among the Free World countries should be restricted as little as possible. Consequently, it is generally accepted that the decision to impose national security restrictions on trade within the West should depend on whether such sales are likely to result, directly or indirectly, in a transfer of militarily significant goods or technology to the Soviet bloc. Thus, the focus of this report is on the effects of national security export controls on the technological development and economic vitality of the Free World countries.

• *Focus on dual use goods and technology*   Soviet military capability can be enhanced by the export of certain dual use goods and technology, as well as directly by military hardware (i.e., munitions). The Export Administration Act, as amended, establishes a system of national security export controls that is intended to regulate the flow of dual use items. Exports of military hardware are controlled under the terms of the Arms Export Control Act; this part of the system appears to function well. The current study focuses primarily on the problems associated with the control of dual use items rather than of munitions.

• *Diversion and espionage*   Items subject to U.S. national security export controls are sometimes diverted from their approved destination or end user, either directly or through intermediaries, to the Soviet bloc. Preventing such diversions is a major objective of U.S. export (and reexport) controls, and this problem is discussed extensively in this report. Espionage is another extremely serious channel for the loss of militarily critical technology and information; it is not, however, addressed in detail here because national security export controls are unlikely to affect directly the outcome of covert operations. The panel is deeply concerned, as are most citizens, about the evidence of serious loss due to espionage; it is clear that Soviet success in espionage can circumvent controls for commercial dual use technology. This report, however, focuses on national security export controls, which are only one element of the broader measures required by the West to protect militarily critical technology.

• *Other limitations*   At least three other important subjects were determined to lie outside the panel's frame of reference. First, although obviously an important determinant of technology lead in military systems, the panel did not examine in detail the problem of deficiencies in the U.S. military procurement process. This matter has received substantial recent attention,[8] and, although the results were considered by the panel, no additional analysis was deemed necessary or feasible. Second, the panel was not charged to consider other applications of export controls, including foreign policy and short supply constraints. Foreign policy export controls in particular may occasionally become intertwined or confused with national security export controls. One example is the case of controls imposed on the export of pipeline technology to the Soviet Union following the imposition of martial law in Poland. Foreign policy controls were not examined by the panel, however, except to the extent that they affect the effective functioning of the national security export control regime. Finally, this report does not address the problems associated with exports to particular nations outside the Soviet bloc such as Libya or Syria.

Despite these necessary limitations in focus, the panel examined the details of the national security export control system, considered a wide spectrum of issues, and heard arguments for both expanded and reduced national security export controls. It has examined these positions carefully with one goal in mind: to discern what types of national security export controls are reasonable and practicable in light of the new economic and technological realities that confront the United States in the final years of the twentieth century.

ORGANIZATION OF THE REPORT

The panel's report comprises eight chapters and eight appendixes. Chapter 2 provides evidence on the technology transfer problem at the unclassified level, while Chapter 3 analyzes the changing global technological and economic environment in which national security export controls must operate. Chapter 4 describes U.S. national security export controls and lays out the dimensions of the multilateral control system. Chapters 5 and 6 in turn assess the effectiveness of the U.S. and multilateral national security export processes. The report concludes by presenting the panel's findings and key judgments in Chapter 7 and its recommendations in Chapter 8, followed by eight appendixes of supplementary materials.

NOTES

1. U.S. Department of Defense, *Soviet Military Power, 1985* (Washington, D.C.: U.S. Government Printing Office, 1985), p. 77.
2. National Academy of Sciences, *Scientific Communication and National Security* (Washington, D.C.: National Academy Press, 1982).
3. National Research Council, Panel on Advanced Technology Competition and the Industrialized Allies, *International Competition in Advanced Technology: Decisions for America* (Washington, D.C.: National Academy Press, 1983).
4. National Research Council, Office of International Affairs, *Technological Frontiers and Foreign Relations* (Washington, D.C.: National Academy Press, 1985).
5. U.S. Department of Defense, Office of the Director of Defense Research and Engineering, *An Analysis of Export Control of U.S. Technology—A DoD Perspective* (Report of the Defense Science Board Task Force on Export of U.S. Technology) (Washington, D.C.: U.S. Government Printing Office, 1976).
6. Stephen A. Merrill, ed., *Securing Technological Advantage: Balancing Export Controls and Innovation* (Washington, D.C.: Center for Strategic and International Studies, Georgetown University, 1985).
7. Business-Higher Education Forum, *Export Controls: The Need to Balance National Objectives* (Washington, D.C., 1986).
8. See in this regard the President's Blue Ribbon Commission on Defense Management (also known as the Packard commission), *A Quest for Excellence: Final Report to the President* (Washington, D.C.: U.S. Government Printing Office, 1986).

2

Evidence on the Technology Transfer Problem

INTRODUCTION

The Intelligence Community* plays a particularly significant role in decision making on national security export controls. This chapter addresses what is known about technology acquisition efforts in the West by the Soviet Union, contributions to Soviet technological advancement (including military systems), the state of Soviet science and technology, and implications for national security export control policy.

No less than in other areas of intelligence, data on these matters are incomplete and fragmentary. For example, evidence provided by the few cases uncovered to date of espionage and diversion of militarily significant technology in all likelihood offers only a limited—and perhaps not fully representative—indication of the overall volume of such activities. Moreover, because intelligence often becomes available relatively late in the development of national security export control policy, it is not yet possible to assess the impact of the changes in national security export controls that have been undertaken during the past few years. Nonetheless, despite the need for judgment and intuition to bridge information gaps, the data do provide a backdrop for assessing the need for and effectiveness of national security export controls.

---

*The *Intelligence Community* is a collective term denoting the director of central intelligence and the U.S. intelligence agencies.

INTELLIGENCE EVIDENCE ON SOVIET TECHNOLOGY ACQUISITION

Intelligence information reviewed by the panel confirms previous reports[1] that the Soviet technology acquisition effort is massive, well financed, and frequently effective. Western technology has flowed to Warsaw Pact countries in recent years through three primary channels:

- *espionage*—theft of classified information and/or items of direct relevance to military systems;
- *diversion*—shipment of militarily significant dual use products and technology to unapproved end users, either directly through the export of controlled products without a license (i.e., smuggling), or indirectly through transshipment using a complex chain of increasingly untraceable reexports; and
- *legal sales*—direct trade with the Soviet bloc, usually after receipt of a license, that also includes some reexports (i.e., the legal transshipment of products or components by firms operating in countries that do not impose controls).

The need for vigilance against unwanted transfer of Western technology was underscored by the so-called "Farewell affair," which occurred in France in 1981.[2] Farewell was the codename for an officer of the Soviet Union's Committee for State Security (KGB) stationed in Paris during the 1960s. In 1981 this officer gave the West detailed information on the plans, organization, and financing of Soviet efforts to target and acquire Western high-technology equipment, blueprints, research and development data, and so on. Farewell provided an extraordinary opportunity to assess the effectiveness of the Soviet acquisition of Western technology as it is perceived by the Soviets themselves—extraordinary because information on Soviet intentions usually has been episodic and of insufficient quality or quantity to allow accurate assessments of the Soviet acquisition program. Although the panel recognizes that internal Soviet documents such as the Farewell papers must be viewed with caution (because of the possibility that the authors had an interest in inflating the successes of the acquisition program in their reports to superiors), the Farewell papers do set out a remarkable record of the scope and success of the Soviet acquisition effort. (The information contained in the Farewell papers, which contributes significantly to our current state of knowledge, was documented in the unclassified white paper *Soviet Acquisition of Militarily Significant Western Technology: An Update*, made public by the Department of Defense in 1985.)

The Farewell papers indicate that, during the Tenth Five-Year Plan (1976-1980), the Soviet acquisition program satisfied more than 3,500 specific collection requirements for hardware and documents for the 12 Soviet industrial ministries. Of the items acquired in the West, the Soviets estimated that approximately 70 percent were subject to national security export controls. This proportion was apparently much the same during the most recent 5-year plan (1981-1985) as it was during the previous 5 years (1976-1980), a period of relatively less restrictive Western controls.

Moreover, the Soviet Union has established an elaborate administrative structure, involving tens of thousands of people, to satisfy its collection objectives. An outline of the Soviet institutional framework was published in 1983 by Henri Regnard, a pseudonym used by a senior French counterintelligence official.[3] Regnard describes a bureaucracy composed of the Military-Industrial Commission (VPK), Chief Directorate of Military Intelligence (GRU), State Committee for Science and Technology (GKNT), the KGB, and the Ministry of Defense.[4] This structure administers the three main arms of the Soviet technology acquisition effort: espionage, diversions, and legal sales.

ESPIONAGE

In the discussion of illegal channels of transfer, it is important to make a sharp distinction between espionage and diversions. Espionage is covert activity to obtain classified information about products and technologies pertinent to military systems. Diversions, on the other hand, are illegal shipments of unclassified dual use items or unclassified military goods to unapproved end users. Diversion activity may occur at any stage of the export process: It includes fraud in prelicense or postlicense documentation, theft during transshipment, and unauthorized postshipment reexport.

There is little doubt that Soviet attempts to obtain equipment and technology in the West by means of espionage are extensive, particularly in light of the quite damaging instances of Soviet success revealed by recent Western counterintelligence efforts (e.g., the Walker espionage case). Indeed, it appears that many of the most significant losses to the Soviet bloc (e.g., look-down/shoot-down radar) were achieved through espionage, which is not effectively countered by export controls and thus was not a subject examined in detail by the panel. Espionage does, however, place limits on the effectiveness of any export control system.

DIVERSIONS

As noted above, diversions are illegal shipments of unclassified commodities and technical data to unapproved end users. Diversion activities are often difficult to detect, in part because they may occur at many stages of the export process and in part because the Soviets have devised sophisticated, multinational diversion mechanisms that frequently escape the attention of counterintelligence services of the countries in which the diversion is taking place. The Export Administration Amendments Act of 1985 gives the U.S. Customs Service primary responsibility for foreign investigation of all commercial export control violations including illegal diversions. In the diversion investigation process, the U.S. Customs Service receives information from all relevant government agencies, and the Intelligence Community assists in verifying charges. The U.S. government also seeks the cooperation of the governments of countries in which it suspects diversions are occurring. It is worth emphasizing that many—perhaps most—diversions occur outside the United States and often involve goods and technology originating in other technologically advanced countries.

The Intelligence Community has developed significant information on attempts by the Soviet Union and its allies to divert exports of Western high-technology equipment. Two recent examples of diversion activity help to illustrate the potential for the illegal flow of militarily useful technology to the Soviet Union.

• In July 1986 the U.S. government uncovered a diversion of a large shipment of computers and related sensitive equipment. (The shipment's estimated value was in the tens of millions of dollars.) The equipment, which is believed to have been destined ultimately for the Soviet Union, had been routed first to Belgium and then to a Turkish buyer in Austria where it was seized. (At the time of seizure, investigators report that some components already had been delivered to the Soviet Union.) Some of the products came from a U.S. company specializing in oscilloscopes, spectrum analyzers, and other scientific measuring instruments. Reportedly, acquisition by the Soviets of the U.S. equipment could enhance their electronic intelligence capabilities. As of January 1987 the investigation was still proceeding.

• Richard Mueller, a West German citizen, is still wanted today in that country and in the United States for a number of cases involving illegal exports to the Soviet Union of CoCom-controlled computers, microelectronics, and other products. Mueller's involvement with illegal technology acquisition on behalf of the Soviet bloc dates back to the early 1970s. For his network, he established numerous "dummy" and "front" firms to purchase products and technology; at one point, he reportedly had more than 75 firms operating in Western Europe and the United States. Between 1978 and 1983, Mueller used these firms to deliver to the Soviets advanced computers, peripherals, and microelectronics manufacturing equipment worth many millions of dollars.

Perhaps Mueller's best-known operation was his attempt to divert to the Soviet Union in late 1983 seven large VAX computers (and related hardware and software) manufactured by the Digital Equipment Corporation. The VAX series of super minicomputers is valuable to the Soviets because of their computer-aided design applications for microelectronics fabrication. Mueller's front firms in South Africa and West Germany had purchased this equipment in the United States for eventual transshipment to the Soviets. Although much of it was seized by Swedish and West German authorities when the diversion was uncovered in 1983, some of the equipment is known to have been received in the Soviet Union.

There is no doubt that many diversions evade detection. Moreover, the level and effectiveness of customs enforcement efforts to prevent diversions differ, both within CoCom and among other technologically advanced Free World countries. There often is little likelihood that customs inspectors will identify violations once goods have left the original shipper and have been manipulated by experienced diverters because the volume of trade is great, the number of inspectors is comparatively small, and the detection of mislabeled equipment requires sophisticated technical skills. Identifying diversions is especially problematic while goods are in transit through the bonded or customs-free zones maintained in most countries. Although there is informal international cooperation among customs officials to detect and prevent the diversion of goods in transit, these officials are reluctant to enter such zones and open bonded shipments without strong evidence of wrongdoing.

In light of these facts, perhaps the most important means for reducing diversions arises from government cooperation with the private sector. U.S. businessmen—and businessmen in firms abroad—are in a position to see inconsistencies in an individual's or company's behavior or the appearance of a suspicious new company that does not fit with their knowledge of the specific commercial context. Government officials for their part can promote a stronger sense of responsibility for reporting such circumstances by requesting information from the private sector. These requests, when presented appropriately, often produce useful cooperation including leads on possible diversionary activities. In general, however, government agencies have failed to alert private industry to the importance of this information and have not encouraged feedback.

LEGAL SALES

Some significant technology may be acquired by the Soviet bloc through legal purchases when foreign availability of the given technology exists. (The issue of foreign availability is discussed further in Chapter 5.)

For example, in light of the dispersion of sophisticated technology throughout the world, the Soviet Union and other Warsaw Pact countries have been (or may be) able to obtain controlled technology in Free World countries that do not participate in the national security export control regime established by CoCom. These countries could include both the industrialized neutral countries of Europe and many newly industrializing countries such as India, Singapore, and Brazil. Many of these non-CoCom countries either do not acknowledge or do not enforce restrictions on the reexport of goods and technology obtained originally in CoCom countries. Moreover, many are striving to or have already become sources of indigenous high technology. Thus, there is an increasing likelihood that the Soviet bloc may be able to purchase certain categories of dual use technology (particularly at the lower end of the CoCom-designated threshold*) in some of the more advanced non-CoCom countries without ever having to resort to the use of covert methods.

THE SIGNIFICANCE OF VARIOUS CHANNELS OF LOSS

Based on the evidence reviewed by the panel, it appears that espionage is the most significant of the channels for technology loss. But as noted earlier, export controls do not represent an effective means to deter— much less prevent—espionage. Therefore, although the success of the Soviet espionage effort serves to reveal Soviet intent, it cannot be used to justify the change in export controls on dual use products. Indeed, an assessment of the policy significance of the Soviet bloc's collection activities, which requires examining the various channels for loss, would be improved by greater discrimination on the part of the Intelligence Community in categorizing different types of Soviet collection activities as espionage, diversion, or open acquisition.

SOVIET UTILIZATION OF ACQUIRED WESTERN TECHNOLOGY

It is only on rare occasions that the Intelligence Community can declare with relative certainty that the application of Western dual use technology has contributed substantially to Soviet military developments.† The

---

*This includes the least-sensitive CoCom-controlled products and technologies (e.g., administrative exception note [AEN] 9/national discretion note items and AEN 12/favorable consideration note items). See Chapter 4 for an explanation of these provisions.

†This discussion deals with recent Soviet utilization of acquired Western technology. It is well known that the Soviets acquired European weapons technology as well as scientific knowledge and technical personnel at the end of World War II.

necessarily fragmentary data used for these assessments most often seem to deal with the introduction of process equipment into manufacturing plants. There are also isolated examples of specific Western components, or copies of them, appearing in Soviet military equipment.

One of the few recent instances in which solid evidence on Soviet technology acquisition was uncovered involved data from the Soviet Military-Industrial Commission (VPK). The VPK produces an annual report based on an evaluation of individual Soviet defense manufacturing ministries whose strategic technology needs have been satisfied through technology acquisition efforts in the West. It includes aggregate statistics on the number of technical documents and samples (hardware) obtained, gross ruble savings, and the number and priority of satisfied requirements. Data from one of these reports (as noted earlier in this chapter) indicate that, during the Tenth Five-Year Plan (1976-1980), more than 3,500 requirements or 50 percent of the total were reported as fully satisfied worldwide. Roughly 60 to 70 percent of these were fulfilled by the Soviet intelligence services (KGB and GRU) and their surrogates among the Eastern European intelligence services. Furthermore, the VPK projected that, during the Eleventh Five-Year Plan, the number of fully satisfied requirements will exceed 5,000.[5]

The report also states that from 1976 to 1980 the Ministry of Defense Industry (armor and electro-optics) and the Ministry of Aviation Industry realized the greatest savings in research project costs. By the Soviets' own calculations, these savings equalled $800 million (in 1980 purchasing power equivalents) worth of comparable research activity. The equivalent Soviet manpower cost of these savings alone translates roughly into over 100,000 man-years of scientific research. These data on savings, however, may be conservative: The ruble figures probably reflect operating costs (e.g., salaries, elimination of test range activity) and exclude capital costs.[6]

Given such uncertainties about available data on Soviet costs and savings, the United States has had no persuasive analysis of either the value of Western technology acquisitions to the Soviet R&D process or the ruble expenditures avoided through such efforts. To supply such an analysis, the Department of Defense commissioned a study to estimate both the ruble savings to the Soviets for R&D expenditures foregone and the additional cost to the West to counter new Soviet military capabilities (discussed further in Chapter 5); the report of this study, *Assessing the Effect of Technology Transfer on U.S./Western Security—A Defense Perspective*, was published in 1985. Although the Defense Department report has been regarded generally as a useful first step, the panel and other experts it consulted have found the methodology employed and the conclusions reached to be unconvincing.

Part of the difficulty in assessment arises from the inevitable problems in putting a product or technology into effective use. The Soviets may attempt to reverse-engineer a product—that is, use an item obtained in the West as a basis for producing the technology themselves for military systems. The panel believes that this strategy is generally unproductive for many types of items (such as high-density semiconductor devices) because often the ability to copy a technology depends more on technological infrastructure and the capability of the manufacturing process than on the observable features of a particular device. Indeed, the experience of U.S. firms in setting up manufacturing facilities in foreign subsidiaries indicates that great care and considerable time are required to duplicate a product successfully—at least in terms of quantity—even with full access to all manufacturing process details and equipment. This fact suggests that a loss through the diversion of a few units of most products is unlikely to have much military significance. Of course, in some cases the Soviets can gain insight into the function of a particular component through reverse engineering, which may aid them in the development of countermeasures or give them confidence that a specific design approach has been successful in the West. But this situation is likely to have significance only with regard to uniquely military items rather than with the dual use products that are the focus of this report.

Nevertheless, there are certain key items of process control or manufacturing hardware (so-called keystone equipment) that *can* provide the Soviets with substantial leverage even if only a few are obtained because they facilitate the production of quantities of other hardware. (Precision ballbearing grinders, which the Soviets acquired legally in the past, have been cited as an example of such equipment.) By the standards of Western productivity the Soviets are generally weak in automated manufacturing techniques. Consequently, a prevalent judgment in the United States, at least since the 1976 Bucy report, has been that the emphasis of national security export control policy should be on constraining the flow of essential technologies and manufacturing equipment—incorporated in some turnkey plants—rather than on the end products of the manufacturing process.

Table 2-1 is one of a number of estimates published by the Department of Defense (DoD) that compare the state of the art of Soviet technology with that of the United States. Although in some cases different conclusions may be drawn, the panel has determined that for most types of dual use technology the Soviet Union is on average approximately 5 to 10 years behind the West and does not appear to be closing the gap.

Despite an extensive acquisition effort, then, the Soviets in general have not succeeded in reducing the West's technology lead. Some of the reasons for this state of affairs are discussed in the next section of this chapter. It should be noted, however, that the situation is different for

TABLE 2-1   Relative U.S. Versus USSR Standing in 20 Militarily
Related Technology Areas

Basic Technologies	USSR Superior	U.S./USSR Equal	U.S. Superior
Aerodynamics/fluid dynamics		X	
Computers and software			X→
Conventional warheads (including all chemical explosives)		X	
Directed energy (laser)	X		
Electro-optical sensor (including infrared)	X		
Guidance and navigation			X
Life sciences (human factors/biotechnology)			X
Materials (lightweight, high strength, and high temperature)			←X
Micro-electronic materials and integrated-circuit manufacturing			X
Nuclear warheads		X	
Optics		X	
Power sources (mobile—includes energy storage)		X	
Production/manufacturing (includes automated control)			X
Propulsion (aerospace and ground vehicles)			←X
Radar sensor			←X
Robotics and machine intelligence			X
Signal processing			X
Signature reduction			X
Submarine detection			←X
Telecommunications (including fiber optics)			X

NOTE: This list is in alphabetical order. Relative comparisons of technology levels depict overall average standing only; countries may be superior, equal, or inferior in subcategories of a given technology. Arrows indicate that relative technology levels are changing significantly in the direction shown.

SOURCE: *The FY1987 DoD Program for Research and Development* (Statement by the Under Secretary of Defense, Research, and Engineering to the 99th Congress, Second Session, 1986).

fielded military systems. Although the West generally remains ahead in the most advanced weapon systems, the strong Soviet emphasis on the development and production of military hardware has resulted in many items or equipment in the field that in many weapon system categories often are as modern as those deployed in the West. Assessing the significance of this fact for export controls is difficult, however; often, the technology in Western military hardware lags behind what is widely available in the commercial sector.[7]

In sum the Soviets generally continue to lag behind the West technologically although they have worked for years to close this gap, in part by obtaining new technology from the West. Instead of advancing the overall state of Soviet technological development, however, this practice, in tandem with problems inherent in the structure of Soviet science and technology, may have resulted in maintaining or perhaps even widening their lag due to dependence on generally outdated Western equipment and technology (particularly in the field of computer science). Although it would be foolhardy for the United States and the other technologically advanced countries of the West to facilitate Soviet access to militarily critical technology, the panel considers it unlikely that an influx of Western technology will enable the Soviet Union to reduce the current gap substantially—as long as the West continues its own rapid pace of innovation.

THE STATE OF SOVIET SCIENCE AND TECHNOLOGY[8]

It has long been known that the organizational structure and rigidities of Soviet science have a strong impact on both the effectiveness and efficiency with which the results of scientific research are transferred into technical application in the Soviet Union and on the assimilation of technical innovations acquired from the West. Soviet science and industry are characterized by:

- an incentive system that does not strongly support technical innovation and implementation;
- research activity that is highly concentrated, both organizationally and geographically;
- rigidly hierarchical lines of authority and communication;
- subjugation to political factors (i.e., party bureaucracy and military priorities); and
- difficulty in incorporating new scientific ideas into a development and production phase.

The restricted communications that derive from the Soviet penchant for secrecy have resulted in the isolation of scientific entities within the system. This in turn has caused reduced cooperation among scientists, duplication of effort despite central planning, slow diffusion of new ideas and technologies, and errors due to inadequate peer review. The severe isolation of Soviet scientific institutes and laboratories—from one another, from the design bureaus that actually use the data they produce, and from the West—and the separation of civilian and military research efforts severely hinder the process of cross-fertilization that has accelerated progress in science and technology in the West.

It is especially difficult for the Soviets to incorporate new scientific ideas into development and production in the civilian sector. Formal review and approval must take place through several levels of management. Moreover, line managers often ignore ministry directives calling for innovation because they fear the consequences of not meeting short-term quotas as specified in the current plan. Recently, additional changes reportedly have been made to encourage risk-taking through the implementation of technical innovations; these changes allow production quotas in the current plan to be reduced for a period of time following the introduction of a new instrument or new process.[9]

Soviet defense projects consistently receive top priority in the allocation of resources to research and development. The military has priority access to the best indigenous technology. It also has the power to encourage innovation and accelerate production. The military's formidable ability to obtain Western technical goods and information further facilitates projects under its sponsorship. When Soviet military equipment designers levy requirements for Western documents, blueprints, and test equipment and other hardware, the VPK reportedly utilizes a national fund of about half a billion rubles* to satisfy them.[10]

The acquisition of particular documents can command funding as considerable as that for hardware items. The Soviets reportedly spent over 50,000 rubles for documents on the U.S. shuttle orbiter control system; the same sum was committed to acquiring information on high-energy laser developments. More than 200,000 rubles was approved for acquiring selected research documents on U.S. antimissile defense concepts.[11]

Besides substantial funding support, Soviet defense projects also appear to command substantial human resources, including those available in the civilian sector. Although the Western Intelligence Community can only estimate the percentage of Soviet civilian scientists involved in military projects, some place the figure above 50 percent. Often, Soviet scientists are recruited temporarily and agree to work for the military simply to acquire access to choice equipment, which they then put to use on their own nondefense-related projects.

A principal uncertainty with regard to the Soviet military's investment in science is whether it could one day present the West with an unexpected "Sputnik-like" surprise. The views expressed by U.S. scientists, Soviet emigré scientists, Western scientists who have worked in the Soviet Union, and Sovietologists, as well as those contained in

---

*The U.S. government calculated that for 1980 the approximate conversion ratio was 1 ruble = $1.47.

unclassified U.S. intelligence assessments, do not yield a consensus on this question.

General-Secretary Mikhail Gorbachev has stressed the role of scientific and technical progress in Soviet economic development.[12] He has spoken of plans to focus Soviet scientific efforts more on applications and less on pure research—aiming at the twin objectives of more rapid economic growth and a stronger military—and he has given priority to computer science and education. Although the defects noted in Soviet science continue to be fundamental to their system and will not be altered easily or quickly, U.S. policy must be formulated in recognition of the possibility of significant change.

IMPLICATIONS OF INTELLIGENCE EVIDENCE

The preceding discussion of the evidence on technology transfer to the Soviets yields a number of important implications for the formulation of an appropriately designed national security export control regime. Among the most significant are the following:

1. In the judgment of senior Western intelligence officials, espionage is the technology acquisition channel that is most valuable to the Soviets in enhancing their military capability, followed (to a lesser extent) by diversion of unclassified but controlled technology. Third in importance is the acquisition of uncontrolled Western technology. The U.S. national security export control regime does not provide solutions to the problem of espionage.

2. Based on its review of Intelligence Community evidence, the panel agrees that a legitimate need for appropriately designed export controls continues to exist. However, the significance of export controls alone in stemming losses should not be overestimated.

3. Because sources of products and technology increasingly exist elsewhere in the world, and because most diversions involve activities in other Western nations, the U.S. export control effort must be multinational. (See Chapter 6.) Attempting to develop an extensive system of controls centered in the United States appears futile in light of the fact that significant losses continue to occur elsewhere. Reduction of "high-end" diversion (i.e., diversion of the most sensitive CoCom-controlled products and technologies) requires the cooperation of CoCom and other non-CoCom Free World countries—cooperation that currently may not exist and that may require substantial diplomatic and private sector efforts to achieve. Nevertheless, improving the effectiveness of export enforcement in the current regime can make a substantial difference with respect to the control of unclassified dual use items.

4. Part of the U.S. concern about the Soviet technology acquisition effort relates to the current status of alternative technology sources around the world. Intelligence evidence indicates that U.S. dominance in various technology areas generally is decreasing (see Chapter 3). The diffusion of technology, the availability of controlled technology from outside the CoCom countries, the impossibility of an absolute embargo on any technology other than that contained in very high-cost items existing in small quantities (e.g., supercomputers) are all factors that contribute to U.S. policy formulation and that require reliable corroborating data.

The Intelligence Community and the Department of Defense have endeavored to make intelligence information on Soviet technology acquisition activity available to the public. For example, various "white papers" have been issued by the Intelligence Community, an effort that is especially valuable because public awareness may be a key to stemming losses through espionage or diversion. There is a similar need for improved dialogue between the U.S. R&D community (industry, academia, and government labs) and government officials charged with staying abreast of important developments in science and technology—particularly those who must make export control decisions on the basis of their understanding of the technologies involved and their knowledge of the state of foreign science and technology capability. The utilization of information derived from such a dialogue can be invaluable in determining specific products or technologies that should be controlled or decontrolled and in promoting a better general understanding of the worldwide state of the art in key technologies.

NOTES

1. U.S. Department of Defense, *Soviet Acquisition of Militarily Significant Technology: An Update* (Intelligence Community white paper) (Washington, D.C., September 1985).
2. Thierry Wolton, *Le KGB en France* (Paris: Editions Grasset & Fasquelle, 1986).
3. Henri Regnard (pseudonym), "The U.S.S.R. and Scientific, Technological, and Technical Intelligence (English translation)," *Défense Nationale* (December 1983), pp. 107-121.
4. Regnard's statements are consistent with descriptions in the "Penkovsky papers" of 1965, which identified KGB participation in the foreign activities of GKNT. (Oleg Penkovsky, *The Penkovsky Papers* [London: Collins, 1965]. This book is based on the testimony of a Soviet double agent.) The white paper *Soviet Acquisition of Militarily Significant Western Technology: An Update* provides extensive discussion of the key Soviet organizations involved in the acquisition of Western technology.
5. U.S. Department of Defense, *Soviet Acquisition*, p. 60.
6. Ibid., p. 6.
7. This topic was thoroughly addressed in the recent Packard commission report, *A Quest for Excellence: Final Report to the President by the President's Blue Ribbon Commission on Defense Management* (Washington, D.C., June 1986).

8. The data on which this section is based were drawn primarily from the 1985 report by the Foreign Applied Sciences Assessment Center (FASAC) entitled *Selected Aspects of Soviet Applied Science*. Coordinated by Science Applications International Corporation, FASAC has produced a number of studies at the request of the U.S. government assessing the state of science and technology in the Soviet Union. The center has drawn on the expertise of more than 100 U.S. scientists and engineers to evaluate available Soviet literature in their fields and summarize the military, economic, and political implications of recent developments in the Soviet Union. The principal focus of the FASAC reports is on Soviet exploratory research, which seeks to translate developments in fundamental research into new forms of technology with important application potential.

9. *A Study of Soviet Science* (Intelligence Community white paper) (Washington, D.C., December 1985), p. 10.

10. U.S. Department of Defense, *Soviet Acquisition*, p. 3.

11. Ibid., p. 4.

12. From a speech to the 27th Congress of the Communist Party of the Soviet Union, March 1986, reported by Gary Taubes and Glenn Garelik in "Soviet Science: How Good Is It?" *Discover* (August 1986), p. 57.

3

The Changing Global Economic and Technological Environment

For more than 35 years the United States and its CoCom allies have sought to deny militarily critical technology to the nations of the Warsaw Pact. Although the objective of denial still underlies U.S. policy, U.S. national security export controls (which are discussed in detail in the following chapter) are, in some respects, out of step with the rapidly changing environment in which they operate. In this regard, three major developments may be noted.[1] First, the character of the international marketplace is evolving in such a way that global diffusion of commercial technology takes place at a rapid rate; with growing frequency the technology being diffused has military applications. Second, the growing importance of trade as a part of U.S. economic activity causes the overall U.S. economy to be increasingly sensitive to policies that affect trade. Third, U.S. dominance over advanced technology is declining; stiff competition from foreign companies has appeared in almost every high-technology sector. In any reconsideration of U.S. national security export control policy, the implications of these developments warrant discussion and review.

CHANGES IN THE INTERNATIONAL MARKETPLACE

The volume of world trade has grown dramatically since World War II; in addition, the value of goods traded has increased manyfold since the 1950s. More and more, Western nations are exporting large proportions of their domestic output and consuming sizable quantities of imported goods. This increased volume of trade has been accompanied by the

54

appearance of new products and by changing business strategies, all of which markedly affect the environment in which national security export controls operate.

Integral to these developments is the phenomenon of information diffusion, which is occurring more and more rapidly, in ever-greater volumes, and to more destinations than ever before. This development is partially due to the improved capabilities offered by new communications technologies such as satellites, fiber optics, and digital switching systems. It is also due to the widespread use of many other technologies—for example, computers—which make expanded global interaction more efficient and less expensive as well.

The current competitive environment promotes information diffusion because it creates incentives for companies to pursue such global production strategies as locating research, development, and manufacturing facilities around the world and entering into joint ventures. As these companies work to coordinate their international efforts, they transfer massive amounts of information. Attempting to control these rapidly growing volumes of data transfers would be an enormous endeavor; moreover, significant interference with this vital flow would disrupt the communications essential for competitive business operations.

The shift to global production has resulted in the emergence of a new type of product, such as the "world car," whose components may cross national borders a number of times during production. It has also greatly expanded the roster of countries capable of mass-producing high-technology products. Even U.S. defense industries now rely on foreign-manufactured components and expertise for such sensitive items as missile guidance systems, radars, communications gear, satellites, and air navigation instruments. Some top-of-the-line U.S. supercomputers, of particular importance to the Intelligence Community, now incorporate high-performance chips made only in Japan. As can well be imagined, this situation has become a source of rising concern among defense planners.[2]

Some of these global products (for example, certain personal computers and memory chips) are produced in large quantities in an ever-greater number of countries; as a result, they have become, essentially, "technological commodities." The increased availability of such products and the rapid diffusion of the means to produce them make the effort to control high technology much more complicated—an effect further intensified by the fact that many of the countries involved are not members of CoCom and therefore are not subject to self-imposed controls.

Another important development in international trade is the expanding commercial market for dual use products, most of which embody advanced technology. To compete successfully in this market and maintain their market share in the face of growing competition from Japan,

Western Europe, and the newly industrializing countries, U.S. firms are experiencing added pressure to export their most technologically sophisticated commercial products.

An important related development in this period has been a growing disparity between the pace of technological progress from privately sponsored (commercial) R&D and that sponsored by the Department of Defense. Early in the postwar era, DoD recognized that technology would be more and more vital to the defense of the NATO alliance and consequently supported research and development in a number of important fields. Defense-funded programs in aeronautics, propulsion, and electronics were particularly successful and ultimately had major impacts on the civilian economy as these new technologies were commercialized. As long as DoD-funded programs remained at the leading edge of technology development, subsequent commercial exploitation presented little threat to U.S. security. New weapon systems could be fully operational in the U.S. military well before commercialization began, thus ensuring a continuing Western lead.

Although overall technological progress in the United States continued throughout the postwar era, a number of factors combined to undermine DoD's early leadership role in the development of militarily significant technologies. For a variety of reasons, the cost of developing new weapon systems incorporating state-of-the-art technology rose dramatically after the late 1960s. Military R&D and procurement expenditures subsequently declined, but the civilian market for high-technology products such as aircraft and consumer electronics experienced explosive growth. Thus, by the late 1970s there were a number of dual use high technologies, such as advanced microelectronics, that were introduced into the commercial sector well before they found application in military systems. As a result the U.S. government was in some cases left in the difficult position of trying to restrict the dissemination of technologies already available in the world marketplace. This dilemma is central to the debate over national security export controls.

As discussed in Chapter 1, control of advanced dual use technology and products is vital to the maintenance of the West's qualitative military advantage. Effective control is growing more difficult, however, because of the increasing rate of information diffusion and the rise of global production capabilities. A further complication is the United States' increasing participation in and reliance on the global economy.

GROWING U.S. INTERACTION IN THE GLOBAL ECONOMY

The United States is the single largest international trader, reporting exports of $360 billion in 1985. Exports thus have assumed growing

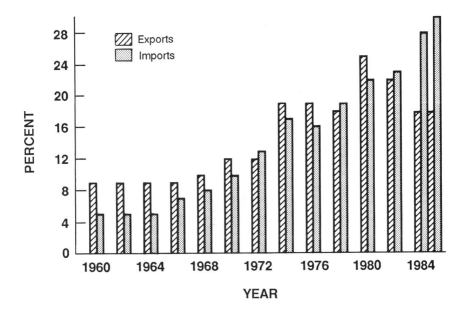

*1976, 1978, and 1980 imports are custom value.

FIGURE 3-1   Manufacturing trade as a percent of gross domestic product per manufacturing (domestic and foreign exports, f.a.s.; general imports, f.a.s.*).

importance to the U.S. economy and in particular to U.S. producers of manufactured goods. Manufactured exports as a percentage of gross domestic product for manufacturing were 9 percent in 1960 and grew to 25 percent in 1980 before declining to 18 percent in 1985.*

Imports of manufactured products as a percentage of gross domestic product for manufacturing exhibit an even more dramatic trend, rising from 5 percent in 1960 to 30 percent in 1985 as shown in Figure 3-1. The size and importance of the manufactured goods component of U.S. exports have also grown steadily; manufactured goods constituted 76 percent of total U.S. merchandise exports in 1985. Because export controls bear most heavily on manufactured goods, such controls can have a serious impact on the overall economic well-being of the United States.

It is also important to keep in mind the character and global distribution

---

*Most European and Asian countries trade a much higher proportion of their total economic output than does the United States. With such high levels of interaction in world markets, it is not surprising that European and Asian countries are sensitive to the negative effects on trade caused by export controls.

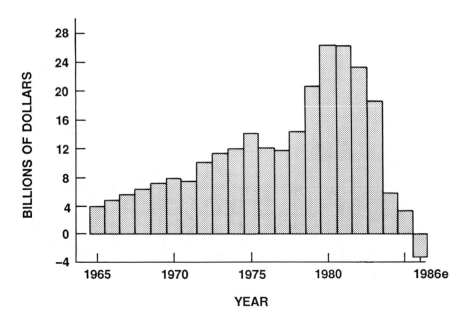

*U.S. Department of Commerce DOC-3 definition.

†1986 figure is estimated.

SOURCE: U.S. Department of Commerce, Bureau of the Census.

FIGURE 3-2   U.S. high-tech* trade balance, 1965-1986e† (domestic and foreign exports, f.a.s.; general imports, c.i.f.). Note: 1978-1980 data exclude trade between U.S. Virgin Islands and foreign countries.

of U.S. exports.[3] For instance, exports to CoCom countries are substantial, representing over 60 percent of total U.S. exports in 1985. By contrast, exports to the Soviet bloc in 1985 represented only 1 percent of U.S. exports. Therefore, trade policies that might diminish West-West trade have greater potential to damage the U.S. economy than do those that might reduce exports to the Eastern bloc.

The high-technology sector[4] is an important component of U.S. exports. It accounted for 30 percent of all U.S. goods exported and 42 percent of manufactured exports in 1985, and contributed to a steadily growing trade surplus from 1965 through 1981 as shown in Figure 3-2. This surplus helped to offset the trade deficit produced by other sectors. But for the past 5 years, the high-technology trade balance has worsened in parallel with the overall U.S. trade balance. Based on trends established in the first three quarters of 1986, the United States will register its first full-year trade deficit in high-technology goods since this category was established. Export controls are not a leading cause of this recent decline in high-technology export performance, but they may tend to exacerbate the U.S. trade deficit by contributing to an environment that discourages export activities by U.S. firms.

THE CHALLENGE TO U.S HIGH-TECHNOLOGY LEADERSHIP

The promotion of high-technology industries is an attractive policy option for many countries because these industries promise high growth, limited degradation of the environment, low natural resource requirements, and international prestige. The promotion of high-technology industries also encourages modernization of a nation's economy and society. Consequently, a number of countries are devoting a great deal of attention to developing and improving their indigenous technical capabilities.

CoCom Countries

Many of the CoCom countries have a long history of advanced technological development. In the post-World War II period, these nations did not offer significant competition to the United States as they worked to rebuild their economies. But several of these countries—notably West Germany, France, and Japan—are now providing significant competition to the United States. The ability to compete is in part the result of long-term efforts to enhance their indigenous technical capability. Rising R&D expenditures in West Germany, France, and Japan are one indication of this effort. In the early 1960s, the proportion of GNP the United States spent on R&D was more than twice that spent by West Germany, France, or Japan; by 1983, however, the expenditures of these countries had reached approximately the same level (2.5 percent) as that of the United States (see Figure 3-3).

It is important to note that, although Japan, West Germany, and the United States all devote an equivalent proportion of GNP to R&D, Japan and West Germany may derive a commercial advantage from these expenditures because they devote a much smaller proportion of their R&D to military development (see Figure 3-4). In 1981 the United States devoted more than half its total government R&D funding to defense-related research; West Germany and Japan, on the other hand, devoted 9 percent and 2 percent, respectively. In 1986 the United States allocated over 70 percent of government R&D funding to defense projects. Although defense-related research can have commercial benefits, some have questioned its efficiency in generating commercially viable products—in comparison to resources targeted specifically for commercial research purposes.

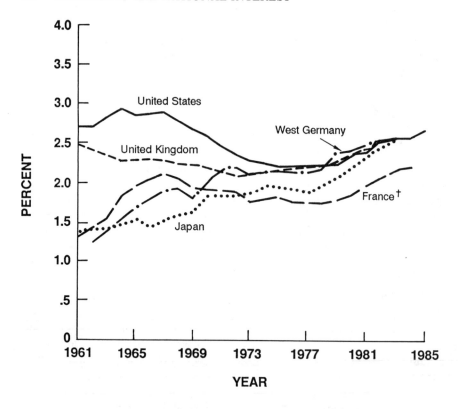

*Gross expenditures for performance of research and develop-
ment including associated capital expenditures (except for the
United States, where total capital expenditure data are not
available). Estimates for the period 1972–80 show that the
inclusion of capital expenditures for the United States would
have an impact of less than one-tenth of one percent for each
year.

†Gross domestic product.

SOURCE: Science Indicators--1985.

FIGURE 3-3   National expenditures for performance of R&D* as a percent of GNP by
country.

Another indication of the long-term commitment by these countries to
enhance their technical capability is their increasing employment of
scientists and engineers. Although the United States still employs the
highest proportion of technical professionals in the Western labor force,
Japan, West Germany, France, and the United Kingdom have all moved
to close this gap as shown in Figure 3-5.

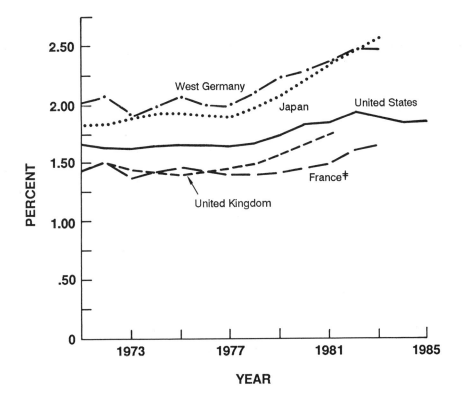

*Gross expenditures for performance of research and develop-
ment including associated capital expenditures (except for the
United States, where total capital expenditure data are not
available). Estimates for the period 1972–80 show that the
inclusion of capital expenditures for the United States would
have an impact of less than one-tenth of one percent for each
year.

[†]National expenditure excluding government funds for defense
R&D.

[‡]Gross domestic product.

SOURCE: Science Indicators—1985.

FIGURE 3-4   Estimated ratios of nondefense R&D* expenditures[†] to GNP for selected
countries.

One indirect measure of the growing technical competence of the
Europeans and the Japanese can be found in patent applications.
(Although patent applications are not an exact proxy for a nation's
technical capability and inventiveness, they do provide a measure of

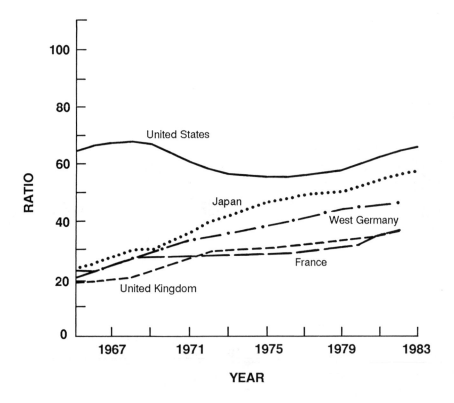

*Includes all scientists and engineers on a full–time equivalent basis (except for Japan whose data include persons primarily employed in R&D).

SOURCE: Science Indicators--1985.

FIGURE 3-5   Scientists and engineers* engaged in research and development per 10,000 labor force population by country.

relative change.) Between 1965 and 1984 the number of U.S. patents granted to U.S. inventors remained relatively constant while the number of U.S. patents granted to foreign inventors nearly tripled. As shown in Figure 3-6 there has also been a sharp decline in the number of U.S. citizens applying for patent protection from foreign governments.

A more concrete assessment of the growing competition faced by the United States is gained from a review of specific technologies. The following case examples help illustrate the tenuous nature of U.S. dominance in several high-technology fields.

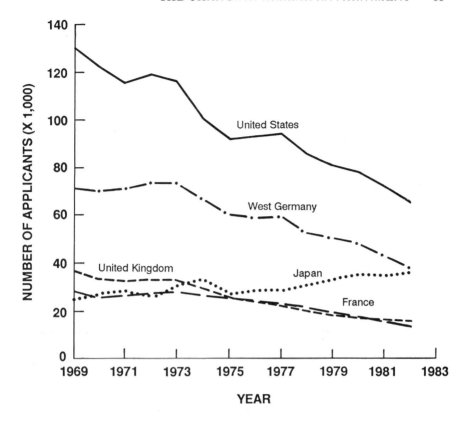

SOURCE: Science Indicators--1985.

FIGURE 3-6   External patent applications by residents of selected countries.

• *Semiconductors:* The United States no longer has the lead in several important areas of semiconductor technology. Japan has an emerging leadership role in metal-oxide semiconductor (MOS) high-density computer memories with well over 50 percent of the world market. Japanese firms are reputed to be leading most U.S. merchant* semiconductor companies in developing reliable, low-cost, 1-megabyte dynamic random access memory (D-RAM) chips and in the early development of 4-megabyte designs. And Japanese companies now are the only source of the highest-quality fused quartz glass required for mass-producing state-

---

Merchant refers to companies that sell their products on the open market—as opposed to producing only for internal consumption (e.g., IBM).

of-the-art chips of all types. Japan also rivals U.S. capability in semiconductor production equipment technology. The erosion of traditional U.S. dominance of semiconductor technology has occurred almost entirely within the last 5 to 10 years.[5]

• *Fiber optics:* Japan is acknowledged to have gained a clear lead in light source technology, one of the main components of fiber optic systems. In addition, Japan is credited with a lead in fiber optic applications and is competitive with the United States in other component technologies.[6]

• *Space:* The U.S. lead in space relative to the European countries is decreasing. The European Space Agency (ESA) has developed civilian unmanned space launch capability, ending NASA's near monopoly. And even before the U.S. space shuttle disaster in January 1986, French economic policies and subsidies had allowed its space agency to take business from NASA. U.S. dominance of satellite production, an area that has enjoyed a long-term advantage due to the tie-in with U.S. launches, is also expected to decline.[7]

• *Aircraft:* U.S. industry traditionally has dominated the world market for civilian aircraft, holding 95 percent of the world's orders for airliners through the mid-1970s. In 1975 related U.S. R&D expenditures began to decline; European expenditures, however, were growing through Airbus Industries, a European consortium designed to challenge U.S. producers. Between 1980 and 1985 Airbus captured 17 percent of the world market.[8]

• *Computer hardware and software:* Although the United States retains broad leadership in computer hardware and software production, the Japanese now match or exceed the capabilities of U.S. producers in important subsectors such as large-scale processors and magnetic disk storage. In addition the Japanese joint government-industry R&D program is attempting to leapfrog U.S. industry with the development of the so-called "fifth generation" computer system.[9]

• *Other areas:* U.S. foreign competitors also have demonstrated success in biotechnology, robotics, and machine tools and in the development of important new materials such as high-performance ceramics.[10]

In reviewing these examples, it is important to keep in mind two important points: (1) the relative decline in U.S. dominance is an expected result of the economic recovery of countries whose industrial capability was destroyed or severely damaged in World War II; and (2) the countries making the most progress in developing or improving their capability are U.S. allies. Although their progress serves to enhance the overall strength of the Western military alliance, it also underscores the vital need to increase the degree to which export controls are implemented through a multilateral system.

The growing challenges to U.S. industrial dominance must be considered carefully by those responsible for U.S. export control policy. If goods comparable to controlled U.S. products are available with little or no control from foreign sources, then a clear incentive exists for buyers to seek those sources. The trend toward non-U.S. sourcing or "de-Americanization" is already evident in Europe. During its European study mission, the panel heard repeatedly from representatives in every country it visited[11] that some of their companies were in the process of switching to non-U.S. sources for items controlled by the United States; in areas in which no non-U.S. source exists, many of these companies are making efforts to develop them. These actions stem not only from concerns about the additional costs and delays imposed by U.S. export controls but even more importantly from a view that the United States is not a reliable supplier—a fear that was given credence by U.S. efforts to control gas and oil equipment in recent years in the face of strenuous opposition by our allies.

In assessing the scope and gravity of the problem of non-U.S. sourcing, an important additional consideration is the long-term consequences of such changes in suppliers. Customers that buy equipment incompatible with U.S. systems may be locked into buying add-on items and spare parts from non-U.S. sources for years after their original purchase. Although this pattern has worked to the advantage of the United States in the past, once non-U.S. sources have been identified, it will be difficult for the United States to regain lost customers in the future.

Any benefits (in terms of enhanced protection of an item from acquisition by the Soviet bloc) that might be derived from more stringent unilateral controls on U.S. products and technology are attainable only in the shrinking number of cases in which the United States is the sole source. In technology areas in which there are non-U.S. sources with less stringent controls, no additional protection is provided and the disadvantages imposed on U.S. goods and technology have no countervailing benefits.

Non-CoCom Countries

Indigenous technical expertise challenging that of the United States also comes from non-CoCom industrialized countries such as Switzerland, Austria, and Sweden (see also Appendix B). U.S. and CoCom export control policies that do not require assurances from such countries that comparable indigenously produced products or technical data also are denied to our adversaries will weaken the CoCom countries and thereby the NATO alliance.

Newly Industrializing Countries

Newly industrializing countries (NICs) such as South Korea, Taiwan, and Brazil have become important world suppliers of manufactured goods in the last 20 years. (For example, the value of manufactured goods exported from South Korea rose by a factor of 200 between 1965 and 1983.) Currently, a large share of these exports are traditional manufactures (e.g., footwear and textiles); but the share of high-technology items, such as computer and communications equipment, is growing. In 1985, 17 percent of the high-technology products imported by the United States came from the East Asian NICs (Hong Kong, Singapore, South Korea, and Taiwan) as shown in Figure 3-7. Due to the presence of foreign-owned multinational corporations, some of the NICs are now producing, in large volumes, items with technical specifications similar to those of

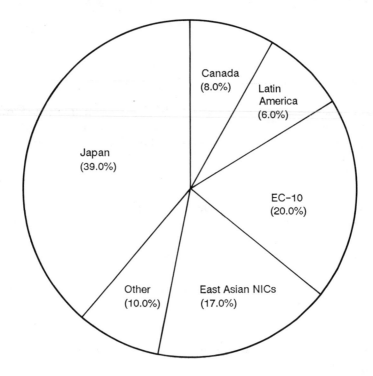

*U.S. Department of Commerce DOC-3 definition.

SOURCES: U.S. Department of Commerce, Bureau of the Census.

FIGURE 3-7 Suppliers of U.S. high-tech* imports, 1985 (domestic and foreign exports, f.a.s.; general imports, c.i.f.).

CoCom-controlled items (such as high-density memory chips and 16-bit microprocessors). They also are committed to developing more advanced indigenous capabilities.

The ability to produce high-technology goods does not necessarily imply that a country possesses the indigenous capability to develop them. Many of the NICs are aware of this fact and are aggressively pursuing greater indigenous technological sophistication. A variety of policies are used to encourage development of indigenous capability:

- requiring multinational companies located in the country to train local employees;
- sending large numbers of students to foreign countries for technical education;
- hiring foreign scientists and engineers;
- licensing production technology with the condition that the company supplying the technology buy back a portion of the output;
- sponsoring domestic research centers to encourage indigenous talent; and
- protecting infant industries.

Industrializing countries vary in their willingness to comply with controls on militarily critical technology. Countries like South Korea and Taiwan—with their close political and economic relationships with CoCom countries—are more likely to cooperate with CoCom's export control policies than are countries less dependent on CoCom such as Brazil and India.

The U.S. government currently is negotiating bilateral export control agreements with several non-CoCom countries. Although the need for such agreements is evident, there is a clear danger associated with an exclusively bilateral approach. An agreement with a non-CoCom country that puts controls on U.S.-origin goods and technical data without controlling them from indigenous or other non-U.S. sources puts U.S. firms at a serious competitive disadvantage. Such a situation is likely to lead to the loss of U.S. sales without enhancing the protection of the technology in question. Agreements with non-CoCom countries would result in more effective control—with less risk to U.S. business—if they were pursued in cooperation with other CoCom countries. Moreover, to be truly effective, any such agreements should also encompass indigenously produced goods and technology.

The changing character of the global economic and technological environment discussed in this chapter has at least one clear implication: Effective control of technology must be pursued in a consistent, multilateral fashion. To the extent that the U.S. control system, discussed in the next chapter, fails to adjust to these changes in the global environment and to consider their implications, it will continue to work to the disadvantage of U.S. exporters and multinational subsidiaries with only modest offsetting national security advantages.

NOTES

1. The various statistics in this chapter are drawn almost entirely from the following sources:

   Richard N. Cooper, "Growing American Interdependence: An Overview" (Paper prepared for a conference at the Federal Reserve Bank of St. Louis, October 1985).

   Charles H. Ferguson, "High Technology Product Life Cycles, Export Controls, and International Markets" (Paper prepared for the National Academy of Sciences Panel on the Impact of National Security Controls on International Technology Transfer, June 1986).

   Lionel H. Olmer, *U.S. Manufacturing at a Crossroads— Surviving and Prospering in a More Competitive Global Economy* (Washington, D.C.: U.S. Department of Commerce, International Trade Administration, 1985).

   U.S. Department of Commerce, Bureau of the Census, *Highlights of U.S. Export-Import Trade*, FT-990 series (Washington, D.C.).

   U.S. Department of Commerce, Bureau of Economic Analysis, *Survey of Current Business* (Washington, D.C., April 1986).

   U.S. Department of Commerce, International Trade Administration, *An Assessment of U.S. Competitiveness in High Technology Industries* (Washington, D.C., February 1983).

   U.S. Department of Commerce, International Trade Administration, Office of Trade and Investment Analysis, *The Rising Trading Power of the East Asian NICs* (Washington, D.C., October 1985).

   U.S. Department of Commerce, International Trade Administration, *U.S. High Technology Trade and Competitiveness* (Washington, D.C., February 1985).

   U.S. Department of Commerce, International Trade Administration, *United States Trade—Performance in 1984 and Outlook* (Washington, D.C., June 1985).

   U.S. Department of Commerce, International Trade Administration, *United States Trade—Performance in 1985 and Outlook* (forthcoming).

2. See, for example, the Committee on Electronic Components, Board on Army Science and Technology, National Research Council, *Foreign Production of Electronic Components and Army Systems Vulnerabilities* (Washington, D.C.: National Academy Press, 1986), which was prepared for the Department of Defense.

3. William F. Finan, Perry D. Quick, and Karen M. Sandberg (Quick, Finan & Associates, Inc.), "The U.S. Trade Position in High Technology: 1980-1986" (Report prepared for the Joint Economic Committee of the U.S. Congress, October 1986).

4. High-technology trade in this report is defined by U.S. Department of Commerce definition DOC-3, which is based on R&D expenditures as a percentage of shipments. Standard industrial classification (SIC) categories included in this definition are: industrial inorganic chemicals (281); plastic materials and synthetic resins, synthetic rubber, and synthetic and other manmade fibers except glass (282); drugs (283); ordnance and accessories except vehicles and guided missiles (348); engines and turbines (351); office, computing, and accounting machines (357); radio and television receiving equipment except communication types (365); communication equipment (366); electronic components and accessories (367); aircraft and parts (372); guided

missiles and space vehicles and parts (376); measuring, analyzing, and controlling instruments; photographic, medical, and optical goods; watches; and clocks (38)—except instruments for measuring and testing of electricity and electrical signals (3825). The trade figures shown in this chapter were calculated using the DOC-3 definition.

5. National Materials Advisory Board, National Research Council, *Advanced Processing of Electronic Materials in the United States and Japan* (Washington, D.C.: National Academy Press, 1986); Ferguson, "High Technology Product Life Cycles"; U.S. Department of Commerce, International Trade Administration, *An Assessment of U.S. Competitiveness*; Committee on Electronic Components, Board on Army Science and Technology, National Research Council, *Foreign Production of Electronic Components*.

6. U.S. Department of Commerce, International Trade Administration, *An Assessment of U.S. Competitiveness*; personal conversation with staff of the Department of Commerce, International Trade Administration, Office of Telecommunications.

7. U.S. Department of Commerce, International Trade Administration, *An Assessment of U.S. Competitiveness*.

8. U.S. Department of Commerce, International Trade Administration, *An Assessment of U.S. Competitiveness*; personal communication with staff of the Department of Commerce, International Trade Administration, Office of Trade Development, Office of Aerospace.

9. Ferguson, "High Technology Product Life Cycles"; U.S. Department of Commerce, International Trade Administration, *An Assessment of U.S. Competitiveness;* Committee on Electronic Components, Board on Army Science and Technology, National Research Council, *Foreign Production of Electronic Components*.

10. Ferguson, "High Technology Product Life Cycles"; U.S. Department of Commerce, International Trade Administration, *An Assessment of U.S. Competitiveness;* Committee on Electronic Components, Board on Army Science and Technology, National Research Council, *Foreign Production of Electronic Components*.

11. Delegations of panel and staff members visited Austria, Belgium, the Federal Republic of Germany, France, Sweden, and the United Kingdom.

4

The Dimensions of National Security Export Controls

Two laws provide the primary mandate for U.S. national security export controls. The Arms Export Control Act of 1976[1] requires government approval for the import and export of military weaponry and services. The Export Administration Act (EAA) of 1979, as amended,[2] controls the export of commercial goods and technologies that would make a significant contribution to the military capabilities of a potential adversary. EAA also authorizes controls to serve U.S. foreign policy goals and to ensure the domestic availability of resources in short supply.

The regulations implementing these laws are extensive and complex. The United States asserts jurisdiction over goods and technology even outside the territorial United States when: (1) the product or technology in question originated in or is to be or has been exported from the United States; (2) the product or technology incorporates or uses products or technology of U.S. origin; and (3) the exporter is a U.S. national or is owned or controlled by U.S. interests. Responsibility for administering the export control system is divided among many federal departments and agencies as is representation in the export control policymaking process.

To some degree, U.S. export controls parallel multilateral or bilateral agreements or understandings with other countries. The United States is a founding member of the Coordinating Committee on Multilateral Export Controls (CoCom), an informal, nontreaty organization comprising all the NATO countries (except Iceland) and Japan.[3] Created in 1949 in the early days of the Cold War, CoCom administers a uniform system of multilateral controls over three categories of products: munitions, nuclear energy, and dual use. All products subject to CoCom control are also subject to U.S. controls. In addition the United States has bilateral agreements or arrangements with a number of non-CoCom nations that provide for varying degrees of cooperation on national security export controls. These countries include Australia, New Zealand, Austria, Switzerland, and Sweden.

This chapter presents an overview of the dimensions of the current national security export control system. It first summarizes the evolution of export controls in the United States to provide a historical context. Next, it examines the mechanisms used by the United States for policymaking and administration. Finally, it reviews the multilateral CoCom framework for controlling strategic goods and technologies and key attributes of the controls maintained by several other nations.

HISTORICAL BACKGROUND

Current controls on the export of commercial dual use products and technologies have their roots in the period leading up to World War II. To understand more fully the current efforts of the United States to impede the flow of these products and technologies to potential adversaries, it is useful to review the evolution of export controls and the historical circumstances that have shaped them.

World War II Origins and the Early Postwar Years

Before 1940 the United States had no legal mechanism for controlling peacetime exports of militarily significant products or information to potential enemies.[4] Consequently, despite the growing military threat posed by fascism and militarism in the late 1930s, there were no legal constraints on exports, and U.S. firms were free to sell almost anything to Germany, Italy, or Japan virtually until the outbreak of hostilities. Japan's military industry in particular seems to have benefited to a considerable degree from free access to technology, strategic materials, and capital from the United States.[5]

By 1940, however, the war had begun in Europe, and Congress moved to give the President authority to control the export of militarily significant goods and technology. Section 6 of Public Law 703 (July 2, 1940 [54 Stat. 714]) gave the President authority to prohibit or curtail the export of "military equipment or munitions or component parts thereof, or machinery, tools, or material, or supplies necessary for the manufacture, servicing, or operation thereof. . . ." The President was required only to determine that his actions were necessary in the interest of national defense and to issue a proclamation describing the articles or materials included in the prohibition or curtailment.

The export control authority provided by the 1940 law originally was intended to expire in only 2 years. But by 1942 the United States was at war, and Congress extended the authority. It was extended again in 1945, in 1946, and in 1947 with only minor revisions. A reading of the hearings accompanying these extensions, together with the fact that each extension was of such limited duration, suggests that Congress regarded export controls as merely a temporary restriction on U.S. trade made necessary by the war. But by 1949, when export controls again came up for renewal, Congress was weighing a somewhat different set of factors in its export control policy equation.

The Export Control Act of 1949 and the Establishment of CoCom

In considering the export control issue in the increasingly tense West-East atmosphere of the late 1940s, Congress sought to avoid the mistakes of the period leading up to World War II; primary among these was providing potential enemies with the wherewithal to make war. By 1949 it was apparent that the Soviet Union and its allies, including the People's Republic of China (PRC), were potential military adversaries. Thus, the lesson of prewar U.S. trade with Japan—trade that had increased that country's military effectiveness—entered into the debate on export controls. Although shortages still played an important role in justifying the continuation of export controls, the 1949 debates included for the first time explicit references to the behavior of the Soviet Union in Eastern Europe and reminders that uncontrolled exports to Japan before the war were "subsequently used against our own people."[6]

When the export control question came to a vote, Congress elected to perpetuate the extraordinary wartime powers extended to the executive branch and to maintain the strict export control regime that had evolved during the war. The new authority, the Export Control Act of 1949, codified the export control procedures that were then being practiced by the executive branch under the terms of the 1940 act (and its subsequent extensions). Two important principles embodied in this legislation have survived the three major, subsequent revisions of the law (1969, 1979, and 1985): (1) the executive branch has broad authority to determine what products or technical data should be subject to export licensing, to administer the licensing system, and to impose penalties for violations; and (2) the rule-making process, including those procedures that apply to the composition of the Control List (of items subject to licensing), is exempt from the usual provisions for public participation and is less likely to be the subject of judicial review.[7] Thus, the export control authority exercised by the executive branch today is substantially unchanged in its basic legal structure from that originally granted by Congress in 1940 as an extraordinary war power.

The renewed international tensions that contributed to Congress' decision to maintain what were essentially wartime export controls also led, in 1949, to the founding of NATO and the other regional treaty organizations. To ensure the effectiveness of NATO and the other regional alliances, the United States transferred military technology (mostly in the form of hardware) directly to its allies. In addition, as Western Europe and Japan recovered from the war, they began to revitalize their industrial capabilities and to challenge what had been virtually a U.S. monopoly on advanced technology (see Chapter 3).

To prevent such technology from reaching the hands of potential adversaries, it became necessary to establish a mechanism to coordinate allied export control policies. That mechanism, which was created in 1949, was the Coordinating Committee on Multilateral Export Controls, or CoCom. From the start, however, the items on which the United States imposed controls differed from those controlled by CoCom: In addition to those items that all CoCom members agreed to control, the United States controlled many items unilaterally. The vast majority of these pertained to areas in which the United States held a virtual monopoly.

To prevent the flow of controlled U.S. technology and information from third (non-CoCom) countries to the Communist world, the United States also imposed controls on the reexport of U.S.-origin goods, controls that were accepted because the United States at that time was the only source of many advanced technology-based products. Furthermore, countries that were the beneficiaries of the Marshall Plan and other U.S. government programs and that were dependent on the United States for their security were not inclined to challenge U.S. export controls.

As with the previous export control acts, the Export Control Act of 1949 was originally scheduled to expire in just a few years, this time in 1953. That it was necessary to extend and strengthen the act repeatedly throughout the next two decades was due not only to continued tense relations with the Soviet Union but also to a fundamental change in the U.S. military posture and strategy in the decade following World War II. The United States and its allies chose to abandon the successful wartime strategy of being prepared to outproduce the adversary and began under the NATO doctrine to rely on superior military technology to offset the numerical advantages achieved by the Soviet military in the postwar decades.

The New Role of Science and Technology in Postwar U.S. Defense Strategy

From the start of the postwar era, U.S. military planners understood that they could not achieve the goal of maintaining military superiority solely with narrowly defined engineering research aimed at meeting a specific military requirement. Before them was the example of the development of atomic weapons—a graphic demonstration that highly speculative ideas at the frontiers of basic research could become militarily decisive in a very short period of time. The lesson inherent in the Manhattan Project was that the U.S. government, in a departure from prewar policy, should continue to promote the early development of technologies with possible military application. Thus, the United States perpetuated parts of the research system that had been created during the war and expanded the role of federal laboratories in the early postwar years. The government also expanded the role of the military services in supporting science and engineering research at both government and private laboratories.

In the 1950s Congress broadened federal research support still further. At the beginning of the decade, it established the National Science Foundation as a source of federal funding for scientific research that was not directed at a specific military or other previously defined national objective. In the late 1950s the coming of the space race resulted in the founding of NASA*; it also provided the impetus for the creation of federal programs to enhance scientific and technical education, which was considered to be a vital part of the infrastructure necessary to support military programs. In the 1960s and 1970s federal support of research and development continued; programs included funding directed toward solving key national environmental, energy, health, and economic problems. Thus, federal support of research and development—a governmental role that originated during the postwar era as a military necessity—ultimately evolved into a permanent recognition of the importance of science and technology to broader national interests.

Detente and the Export Administration Act of 1969

When export control legislation again came up for renewal in 1969, the mood of Congress and of the nation was far different from what it had been at the time of the previous reauthorizations. Detente was the

---

*NASA incorporated the National Advisory Committee for Aeronautics, an aeronautical research agency established in 1914.

operative principle, and there were calls in Congress for a relaxation of West-East trade restrictions. According to Henry Kissinger, even as the debate over the renewal of export controls went on in Congress, the National Security Council issued a directive: The list of items controlled by the United States should be brought in line with the less extensive CoCom list, except for those items over which the United States held a monopoly.[8]

In the legislation Congress finally adopted, the substitution of "administration" for "control" in the title of the 1969 Export Administration Act reflected the political mood of the time and implied a far more liberal export control policy than was embodied in the previous acts. The act included language advocating expanded trade with the Soviet Union and Eastern Europe, recognized the economic cost of excessive controls, and required the executive branch to provide Congress with explicit justification for the continued control of products and technical data available to potential enemies from suppliers outside the United States. Believing, however, that improved Soviet attitudes on other issues should be a quid pro quo for improved trade relations, President Nixon blocked a number of efforts made by the Department of Commerce to reduce the number of items controlled for export to the Soviet bloc. Nevertheless, the atmosphere of detente ultimately did bring some relaxation, albeit only briefly, in the U.S. export control regime. The United States and its allies approved the export of major automotive and semiconductor manufacturing facilities to the Soviet Union, and U.S. companies sold to the Soviets some highly advanced machine tools, computers, and communications equipment.

During this same period there were shifts in the economies of the Western nations that significantly changed the dynamics of export controls. Most important was that for many areas of advanced technology the civil sector began to lead the military, and sophisticated dual use items increased in relative importance in international trade. As a result, export controls reached an ever-growing share of U.S. commercial exports.

U.S. NATIONAL SECURITY EXPORT CONTROLS

Figures 4-1 and 4-2 illustrate the structure of current U.S. national security export controls. The complexity illustrated by these figures is partly a function of the multifaceted task of controlling the exports of militarily significant products and technology and partly a result of the long evolution of U.S. controls as described above. Although the enabling legislation has been amended many times, there has never been a complete overhaul of the controls or of the list of controlled items since the system was initiated in the days preceding World War II.

76

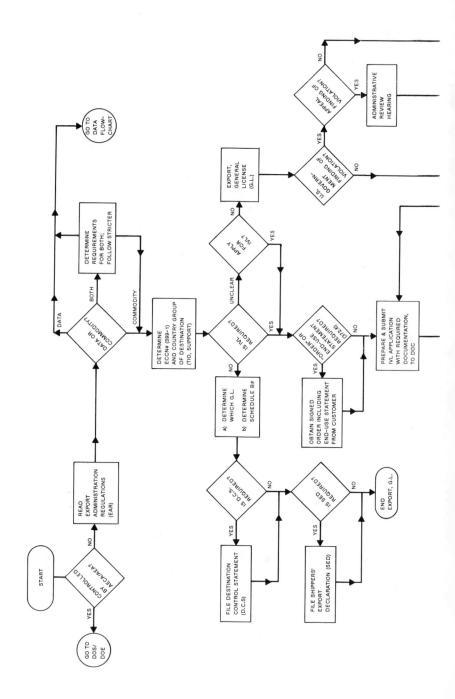

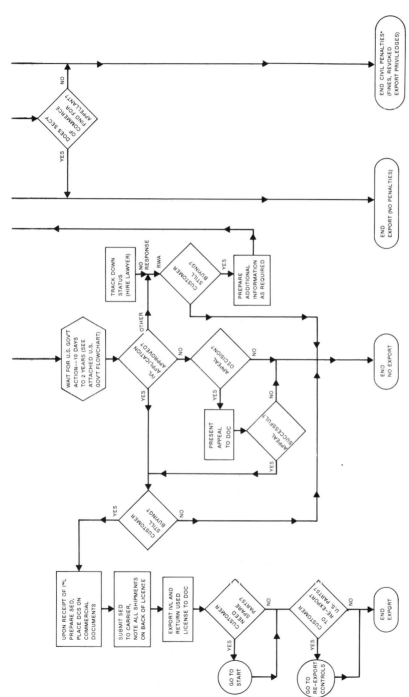

FIGURE 4-1 Exporters' individual validated license (IVL) flowchart.

THIS CHART IS FOR ILLUSTRATIVE PURPOSES ONLY AND IS BASED ON THE BEST INFORMATION AVAILABLE TO THE PANEL AT THE TIME OF PUBLICATION. CHARACTERISTICS OF SOME INFORMAL REVIEW MECHANISMS SHOULD BE CONSIDERED SUBJECTIVE. NOT TO BE USED AS A SUBSTITUTE FOR CAREFUL READING OF EXPORT ADMINISTRATION REGULATIONS (EAR).

*INTENTIONAL VIOLATIONS ALSO PUNISHABLE BY IMPRISONMENT.

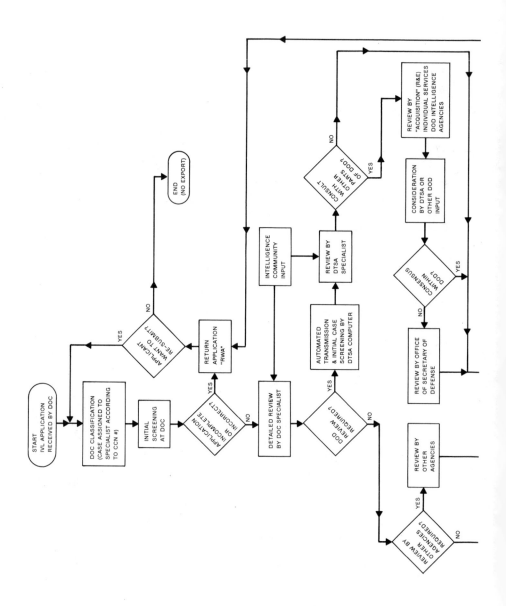

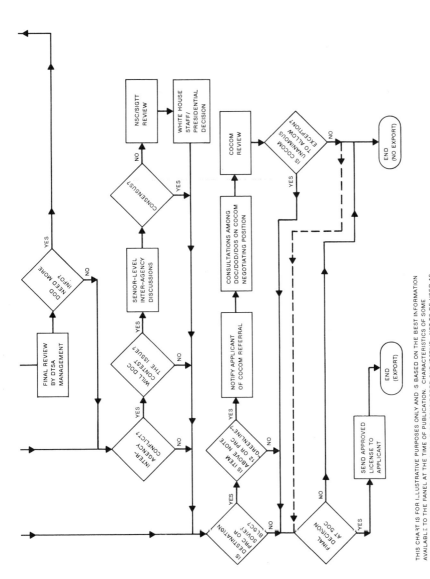

FIGURE 4-2 U.S. government IVL review flowchart.

THIS CHART IS FOR ILLUSTRATIVE PURPOSES ONLY AND IS BASED ON THE BEST INFORMATION AVAILABLE TO THE PANEL AT THE TIME OF PUBLICATION. CHARACTERISTICS OF SOME INFORMAL REVIEW MECHANISMS SHOULD BE CONSIDERED SUBJECTIVE. NOT TO BE USED AS A SUBSTITUTE FOR CAREFUL READING OF EXPORT ADMINISTRATION REGULATIONS (EAR).

Controls on Munitions

Under the 1976 revision of the Arms Export Control Act, the U.S. government strictly controls the import and export of defense articles (arms, ammunition, and implements of war), defense services, and directly related technical data. The International Traffic in Arms Regulations (ITAR)[9] implement the law; the Office of Munitions Control (OMC) in the Department of State administers the regulations. Through its role as adviser to OMC, the Department of Defense is largely responsible for determining the defense items to be controlled.

ITAR defines a defense article as any item specifically designated on the U.S. Munitions List, which is part of ITAR. Defense service means "the furnishing of assistance, including training, to foreign persons in the design, engineering, development, production, processing, manufacture, use, operation, overhaul, repair, maintenance, modification, or reconstruction of defense articles."[10] If an article or service is on the Munitions List, ITAR regulates its export and reexport exclusively. To supplement the published Munitions List, OMC determines on written request whether particular articles or services are controlled by ITAR or whether they are subject to the Commerce Department's controls on dual use items.

Before an article or a service subject to ITAR can be exported, OMC, with DoD advice, must formally approve the transaction. No approvals are granted for exports or reexports to actual or potential adversaries. And unlike the Commerce Department's Export Administration Regulations (see below), there are no general licenses or "bulk" validated licenses covering multiple transactions. The written approval of the State Department also must be obtained before an end user abroad may resell or dispose of an ITAR-controlled item to another party in his country or in any other nation.

Most other Western nations maintain similar controls on the import and export of munitions. And, as noted earlier, CoCom also maintains a munitions list specifying the items that all its member countries control. For most nations, including the United States, munitions controls are relatively straightforward. The control system for dual use products and technologies is more complex.

Controls on Dual Use Products and Technologies

The Export Administration Act (EAA) of 1979, as amended, authorizes the control of exports of commercial goods and technologies that would make a significant contribution to the military capabilities of a potential adversary. It also authorizes controls to achieve U.S. foreign policy goals and to ensure the domestic availability of resources in short supply. Most export controls imposed under EAA for national security reasons have been agreed to multilaterally within CoCom. Although these national security controls are directed primarily at the Soviet Union and its Warsaw Pact allies, the control scheme regulates exports to many other nations because of concern about possible diversions or uses that might be detrimental to U.S. security or to the security of U.S. allies or other friendly nations.

Export Administration, which is an element of the International Trade Administration of the Department of Commerce, administers these controls over U.S. exports and over reexports of U.S.-origin commodities from foreign countries. The extensive, complex instrument that provides the framework for this control is the Export Administration Regulations (EAR),[11] which Export Administration publishes and updates frequently. Products and technical data are addressed separately in the regulations, a division paralleled in this report.

DUAL USE PRODUCTS

A major EAR component is a list (i.e., the U.S. Control List) specifying the characteristics of each commodity subject to control. The current list of 128 pages contains 240 entries divided into 10 categories:

- Metal-working machinery
- Chemical and petroleum equipment
- Electrical and power-generating equipment
- General industrial equipment
- Transportation equipment
- Electronics and precision equipment
- Metals, minerals, and their manufactures
- Chemicals, metalloids, petroleum products, and related materials
- Rubber and rubber products
- Miscellaneous

The entries or commodity classification descriptions range from the very specific (e.g., "pulse modulators capable of providing electric impulses of peak power exceeding 20 MW or of a duration of less than 0.1 microsecond, or with a duty cycle in excess of 0.005. . . .") to the very general* (e.g., "other electronic and precision instruments, including

---

*These very general or "basket" categories serve to "catch" new products with important characteristics not yet reflected on the U.S. Control List. They also ensure that no exports are made to certain countries such as Cuba, North Korea, Kampuchea, and Vietnam without specific U.S. government approval.

photographic equipment and film, n.e.s. [not elsewhere specified], and parts and accessories, n.e.s.'').

The commodity classifications have different broad levels of restrictions, which depend on the military importance of items in that category, the ultimate country of destination, and in some cases the dollar value of the proposed shipment. For control purposes, Export Administration separates the nations of the world, except Canada, into country groups (see Figure 4-3, pp. 84–85). Of particular importance with regard to national security export controls are country groups W (Hungary and Poland), Y (other Eastern European nations and the USSR), and Z (North Korea, Vietnam, Cambodia, and Cuba).

Canada does not fall into any country group and is the only destination for which licenses for most U.S. exports are not required. The Hyde Park Declaration of 1941, negotiated by President Franklin D. Roosevelt and Prime Minister Mackenzie King along with an Exchange of Notes in 1945, began a course of collaboration between the two countries relating to hemispheric defense. As a result, Canada and the United States have eliminated licensing in either direction for all exports except a few nuclear-related, communications countermeasures, and short-supply items. This unique relationship does not apply to any other U.S. ally.

To export products, U.S. firms must use a general license or obtain a validated license (see Figure 4-4). Moreover, if reexport approvals are not authorized by EAR or the terms of a validated export license, U.S. exporters must obtain them if, prior to the time of shipment, they know or have reason to believe that the person or firm receiving the item will reexport it to another destination. The complexity of the system becomes apparent in considering the types of licenses that may be required for an export.

GENERAL LICENSES

A general license authorizes the export of certain products on the EAR control list that have been approved in advance by Export Administration for shipment. (An exporter must determine that certain conditions are met but need not apply to the government for permission.) These products have been so identified because of their low sensitivity, minimal value, country of destination, or other elements of control. G-DEST, a general license available for shipments of products to destinations not requiring a validated license, is the most commonly used general license; but there are also 17 other general licenses available for such circumstances as shipments of limited value, temporary exports, the return of products to countries from which they were imported, and the replacement of defective parts.

To reduce the volume of formal license applications and the need for specific approvals, the Export Administration Amendments Act (EAAA) of 1985[12] created a special type of general license available to CoCom member nations for goods that would ordinarily require a validated license to non-CoCom destinations. General license G-COM covers shipments of less-sensitive controlled items to CoCom member nations. "Less-sensitive items" are items on the CoCom control list that a member country, at its discretion, may approve for shipment to proscribed destinations.

In 1986 Export Administration proposed to establish general license G-CEU (certified end user),[13] which would authorize exports of most products that ordinarily require validated licenses to precertified foreign end users located in CoCom member nations. Upon application to the Department of Commerce, certification would be provided to foreign firms that consistently demonstrate and maintain compliance with U.S. export and reexport control regulations. A certified end user would be required to use and retain the commodities obtained under G-CEU at its own facilities or dispose of them only to other certified end users. Any other disposition would require prior individual authorization.

VALIDATED LICENSES

A validated license grants limited permission to make exports, either on a single- or a multiple-transaction basis. Validated licenses are also used to authorize the reexport of U.S.-origin commodities under certain circumstances to new destinations abroad. U.S. exporters of products that do not qualify for shipment under a general license must apply to Export Administration for a validated license.

Exporters most often use two types of validated licenses—individual and distribution. A typical individual validated license authorizes the export of a specified quantity of products during a 2-year period to a single recipient. A distribution license, which is also a 2-year authorization, permits an approved U.S. exporter to ship unlimited quantities of specified commodities to approved distributors or customers in Free World countries. With a distribution license a U.S. firm can ship its controlled products to foreign distributors; the distributors are then permitted to resell the products to responsible parties within their approved sales territories without obtaining individual approvals for each sale. Other types of multiple or bulk approvals include project licenses, which authorize the export of products for up to 1 year for use in specific projects (such as building, equipping, and/or supplying a manufacturing facility); and service supply licenses, which authorize the export of spare and replacement parts for servicing equipment abroad.

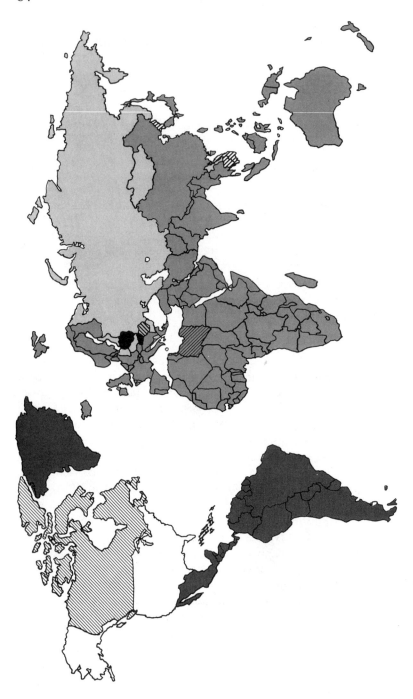

85

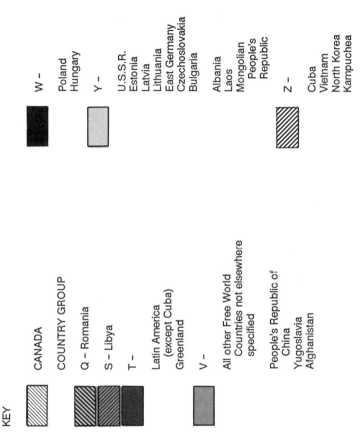

KEY

CANADA

COUNTRY GROUP

Q – Romania

S – Libya

T –

Latin America
(except Cuba)
Greenland

V –

All other Free World
Countries not elsewhere
specified

People's Republic of
China
Yugoslavia
Afghanistan

W –

Poland
Hungary

Y –

U.S.S.R.
Estonia
Latvia
Lithuania
East Germany
Czechoslovakia
Bulgaria

Z –

Albania
Laos
Mongolian
People's
Republic

Cuba
Vietnam
North Korea
Kampuchea

FIGURE 4-3 Department of Commerce country groups.

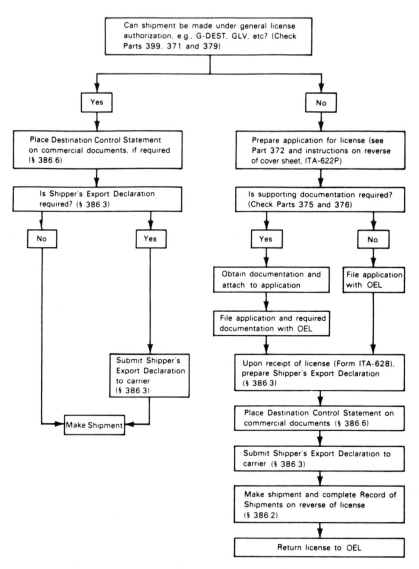

EXPORT CONTROL FLOW CHART—This is intended as a general guideline for exports of commodities under Department of Commerce jurisdiction. However, it is not comprehensive. You should review other parts of the Regulations, for example, for special commodity restrictions and special country restrictions. Also, you should consult the "Table of Denial Orders Currently in Effect" (see Supps. Nos. 1 & 2 to Part 388) to be sure your proposed export does not involve a party currently denied export privileges.

FIGURE 4-4   Export control flowchart.

To speed up the export licensing process, EAAA made a number of changes in the control regulations in addition to instituting the G-COM license. The amendments now require that individual validated license applications for most exports to CoCom nations either be rejected or approved automatically within 15 working days after filing—unless the applicant is notified that more time (not to exceed 15 additional working days) is required. At the end of the 15- (or 30-) working-day period, the export request must be rejected or it is deemed to be licensed even if no document or communication to that effect has been sent or received. In addition, EAAA amended Section 5(k) of the 1979 act to extend this automatic licensing procedure and the provisions of general license G-COM to exports to those non-CoCom nations that enter into agreements imposing export restrictions comparable to those agreed to within CoCom.

Applications for distribution licenses and other special licenses must be accompanied by extensive documentation and may require months to process for first-time applicants. Applications for exports to proscribed destinations including the Soviet bloc are subject to interagency review and may also require lengthy processing.

Controls on Technical Data

The regulations that govern exports of technical data are similar but not identical to those for exports of products. Separate EAR control procedures govern the export of technical data.

EAR defines *technical data* as "information of any kind that can be used, or adapted for use, in the design, production, manufacture, utilization, or reconstruction of articles or materials." The data can be tangible (a prototype, blueprint, or operating manual) or intangible (technical advice). Figure 4-5 is a flowchart of the procedures for controlling technical data.

An "export" of technical data is defined broadly to include not only the actual shipment or transmission of data out of the United States but also visual inspection by foreign nationals of U.S.-origin equipment and facilities, oral exchanges of information with foreigners in the United States or abroad, and the application to situations abroad of personal knowledge or technical experience acquired in the United States. Most technical data can be exported under one of two general licenses: GTDA (technical data available) or GTDR (technical data restricted).

General license GTDA principally covers technical data that have been made generally available to the public (i.e., released in readily available publications and at open conferences, lectures, trade shows, etc.). It also covers scientific and educational data "not directly and significantly related to design, production, or utilization in industrial pro-

88

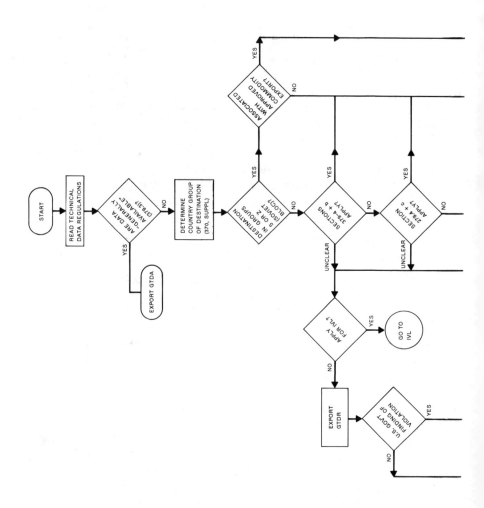

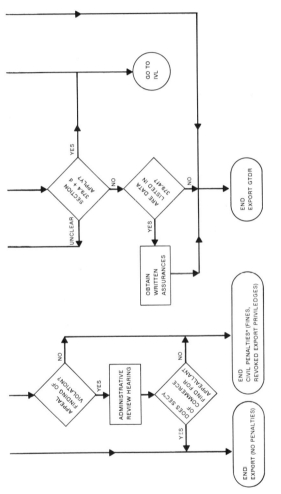

FIGURE 4-5 Technical data export flowchart.

*SECTIONS 379.4b, c, AND d DEFINE TYPES OF DATA THAT CANNOT BE EXPORTED UNDER GENERAL LICENSE GTDR TO THREE DIFFERENT CLASSES OF COUNTRY GROUPS.

*INTENTIONAL VIOLATIONS ALSO PUNISHABLE BY IMPRISONMENT.

THIS CHART IS FOR ILLUSTRATIVE PURPOSES ONLY AND IS BASED ON THE BEST INFORMATION AVAILABLE TO THE PANEL AT THE TIME OF PUBLICATION. CHARACTERISTICS OF SOME INFORMAL REVIEW MECHANISMS SHOULD BE CONSIDERED SUBJECTIVE. NOT TO BE USED AS A SUBSTITUTE FOR CAREFUL READING OF EXPORT ADMINISTRATION REGULATIONS (EAR).

cesses. . . ."[14] The license permits U.S. firms and individuals to disseminate these kinds of data to all destinations without requesting U.S. government approval.

U.S. companies export most proprietary technical data under general license GTDR. Like GTDA data, exports covered by this license do not require specific U.S. government approval; but for the most part they can only be sent to Free World destinations. Specific permission is required in the form of a validated license to export most nonpublic data to country groups S, Q, W, Y, and Z[15] and to the People's Republic of China. Before using the GTDR license for data related to products subject to CoCom control and certain other sensitive data categories, the exporter must receive written assurance from the foreign recipient of the data that the recipient will not reexport the data—and in many cases the direct products of the data—to proscribed destinations without the approval of the U.S. government. This requirement applies to the exchange of technical data between U.S. and foreign nationals,* whether that national resides overseas, is living in the United States, or is a visitor (e.g., at a U.S. university).

Certain more-sensitive technical data do not qualify for the GTDR license at all; these data relate to such areas as civil aircraft, airborne electronic direction-finding equipment, hydrofoil and hovercraft watercraft, and infrared-imaging equipment. To export such data to any destination (except Canada), an exporter must obtain a validated license. The export of some technical data, particularly nuclear-related, requires a validated license even to Canada.

Congress anticipated that certain products and technologies (both tangible and intangible) would be identified during the development of the Militarily Critical Technologies List (MCTL) as particularly "critical" and thus subject to more stringent licensing requirements. (Mandated originally by Congress, the MCTL is a document listing technologies that the Department of Defense considers to have present or future utility in military systems.) Accordingly, EAAA authorized the creation of a comprehensive operations license (COL) for such products and technical data. Although it has not yet been implemented and U.S. firms continue to use general license GTDR, this license is intended to be a technology counterpart to the distribution license available for commercial products. It would allow for multiple exchanges of technical data within a multinational company or network over a given period of time without the requirement for validated licenses for each transfer. The multinational

---

*A *foreign national* is any person who is not a citizen of the United States and who has not been lawfully admitted for permanent residence in the United States.

company or network would have to demonstrate an internal capability, which would be audited periodically by the Department of Commerce, to protect such exchanges. The license would be available only to demonstrably reliable U.S. exporters for use with eligible consignees in Free World countries with which they have ownership affiliations or long-term contractual relationships.

The export of technical data in patent applications is controlled by the Patent and Trademark Office (PTO) within the Department of Commerce and may be restricted through secrecy orders. Patent applications that must by definition contain sufficient detail to allow skilled readers to practice the invention may contain useful technical data that would otherwise be subject to validated licensing requirements under ITAR or EAR. In the United States, an application is published when the patent is issued; in most of the rest of the world, an application is published a year or two after filing, whether or not a patent ultimately will be issued. A secrecy order can be used to delay issuance of a U.S. patent and restrict the dissemination of technical data contained in the application. Secrecy orders are issued by the commissioner of patents at the request of a defense agency.

Under current law,[16] an inventor or his designee may file for patent protection on any invention in a foreign country—thus transferring or "exporting" technical data to that country in the application process—without requesting U.S. governmental approval if two conditions are met: (1) the U.S. application has been on file 6 months or longer, and (2) no patent secrecy order has been imposed. If the patent application has not been on file in the United States for at least 6 months, or if a secrecy order is in place, the inventor must obtain a license or permit from the Patent Office prior to the foreign filing. Thus, compliance with these rules permits an inventor to foreign-file a patent application without applying to the appropriate U.S. licensing agency (the State Department, for an export license under ITAR, or the Commerce Department, for a license under EAR).

There are now three types of secrecy orders. One of these is specifically available to PTO when the Department of Defense determines that unclassified technical data in a patent application should be subject to export controls.[17] This order permits disclosure of the data for business purposes to U.S. nationals within the United States and authorizes the filing of foreign applications in Canada, Australia, and most of Europe—but not in Japan or in any newly industrializing or developing nation where there are no applicable patent secrecy provisions. The order further authorizes both selling or producing products for the commercial domestic marketplace based on the innovation contained in the application and sales abroad—provided an appropriate export license is obtained.

Reexport Controls

In addition to export controls, EAR specifies a comprehensive control system for reexports of U.S.-origin products and technical data from foreign countries. These reexport controls encompass finished end products and, under certain circumstances, U.S.-origin parts and components incorporated into end products that are manufactured abroad. They are similar to controls for direct exports: An exporter in another country must obtain specific approval from the Department of Commerce for a reexport if the product or technical data involved would have required a validated license for shipment directly from the United States to the country of final destination (see Figure 4-6). Under a 1986 Commerce Department proposal published in the *Federal Register*, no reexport approval would be required for foreign-manufactured products that are exported to most Free World nations if the U.S.-origin controlled parts and components constitute 20 percent or less of a product's value.[18]

In certain instances, exports of foreign end products that are manufactured with U.S.-origin technical data are controlled by EAR even if these products are entirely of foreign content. Controls on foreign-made "direct products" of U.S.-origin technology apply primarily to exports to Soviet bloc or other embargoed countries of products in categories that are subject to CoCom export regulation. These controls have their principal impact on exports from industrialized countries outside CoCom such as Switzerland, Sweden, Austria, South Korea, Taiwan, and Singapore, countries that do not themselves have comparable export control systems.

Penalties for Violations

The U.S. government is authorized to impose several types of administrative sanctions for EAR violations. First, the Commerce Department has discretionary authority to impose fines of up to $100,000 per violation in cases involving national security controls and up to $10,000 per violation in other cases. Second, the department may suspend or revoke a company's privilege to participate in all types of export transactions—those carried out under general licenses as well as those covered by validated licenses. In invoking this type of sanction, the department may suspend or revoke a company's or an individual's existing export licenses, it may deny future license applications, and it may prohibit export transactions that would be covered by a general license. Third, the U.S. Customs Service may require the forfeiture of goods that have been seized during the course of an unauthorized export.

Companies and individuals whose export privileges have been suspended or otherwise impaired are listed by the Department of Commerce in the Table of Denial Orders, which is published in the *Federal Register*. Any company that engages in an export transaction with these companies or individuals in violation of the denial order is itself subject to all the penalties available under the act. These civil sanctions apply even to unintentional violations.

The Justice Department enforces criminal provisions of the Export Administration Act in the federal courts. Under these provisions, individuals may be imprisoned for up to 10 years and/or fined up to $250,000 for each willful violation. Companies may be fined up to five times the value of the exports involved or $1 million, whichever is greater. Unintentional violations generally are not subject to criminal prosecution.

ADMINISTRATION OF U.S. CONTROLS

The spectrum of administrative, investigatory, and enforcement activities related to export controls involves a broad array of departments and agencies within the executive branch. Various instruments—legislation, regulations, and executive orders—define the roles of these departments and agencies. In general, the Commerce Department regulates exports of commercial equipment and technology, and the State Department oversees exports of military equipment and technology. The Defense Department plays a key advisory role for both commercial and military exports. In addition to these departments, a number of other governmental entities maintain a special interest in controlling the transfer of militarily important technology; these include the Departments of Treasury (U.S. Customs Service), Energy, and Justice, as well as NASA, the Nuclear Regulatory Commission, and the intelligence agencies. The Department of Commerce and the U.S. Customs Service share responsibility for the enforcement of export controls and are now directly linked by computer for more efficient case processing. The latter agency is empowered to seize unauthorized shipments or suspected diversions, which are subject to forfeiture. It also has an extensive enforcement program known as Operation Exodus that includes random checks of outgoing shipments for license authority. The existence of such a program indicates the increased enforcement emphasis within the U.S. government and has helped to focus public attention on the need to uncover and prevent illegal shipments.

By law the interagency process for deciding export control issues for dual use commodities and technologies centers in the Department of Commerce; recently, however, the Department of Defense has dominated the national security aspects of the procedure. The Reagan administration came into office convinced that Soviet acquisition of U.S. military and

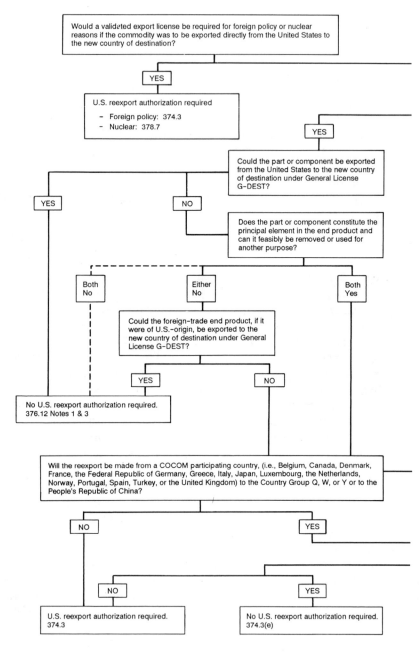

Would a validated export license be required for foreign policy or nuclear reasons if the commodity was to be exported directly from the United States to the new country of destination?

YES

U.S. reexport authorization required

- Foreign policy: 374.3
- Nuclear: 378.7

YES

Could the part or component be exported from the United States to the new country of destination under General License G-DEST?

YES   NO

Does the part or component constitute the principal element in the end product and can it feasibly be removed or used for another purpose?

Both No   Either No   Both Yes

Could the foreign-trade end product, if it were of U.S.-origin, be exported to the new country of destination under General License G-DEST?

YES   NO

No U.S. reexport authorization required. 376.12 Notes 1 & 3

Will the reexport be made from a COCOM participating country, (i.e., Belgium, Canada, Denmark, France, the Federal Republic of Germany, Greece, Italy, Japan, Luxembourg, the Netherlands, Norway, Portugal, Spain, Turkey, or the United Kingdom) to the Country Group Q, W, or Y or to the People's Republic of China?

NO   YES

NO   YES

U.S. reexport authorization required. 374.3

No U.S. reexport authorization required. 374.3(e)

THIS CHART IS FOR ILLUSTRATIVE PURPOSES ONLY
Not to be used as a substitute for careful reading of Export Administration Regulations (EAR)

FIGURE 4-6 U.S. reexport licensing decision chart. Basic steps required of foreign reexporters to comply with unilateral U.S. reexport regulations.

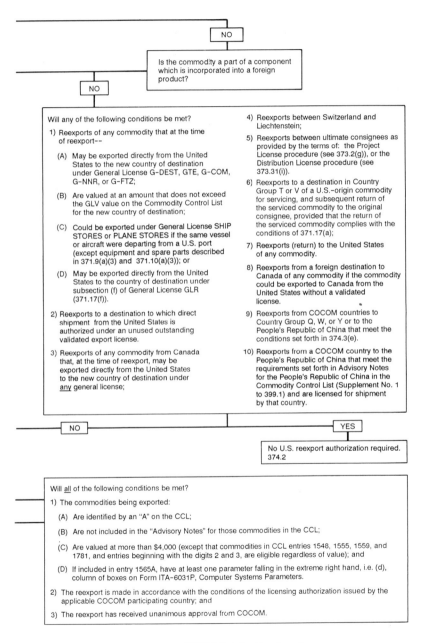

NO

Is the commodity a part of a component which is incorporated into a foreign product?

NO

Will any of the following conditions be met?

1) Reexports of any commodity that at the time of reexport--

   (A) May be exported directly from the United States to the new country of destination under General License G-DEST, GTE, G-COM, G-NNR, or G-FTZ;

   (B) Are valued at an amount that does not exceed the GLV value on the Commodity Control List for the new country of destination;

   (C) Could be exported under General License SHIP STORES or PLANE STORES if the same vessel or aircraft were departing from a U.S. port (except equipment and spare parts described in 371.9(a)(3) and 371.10(a)(3)); or

   (D) May be exported directly from the United States to the country of destination under subsection (f) of General License GLR (371.17(f)).

2) Reexports to a destination to which direct shipment from the United States is authorized under an unused outstanding validated export license.

3) Reexports of any commodity from Canada that, at the time of reexport, may be exported directly from the United States to the new country of destination under any general license;

4) Reexports between Switzerland and Liechtenstein;

5) Reexports between ultimate consignees as provided by the terms of: the Project License procedure (see 373.2(g)), or the Distribution License procedure (see 373.31(i)).

6) Reexports to a destination in Country Group T or V of a U.S.-origin commodity for servicing, and subsequent return of the serviced commodity to the original consignee, provided that the return of the serviced commodity complies with the conditions of 371.17(a);

7) Reexports (return) to the United States of any commodity.

8) Reexports from a foreign destination to Canada of any commodity if the commodity could be exported to Canada from the United States without a validated license.

9) Reexports from COCOM countries to Country Group Q, W, or Y or to the People's Republic of China that meet the conditions set forth in 374.3(e).

10) Reexports from a COCOM country to the People's Republic of China that meet the requirements set forth in Advisory Notes for the People's Republic of China in the Commodity Control List (Supplement No. 1 to 399.1) and are licensed for shipment by that country.

NO

YES

No U.S. reexport authorization required. 374.2

Will all of the following conditions be met?

1) The commodities being exported:

   (A) Are identified by an "A" on the CCL;

   (B) Are not included in the "Advisory Notes" for those commodities in the CCL;

   (C) Are valued at more than $4,000 (except that commodities in CCL entries 1548, 1555, 1559, and 1781, and entries beginning with the digits 2 and 3, are eligible regardless of value); and

   (D) If included in entry 1565A, have at least one parameter falling in the extreme right hand, i.e. (d), column of boxes on Form ITA-6031P, Computer Systems Parameters.

2) The reexport is made in accordance with the conditions of the licensing authorization issued by the applicable COCOM participating country; and

3) The reexport has received unanimous approval from COCOM.

FIGURE 4-6 *Continued.*

dual use products and technology was a serious problem. The Department of Defense took the lead and acted with vigor in a number of areas, either directly or by pushing Commerce, State, or other organizations to take action. At the behest of DoD, the U.S. Customs Service has intensified its enforcement efforts and the Departments of Commerce and State have encouraged the CoCom member countries to improve their enforcement programs. The Department of Defense has had a statutory obligation for many years to review license applications for selling controlled items to proscribed destinations; this obligation is now being fulfilled by the Defense Technology Security Administration (DTSA), created under DoD Directive 5105.51. DTSA has assumed primary responsibility for license reviews, which was formerly held by the Office of the Under Secretary for Research and Engineering. Now, as a result of a presidential directive issued in January 1985, DoD also reviews license applications for certain commodities to 15 Free World destinations from which the risk of diversion to the Soviet bloc is considered particularly high.

During both the first and second Reagan administrations, the National Security Council (NSC) evolved and modified a structure for export control policy and decision making. From 1981 to mid-1982, the Senior Interagency Group on Foreign Policy (SIG-FP) coordinated the implementation of policy decisions on unilateral and multilateral control of dual use high-technology exports. This group also dealt with other international foreign policy and economic issues such as the export of oil and gas equipment and U.S. policy toward construction of the Siberian natural gas pipeline. The State Department chaired the SIG-FP and its lower-level working groups. Staffing within the SIG-FP on high-technology exports was thin, however, and policymaking reportedly was slow and indecisive, primarily because of three factors: (1) the State Department's desire to focus on other foreign policy issues that it considered to be of higher priority; (2) State's reluctance to antagonize other Western allied nations; and (3) disagreement within the SIG-FP over the issues.

In June 1982 following the imposition of U.S. sanctions against its European allies over the Siberian pipeline,[19] NSC created a new Senior Interagency Group on International Economic Policy (SIG-IEP). The main objective of this new group was to improve NSC attention to issues such as high-technology exports, issues that have overlapping diplomatic, economic, and military implications. During the second half of 1982, when attention remained focused on the Siberian pipeline and the resistance to U.S. controls by the allies, the secretaries of treasury and state cochaired the SIG-IEP. The United States and its allies finally resolved the pipeline issues in December 1982 through an agreement within NATO: The United States agreed to lift the sanctions in exchange for a thorough review of West-East trade questions.

In early 1983 under National Security Decision Directive 83-1, NSC relegated export control policy to a lower "working-level" SIG, which was established officially as the Senior Interagency Group on Transfer of Strategic Technology (SIG-TST). This group continues to function and has become known more commonly as the SIG-TT (Technology Transfer). A primary purpose of the SIG-TT is to expedite decision making in connection with the CoCom list review process. The under secretary of state for security assistance, science, and technology chairs the SIG-TT; the assistant secretary of defense for international security policy or the deputy under secretary of defense for policy represents DoD; and the assistant secretary of commerce for trade administration or the deputy assistant secretary for export administration represents the Department of Commerce.[20]

Since 1983 some of SIG-TT's major activities have focused on export policy vis-à-vis the People's Republic of China, the development of an administration position on the renewal of the expiring Export Administration Act of 1979, and the allocation of enforcement responsibility between the Treasury and Commerce Departments. SIG-TT also has devoted attention to U.S. proposals for strengthening multilateral national security controls through CoCom.

MULTILATERAL NATIONAL SECURITY EXPORT CONTROLS

Based in Paris, the Coordinating Committee on Multilateral Export Controls (CoCom) administers uniform multilateral national security export controls on munitions, products and technologies related to nuclear energy, and dual use products and technologies. Items in each of these categories are placed on control lists maintained by CoCom if there is unanimous consent among the member nations for control. Many of the items on the U.S. Control List parallel items found on the CoCom dual use list, which is known as the International List. The International List covers three types of goods:

• items designed specially or used principally for development, production, or utilization of arms, ammunition, or military systems;
• items incorporating unique technological know-how, the acquisition of which might give significant direct assistance to the development and production of arms, ammunition, or military systems; and
• items in which proscribed nations have a deficiency that hinders development and production of arms, ammunition, or military systems, a deficiency they are not likely to overcome within a reasonable period.

CoCom groups the items on the International List into various categories. Some categories, such as those covering measuring instruments (category no. 1529) and computers (category no. 1565), include products whose technical characteristics range across several levels of sophistication. The degrees of control, which are outlined in Table 4-1, depend on various technical parameters specified in the list or in notes appended to the list. There must be unanimous approval by CoCom members for the export to proscribed destinations of items representing the highest level of technological sophistication; at the lowest level any CoCom government can approve an export based solely on national discretion.

This method of operation reflects the fact that, although there is strong support among CoCom members for a system of common national security export controls, there is considerable disagreement about the scope of items subject to control and the degree to which control is necessary and practical. For example, Canada, the United Kingdom, France, West Germany, and Japan have for years actively advocated major reductions in the scope of coverage. They subscribe to the view that the current multilateral CoCom control list is too extensive and that it would be more credible—and more enforceable—if widely available items were removed.

Prior to 1985, CoCom conducted reviews of the dual use and other control lists every 3 years. In 1985 it initiated a process of annual reviews covering one-fourth of the list every year. (This spreads out the review process and alleviates administrative requirements at the CoCom secre-

TABLE 4-1 CoCom Procedures

- *General embargo*—covering items that must be submitted to CoCom for a general exception to the embargo with approval to export requiring unanimity among the members.

- *Favorable consideration*—covering items falling below the general embargo line that will be considered favorably for export on a case-by-case basis if they meet certain conditions specified in the accompanying notes.

- *One-time review and listing or the "45-day" procedure*—covering items for which a decision to approve their export as a category of product will be made within 45 days; in this case, the question period lasts only 30 days (as compared to 8 weeks for general exception cases). If a product is listed (by make and model number), subsequent exports are controlled under administrative exception note procedures or are free from controls depending on the procedure specified.

- *Notification*—covering items that have been nationally approved for export for which notice must be given to CoCom 30 days in advance of shipment but that do not require CoCom approval.

- *Administrative exception notes (AEN)*—covering items that may be exported at national discretion with only the requirement to report statistics to CoCom monthly (after the fact unless stipulated otherwise).

---

tariat.) Although CoCom now reviews list items on the average only once every 4 years, it publishes the results of the review (i.e., additions and deletions to the list) at the end of each year—instead of waiting until *all* items have been reviewed. In practice, this puts changes into effect more quickly than under the old procedures. Moreover, the practice of reviewing only a portion of the list each year does not preclude any CoCom member government from proposing *essential* changes—additions, modifications, etc.—to portions of the list not under review.

Not all proscribed destinations are treated by CoCom in the same way. At the end of 1985, CoCom agreed to treat the People's Republic of China more liberally than the other CoCom-proscribed destinations. As a result, it added certain equipment (i.e., equipment that falls within agreed-upon technical parameters in each of 27 International List categories) to the national discretion level of control for the PRC. This equipment now can be shipped to that country without prior multilateral CoCom review.

Currently, CoCom follows a policy of not permitting exceptions to the general embargo for proposed exports to the Soviet Union. This policy, which was adopted after the Soviet invasion of Afghanistan, does not apply to other CoCom-proscribed destinations—that is, nations in Eastern Europe.

THE CONTROL SYSTEMS OF OTHER WESTERN NATIONS

The panel reviewed in detail the export control systems of five CoCom countries that maintain control lists substantially parallel to the CoCom list: Canada, France, Japan, the United Kingdom, and West Germany. All five nations have objected to the U.S. assertion of jurisdiction over the following: (1) the reexport of U.S.-origin items; (2) the export of foreign-made products that contain U.S. parts and components or that are based on U.S. technology; and (3) the export of non-U.S.-origin items by U.S. subsidiaries located in their countries. None of the five administers the type of reexport controls listed above on their own dual use items. Moreover, Canada, France, and the United Kingdom have adopted legislation that is specifically designed to protect their sovereignty from the reach of extraterritorial U.S. controls.

All five nations support the international import certificate/delivery verification (IC/DV) system. Under this system the government of the nation importing controlled items from a CoCom country assumes the responsibility for preventing diversionary reexports to proscribed destinations.

With limited exceptions, none of the countries imposes controls that extend beyond the CoCom lists. Certain chemicals make up the only category of items controlled unilaterally by Canada for other than short-supply reasons. West Germany controls a few munitions and nuclear energy items unilaterally.

There is little similarity among countries with respect to technical data controls. Some restrict the export of intangible data; others limit controls to tangible forms of information.

Generally speaking, each CoCom country requires export licenses for CoCom-controlled commodities shipped to non-CoCom, nonproscribed destinations or "third countries." These third countries, however, are not dealt with uniformly. Several of the nations require consignee assurances from Third World countries, a practice that does not mirror U.S. policy. Even within the United States there is no uniformity. For example, the Commerce Department requires import certificates from some non-CoCom nations (e.g., India and Hong Kong); in the case of other countries, it requires consignees merely to sign and submit supporting end use statements. From still other consignees—in some nations in Central and South America—the United States does not require any such assurances.

As part of the special relationship with Canada discussed earlier, Canada abides (albeit somewhat reluctantly) by U.S. national security reexport regulations requiring authorization for U.S.-origin items that are originally shipped to Canada but are being supplied finally to third countries. Canadian cooperation also includes restricting reexports of U.S.-origin items pursuant to U.S. foreign policies not shared by Canada. However, Canadian and U.S. views differ on whether or not an item is of U.S. origin. Although the United States essentially contends that U.S. identity is never lost, Canada maintains that a U.S. item loses its identity if it is materially changed in Canada and the proportion of U.S.-origin parts and components in the resulting new product is less than 80 percent.

The panel also reviewed in detail the export controls of one non-CoCom nation in Europe and one non-CoCom nation in the Far East—Austria and South Korea, respectively. As a neutral nation, Austria approaches export controls from a different perspective than the CoCom countries. Because it desires to maintain good commercial relations with the West without violating its neutrality, Austria maintains controls on reexports as specified by the original country of origin. Austrian-origin goods, however, are restricted only to prevent shortages or price fluctuations.

Austria requires licenses for exports of items that are imported with import certificates, a system based on voluntary agreements between Austrian firms and the Austrian government. Under this system, firms certify that they will abide by the conditions in the export license or reexport license governing items they import from other nations.

Because of its hostility toward North Korea, the Republic of Korea engages in no direct trade with CoCom-proscribed destinations—on the presumption they are conduits to North Korea. Otherwise, Korea does not control the export of any dual use items for security purposes. Except for munitions, Korean export control lists include no items on the CoCom list. The lack of Korean controls on exports of dual use strategic items to other Western destinations concerns many CoCom countries; they fear Korea will become a source of diversion as it proceeds with its rapid technological development.

Both nations—Austria and Korea—also object to U.S. assertions of extraterritorial jurisdiction and support the use of import certificate/delivery verification systems.

The U.S. national security export control system, the multilateral agreements administered by CoCom, and the control systems of other nations are all essential components of the effort to restrain the flow of military and dual use products and technologies to potential adversaries. The next two chapters assess in turn the administration of controls by the United States and the larger multilateral control regime.

NOTES

1. 50 U.S.C. App. 2401 et seq.
2. 22 U.S.C. App. 2778 et seq.
3. The members of CoCom are Belgium, Canada, Denmark, the Federal Republic of Germany, France, Greece, Italy, Japan, Luxembourg, the Netherlands, Norway, Portugal, Spain, Turkey, the United Kingdom, and the United States.
4. Under the provisions of the Neutrality Acts of 1935-1939, exports of goods with potential military application such as advanced aircraft and parts did require a license from the State Department. But State could not withhold such licenses until the President invoked the full provisions of the act and embargoed all such exports to both parties in the war in question—an action he consistently resisted. In particular, the Roosevelt administration opposed efforts to apply this act to the Sino-Japanese conflict in 1937 because it would have hurt China far more than Japan.
5. Japan had the highest level of U.S. investment of any Asian nation during the early 1930s (see Mira Wilkins, "The Role of U.S. Business," *Pearl Harbor as History*, ed. Borg et al. [New York: Columbia University Press, 1973], p. 353). The Munitions Control Board did restrict exports of tin scrap to Japan beginning in 1936 for reasons of short supply and military criticality (Ibid., p. 348). On the other hand, in 1937 the U.S. government had no legal means to prevent an American aircraft company from selling Japan a complete advanced aircraft that had been withdrawn from a U.S. Army procurement contest 2 years earlier. Many key design features of this aircraft later turned up in the famous Japanese "Zero" (see Eugene E. Wilson, *Slipstream* [New York: McGraw-Hill, 1950], pp. 192-193).
6. U.S. Congress, House Committee on Banking and Currency, *Hearings on House Resolution 1661* (January 31, 1949), p. 7 (H.1224-2).
7. The Export Control Act of 1949 and the Export Administration Act of 1969 both specifically exempted penalties assessed for violations of the export regulations from judicial review under the Administrative Procedures Act. The Export Administration Act of 1979 modified this provision by allowing some judicial review of penalties, but the 1985 amendments gave the secretary of commerce final authority in such disputes. None

of these acts provided for judicial review of export regulations or individual licensing decisions.

8. Henry Kissinger, *White House Years* (New York: Little, Brown and Co., 1979), pp. 153-154.

9. 10 C.F.R. 120-130.

10. 10 C.F.R. 120.8.

11. 15 C.F.R. 368-399.

12. Public Law 99-64, 99th Congress, July 12, 1985.

13. See "Notice of Proposed Rulemaking: General License for Certified End-User Procedure," *Federal Register* 51, no. 120, pp. 22826-22829.

14. 15 C.F.R. 379.3. The Department of Commerce has proposed modifying the terms of the GTDA license; see *Federal Register* 51, no. 95, pp. 17986-17989.

15. Romania, Libya, Hungary, Poland, Albania, Bulgaria, Czechoslovakia, Estonia, the German Democratic Republic, Laos, Latvia, Lithuania, the Mongolian People's Republic, the Union of Soviet Socialist Republics, Cuba, Kampuchea, North Korea, and Vietnam fall within these five country groups.

16. Invention Secrecy Act of 1951: 35 U.S.C. 181 et seq.; 37 C.F.R. Part 5.

17. See *Federal Register* 51, no. 180, pp. 32938-32939. This notice appears to imply that only technical data whose export is controlled by the Department of Defense according to guidelines contained in DoD Directive 5230.25, dated November 6, 1984 (32 C.F.R. Part 250), may be subject to the "Secrecy Order and Permit for Foreign Filing in Certain Countries." The commissioner of patents and trademarks, however, in correspondence to the American Association for the Advancement of Science dated March 13, 1986, has asserted that this secrecy order may be used in connection with patent applications arising from privately sponsored research.

18. See "Notice of Proposed Rulemaking: Revision of Controls on Foreign Products Incorporating U.S. Origin Parts, Components, and Materials," *Federal Register* 51, no. 129, pp. 24533-24535.

19. In 1978 the Soviet Union proposed building a large-diameter natural gas pipeline from Siberia to Western Europe. Beginning in 1981 the United States sought to block cooperation by Western European nations and Japan. On June 18, 1982, President Reagan extended a previous order prohibiting direct exports from the United States of oil and gas equipment for the project to include sales by overseas subsidiaries of U.S. firms and by foreign firms producing such equipment under U.S. license. This order was rescinded on November 13, 1982.

20. Membership of the Senior Interagency Group on Transfer of Strategic Technology includes representatives from the Departments of Commerce, Energy, Justice, State, and Treasury, the Arms Control and Disarmament Agency, the Central Intelligence Agency, the Federal Bureau of Investigation, the Joint Chiefs of Staff, the National Aeronautics and Space Administration, the National Security Agency, the National Science Foundation, the National Security Council, the Office of Management and Budget, the Office of the Secretary of Defense, the Office of Science and Technology Policy, the Office of the Vice President, the U.S. ambassador to the United Nations, the U.S. Customs Service, and the U.S. trade representative.

5

An Assessment of U.S. National Security Export Controls

INTRODUCTION

U.S. policy on national security export controls should result from a process that weighs the benefits of controls to the United States in its relations with adversaries against the costs of controls in relations with allies and trading partners. The purpose of controls is to prevent or delay improvements in Warsaw Pact military capabilities that can be accomplished through the acquisition and use of Western technology and goods. Military capabilities can be enhanced directly, through better weapons performance, or indirectly, through improved capability to manufacture military equipment. In peacetime the United States and its allies can counter such advances by the Soviet bloc, albeit by incurring higher military expenditures that impose additional costs on Western economies. The benefits of controls, therefore, are measured by the degree to which Soviet military advances are prevented or delayed and the extent to which savings to the West are realized.

The adverse effects of controls are harder to measure because they derive primarily from a complex web of competitive and cooperative relationships among Western countries. Of principal concern are the sales and market share that U.S. producers of goods and technologies may lose or forego as a result of how the U.S. control system is designed and administered and how it compares with the control systems of other countries with competitive suppliers. Reduced revenue may translate into less investment, a lower growth rate, and reduced innovation, the effects

103

of which could be important to the military as well as the commercial sector. To the extent that private firms anticipate that controls will have an adverse effect on their ability to exploit new technologies, innovation may be directly discouraged. Export controls can also cause friction between the United States and its allies and may interfere with their collaboration on technology security; on weapons development, production, and standardization; or on other matters bearing directly on West-East relations.

The advantages to the West of controlling technology transfers to the East are not simply strategic; controls may yield savings in Western defense expenditures that could be devoted to nonmilitary uses including private investment. Similarly, the costs of controls are not strictly commercial; they too have implications for the military balance of power as well as for West-East competition in political spheres. Thus, assessing U.S. export controls solely in terms of military security gains versus commercial costs is inappropriate because the basis of comparison is incomplete.

It follows that a strictly quantitative benefit-cost assessment of export controls is not feasible. Not all, perhaps not even the most important, advantages and disadvantages of controls can be precisely quantified or compared. They derive from a rapidly changing context and rest on qualitative judgments. The panel affirms that there is a compelling justification for national security export controls. Nevertheless, certain features of the control system impose excessive costs or have little effectiveness. In these cases, it is the panel's judgment that changes in the control system are warranted.

This chapter addresses three basic questions. First, how effective are U.S. national security export controls in denying or delaying Soviet acquisitions of Western dual use technology? Second, how efficiently are they administered? And third, what costs to the economy and the research enterprise are associated with current controls and their administration? Because knowledge about the effects of controls on commercial markets as well as on national security will never be complete, and because judgments will be affected by changes in West-East relations, economic conditions, and technology, this chapter also addresses a fourth, procedural issue: Is the current U.S. policy process capable of generating adequate information, weighing the competing considerations, and balancing U.S. interests over the long term, during which it will be necessary to maintain some type of export control system?

Detailed answers to these questions have eluded previous assessments of the export control system. Not only are the effectiveness and costs of controls uncertain, but there is a dearth of reliable data even on such basic points of reference as the value, composition, and share of U.S. export trade affected by national security export controls.

The Department of Commerce, for example, publishes aggregate figures for individual validated license (IVL) applications—the total number of applications and their total value. It compiles but does not publish breakdowns of the number and value of IVL applications by Control List category (ECCN). But the department's published or prepared data do not distinguish between items controlled for national security reasons and those controlled for foreign policy, nuclear nonproliferation, or other reasons; nor do they distinguish between applications for exports and those for reexports. The department does not examine individual licenses that are returned after use to determine what proportion of the value of goods authorized for export was actually shipped. Nor does the department routinely obtain from qualified exporters or other government sources (e.g., the Bureau of the Census) reports on the volume and value of transactions made under bulk licenses.

Furthermore, the Commerce Department data base does not provide the percentages of reexport applications that are submitted by U.S.-headquartered and independent foreign-based companies even though reexport approval requirements, especially as they affect independent foreign manufacturers and distributors, are a highly controversial feature of the U.S. export control system both in the United States and abroad. Perhaps most importantly, there is no correspondence between Control List categories and the product statistical classifications under which exports are reported to and by the government—a linkage essential to any quantitative analysis of the effects of controls on U.S. export performance.

As a result of congressional and business community pressures to increase the speed of individual licensing decisions, data are available on the processing of IVLs. Although this information is useful, Commerce Department officials have otherwise received little encouragement and few resources to analyze the scope and consequences of their activities. This information deficit impedes informed policymaking and efficient administration as much as it does independent evaluation. The panel attaches high priority to correcting these deficiencies.

In making its own assessment of the operation and effects of export controls, the panel took a variety of steps to fill the information void. In addition to the briefings presented by government officials and business representatives and its study missions to Western Europe and Asia, the panel commissioned two types of studies, each with several components.

First, the panel requested and was granted a "national interest" exception under Section 12(c) of the Export Administration Act, permitting its consultants unprecedented access to Commerce Department license files and data bases subject to strict observance of the confidentiality of business information. The consultants' study included analyses of a randomly selected sample of recently approved individual license applications; a random sample of license applications returned without action; a sample of reexport authorization applications submitted during a recent period; and more than half of the license applications, categorized by administrative criteria corresponding to levels of military criticality, for which processing was completed in a recent 1-week period.

Second, the panel commissioned two surveys of U.S.-based companies affected by national security export controls. The first survey focused primarily on experience in applying for and using individual validated licenses. The second survey was designed to ascertain how the distribution license is used and what have been the effects of recent changes in the Export Administration Regulations governing such licenses.

The conclusions and judgments reached by the panel following these fact-finding efforts are discussed below.

EFFECTIVENESS OF NATIONAL SECURITY EXPORT CONTROLS

Intelligence and Enforcement Evidence

Direct evidence of the effectiveness of national security export controls is confined to the results of enforcement activities and fragmentary intelligence data (see Chapter 2). The former presents a mixed but narrow picture from which only tentative conclusions can be drawn. Some investigations, as in the VAX case, have documented the elaborate, unpredictable, and presumably costly lengths to which the Soviets have gone in the pursuit of certain embargoed items; but other cases suggest that the scale and complexity of international marketing and distribution activities afford ample opportunities to evade controls.

Intelligence sources estimate that the Soviets are paying twice the market price or more to obtain dual use technology illegally, which suggests that controls are raising the cost to the Soviets of their reliance on Western sources. By the Soviets' own estimate, however, contained in the Farewell documents obtained by French intelligence, 70 percent of the Western items that they target and succeed in acquiring are subject to some form of national security export control. The proportion was the same during the most recent Soviet 5-year economic plan (1981-1985) as it was in the previous 5 years (1976-1980), a period of relatively looser Western controls.[1] On the other hand, according to the same sources the Soviets fulfill only about one-third of their requirements annually, suggesting that they encounter some delays in obtaining what they want when they want it.[2] The extent to which such delays have in turn delayed Soviet deployments of advanced military equipment is not known.

It is reasonable to surmise on the basis of this limited evidence that the control system, relative to a free market, inhibits and raises the cost but rarely foils completely technology acquisition efforts as sophisticated and well-financed as those mounted by the Soviet Union. Nevertheless, the question of which controls are relatively more or less effective remains unanswered.

Compliance

An indirect indicator of the effectiveness of controls is the level of corporate compliance. Although this level cannot be determined precisely, there is substantial evidence that compliance has increased in recent years as the government has committed more resources to enforcement. Between FY1981 and FY1985 the number of IVL applications increased more than 70 percent (from 71,369 to 122,606), exceeding the rate of increase in U.S. high-technology exports. Interviews conducted for the panel confirm what has been widely suspected. For years, many small exporters had been doing business unaware that their products required validated licenses. Directly and as a result of the publicity surrounding it, the U.S. Customs Service's Operation Exodus, which resulted in the seizure or detainment of numerous shipments lacking proper authorization, brought about a greater awareness of the Export Administration Regulations and thus a significant improvement in formal compliance. It is not known whether the enforcement campaign has reduced the number of intentional diversions.

Meanwhile, reexport license applications received by the Department of Commerce increased at an even faster rate, nearly doubling between FY1983 and FY1985. In this case, however, the increase in compliance has been one-sided. The overwhelming majority (about 90 percent by value) of reexport applications are from U.S.-headquartered companies and their foreign affiliates, a rate double or triple the estimated share (30 to 40 percent) of U.S. exports represented by intrafirm trade. Unrelated foreign firms initiate only 10 percent of reexport authorizations.

The disparity in the shares of reexport authorization applications of U.S. affiliates and foreign-owned firms is greatest in the case of CoCom member countries, which are the source of more than 80 percent (more than 90 percent by value) of all reexport applications. In a representative sample of recent applications from three major CoCom trading partners, between 87 percent and 98 percent of the submissions were traced to U.S. affiliates. The data strongly suggest that independent foreign companies are either ignorant of or casual in their compliance with U.S. reexport controls—except in the few countries, such as Switzerland, that require their firms to follow the rules of the country of origin when exporting imported products.

These findings are not surprising in view of the fact that most CoCom countries, for reasons of national sovereignty, refuse to cooperate in the enforcement of U.S. reexport controls and are prepared to resist any systematic effort by the United States to penalize noncomplying foreign companies. Of course the export of all but unilaterally controlled U.S.-origin items to proscribed destinations from CoCom countries is subject to licensing by other governments. In these cases, U.S. reexport requirements are not only problematic but also redundant.

Discrimination in Licensing and Enforcement

In addition to the level of formal compliance, the effectiveness of export controls depends on the government's allocation of resources and effort in licensing and enforcement. Controlled products and technologies are of varying military significance, and countries and customers are of varying reliability in preventing their diversion to the Soviet bloc. It follows that exports of the most critical technologies and exports to countries with no or ineffective controls should receive the most scrutiny.

Discrimination, or the lack of it, is a function both of how much is swept into the control system and how it is treated. In the first instance the panel estimates that a very large percentage of U.S. exports—as much as one-half of all nonmilitary manufactured goods shipped in 1985—is covered by one or another type of validated license.* Because exports that the Department of Commerce considers "high technology" constitute about two-fifths of U.S. manufactured exports, it is apparent that controls extend to products embodying relatively low technology.

The panel analyzed a sample of licenses† for goods classified by level of military sensitivity, using administrative criteria developed by the U.S. government and/or in the course of CoCom negotiations. The analysis showed that the broad control net is heavily weighted with transactions in less-sensitive items with allied and other friendly Western countries. Ninety percent of license applications are for exports to Free World countries. One-third of these applications are for items that may be exported to CoCom countries under a general license and even to Soviet bloc destinations

---

*See pp. 116–117 for a detailed explanation of this estimate.

†The analysis was of a sample of 1,618 processed license applications categorized by Department of Commerce license officers. In each case, the officer identified, independent of the intended destination, the item being exported as either within the administrative exception note (AEN) 9 level, within the level of goods that can be exported to the PRC without CoCom approval, eligible for shipment under a distribution license, or ineligible for shipment under a distribution license. The first three of these categories are stepwise inclusive rather than mutually exclusive. The four categories represent progressively higher levels of military criticality.

without prior CoCom approval. According to the sample, the United States rarely refuses a license to export these so-called "national discretion" items to any destination including the Eastern bloc. Two-thirds of the individual license applications were for items sufficiently lacking in military importance that they can be shipped from any CoCom country to the People's Republic of China without prior CoCom approval.

The large volume of cases involving exports of less-critical items to friendly countries severely limits the degree to which licensing officials are able to focus their efforts on the most-critical items. Nevertheless, in 1985 there were two major attempts to sharpen that focus, primarily with respect to country destinations. First, as discussed in Chapter 4, the Export Administration Amendments Act authorized the export of AEN 9-level items to CoCom countries under a general license (G-COM). Although this afforded some relief, the anticipated 15 percent reduction in IVL applications has yet to be realized, evidently because of ignorance or caution on the part of some exporters.* Second, President Reagan directed the Department of Defense, concurrently with the Commerce Department, to review license applications for selected products to 15 Western countries that are not parties to multilateral control agreements and that are regarded as potential points of diversion. This greater attention to so-called "third countries" is reflected in longer processing times and slightly higher denial rates than for exports to CoCom destinations—although it entails an additional layer of review whose independent contribution to the quality of the review process has been questioned by the General Accounting Office.[3]

Although more-sensitive technology items are excluded from distribution license coverage, the panel found little evidence that in the individual licensing process more attention is devoted to products of greater strategic importance than to those of lesser importance. License processing times for applications to Free World destinations do not vary significantly among categories that the Export Administration Regulations treat as more or less militarily critical. Similarly, on the panel's study missions to Europe and Asia, panel members heard frequent complaints from U.S. and foreign enforcement officials that on direction from Washington they devote much of their effort to seeking out diversions of low-technology, widely available products—instead of concentrating on goods of more strategic importance. One foreign-based U.S. Customs officer commented, "We spend most of our time chasing after PCs [personal computers]." The evidence strongly suggests that a greater focusing of efforts could enhance the effectiveness of the control system.

---

*See pp. 112–113.

Benefits of Controls

A 1985 study sponsored by the Department of Defense[4] is the only major attempt to date to quantify the benefits of export controls. Using a sample consisting mainly of rejected 1983-1984 license applications for exports directly to the Soviet bloc, the study estimated that the Soviets could have saved $0.5 billion to $1 billion a year over a 13-year period if the applications in the sample had been approved and the acquired technology exploited. Under the same assumptions, the study projected additional U.S. and NATO defense expenditures of roughly the same magnitude to counter the improved Soviet capabilities.

These conclusions are based on 79 cases (from a universe of 2,000 applications) that were judged by a panel of military and technical experts to involve militarily "important" state-of-the-art technology with high reverse engineering potential. In other words, these 79 rejected applications represent the type of control on exports directly to Warsaw Pact countries of highly sensitive dual use items whose effectiveness and cost are *least* likely to be questioned. These cases further suggest that most of the benefits of controls, if they can be realized, are probably concentrated in a relatively narrow range of products and technologies.

Otherwise, the study's conclusions provide little policy guidance. The claimed benefits of controls are hypothetical in several respects. No attempt was made to determine whether the Soviets did or could acquire the technologies by other means nor to determine if the Soviets did or were capable of exploiting what they might have acquired. The study also assumed that disapproval implied denial, an assumption that is unrealistic for many technologies and, for any particular technology or product, less and less realistic as time goes by.

The study's estimates that the Soviet Union could have saved $6.6 to $13.3 billion over a 13-year period by acquiring the items specified in the sample of license applications, and that additional allied expenditures of $7.3 to $14.6 billion would be required over the same period to compensate for such gains, are the judgments of a group of military experts, but their criteria and assumptions are only partially stated. The more widely quoted assertion that "the cumulative costs of the Soviet long-term acquisition program are much higher—perhaps $20-50 billion per year"[5] is not supported in the text of the report. In view of these uncertainties and lacking access to information that might resolve them,* the panel must question how much weight these estimates should be accorded.

---

*The panel requested from DoD but did not receive back-up data for both sets of estimates.

THE EFFICIENCY OF EXPORT CONTROL ADMINISTRATION

The Export Administration Regulations have evolved over a long period and currently fill more than 570 pages of the Code of Federal Regulations. Understanding and applying the rules are difficult tasks even for full-time, experienced, technically trained, English-speaking export licensing specialists. The system's complexity alone imposes considerable costs on and often undermines compliance by exporting firms. The burden is heaviest on small- and medium-sized companies that are unable to spread the costs over a large volume of export business.

For the exporter, obtaining, using, and (in the case of distribution licenses) keeping export licenses entail an elaborate series of procedures, some of them requiring sophisticated technical judgments. The scope and mechanics of a compliance program will vary with the commodities being exported, the size of the company, and the type of validated license employed. Nevertheless, certain activities are required of all companies that export controlled goods:

• The exporter must properly classify each export product within a category on the U.S. Control List, normally with assistance from in-house technical experts and sometimes from outside consultants.

• If prior government approval is needed for exports of its products, the exporter must prepare and submit license applications, each of which may require at least several hours of effort. Individuals must be trained in how to prepare applications and must be prepared to monitor their progress to ensure that the applications are not lost or delayed by the U.S. government. Assistance from outside consultants is sometimes required.

• The exporter must keep careful records of each individual shipment under an export license; submit to U.S. Customs a shipper's export declaration listing the license authority for each shipment; and ensure that all shipping documents contain the required destination control statements.

• The exporter must monitor additions to the Table of Denial Orders (the list of parties denied the privilege of purchasing U.S.-origin goods or technology) as well as changes in the Export Administration Regulations. Commerce Department notices of amendments to the regulations—ranging from major changes in the rules governing particular types of licenses to revisions of Control List entries to minor technical corrections—appear in the *Federal Register* on an average of about once a week.

• The exporter must review all of its "exports" of technical data including international telephone conversations, servicing and installation activities abroad, and employment of foreign nationals to ensure that any necessary license authority has been obtained. In many cases the exporter must obtain prior U.S. government approval for a technology transfer or obtain a written assurance of compliance with U.S. law from the recipient of the technical data.

• The exporter must maintain tight controls over servicing activities including exports of spare and replacement parts to ensure that proper license authority has been obtained.

• The exporter may need to advise or assist its foreign affiliates and customers in obtaining license authority for reexports of U.S.-origin products from one foreign country to another or for exports from a foreign country of a foreign-made end product containing U.S.-origin parts and components.

Distribution license holders and their approved foreign consignees are required in addition to implement a series of internal control measures that are unique to that type of license. These measures include designating and training employees with export control responsibilities; screening customers against the denial list, nuclear end use restrictions, and a profile of potential diverters; screening transactions against product and country restrictions on the use of the license; and maintaining extensive records to enable the Commerce Department to conduct periodic audits. In addition, distribution license holders are required to inform, train, and audit their approved foreign consignees and to correct and report instances of noncompliance.

In addition to incurring administrative costs, exporters have difficulty interpreting the regulations and obtaining authoritative advice and clarification. For example, proper classification of a product is obviously crucial to compliance; but even engineers often find the U.S. Control List performance specifications, exceptions, and qualifications highly confusing because the terms and measurements often differ from those conventionally used in industry. The Commerce Department will issue a classification decision in response to a written request. Such determinations have been given low priority, however, and commonly have taken several weeks or even months to process. Personnel assigned by the Commerce Department to respond to telephone inquiries are typically of little help on technical matters. Abroad, U.S. embassy officials are frequently ill-informed about even general EAR requirements. Neither in any case can render advice that binds the government.

In circumstances of confusion, uncertainty, or ignorance, many exporters err on the side of caution, submitting unnecessary applications for validated licenses. Seventeen percent of all processed applications in the sample of licenses taken 6 months after the introduction of the G-COM license were found to be eligible for this general license for low-level technology to CoCom-member countries—and therefore need not have been filed and reviewed at all. Instead of returning such filings with a notation that they are eligible for a general license, the Commerce Department finds it easier simply to process license applications that are submitted in error. Even so, exporters who take elaborate precautions frequently find that their submissions are not in strict compliance with the regulations.

There is a pressing need to rewrite, simplify, and condense the Export Administration Regulations and to upgrade the competence of Exporter Services and diplomatic personnel to provide timely, accurate assistance.

Processing Times

A perennial concern of Congress, the business community, and the responsible agencies has been the time it takes to process licenses, especially IVLs. Some improvements have been made in response to statutory deadlines and other congressional pressures and as a result of partial automation and decontrol actions. Nevertheless, licensing delays and uncertainties remain a problem for a significant percentage of export transactions.

Shipping delays impose immediate financial costs on the exporter as well as a longer-term cost in customer confidence. When a product is available but cannot be shipped on receipt of an order, warehousing and other carrying costs are incurred. More expensive means of transportation may need to be used to make up for the delay in obtaining a license, and the exporter may have to pay contract penalties to the purchaser and to subcontractors who supply components and assemblies. In some cases, sales are lost altogether.

The objective of efforts to improve licensing efficiency has been to reduce *average* processing times. In contrast to the 27-day average reported by the Commerce Department, respondents to the survey commissioned by the panel reported a 54-day average processing time. This discrepancy is explained in part by a difference in definition. For the department, the clock starts when the application is recorded and stops with final issuance of the license or other action. For the exporter, the time extends from the mailing of an application to the receipt of a license or adverse decision, not counting the time spent in license preparation, obtaining end use statements, and other steps preparatory to submission. As far as the exporter's ability to ship is concerned, the latter or total processing time is of course determinative.

In contrast, license application turnaround times by the governments of other CoCom countries are generally much shorter. In Japan, for example, the Ministry of International Trade and Industry (MITI) usually responds within 2 or 3 days to applications for exports to Free World destinations. But the important difference is not the number of days. Rather, it is the pattern, in Japan and elsewhere, of consultation between companies and government officials prior to the submission of applications and coincident with negotiations between exporters and their customers. The licensing agency signals its likely approval or disapproval early on in these discussions, removing or at least minimizing uncertainties as to timing and outcome—uncertainties that U.S. exporters frequently experience and that complicate their business dealings.

U.S. averages obscure, moreover, the highly skewed distribution of processing times. In the first quarter of 1986, the average processing time (according to the Commerce Department's definition) was 27 days, with roughly three-quarters of the cases completed in less than that time. But the distribution has an extended "tail" stretching as long as several months and in a few instances even years.* It is the cases in this tail that absorb a large proportion of the corporate resources devoted to working the system and that create uncertainty in the market. The number of such cases is not insignificant; for approximately 5 percent of cases the processing time extends beyond 100 days. Several U.S. companies report that their customers are now insisting that sales contracts contain contingency clauses permitting abrogation of agreements that do not receive approval within a reasonable period of time.

The panel concludes that more effort should be devoted to minimizing or eliminating the uncertainties of the licensing process. Reducing further the average time a license application is under Commerce Department or interagency review is a worthy objective, but it would not necessarily have a significant effect on total processing times, the predictability of the process, or the skewed distribution of processing times.

For many types of transactions, primarily those involving sales of most types of products to allied countries, the licensing system *does* operate

---

*One U.S. company prepared for the panel a detailed chronology of a license application that was ultimately approved after 910 days extending from March 1983 to November 1985. The application was for the sale of a $450,000 nuclear magnetic resonance (NMR) spectrometer to a medical research institute in Eastern Europe. Although U.S. firms pioneered the development of NMR technology, German and Japanese companies now hold two-thirds of the world market for instruments incorporating it. In fact, during the review period a German competitor sold several similar systems to bloc customers. NMR instruments do not appear on the U.S. Control List, but the equipment in question was subject to validated licensing requirements because it incorporated 32-bit array microprocessors and 30-megabyte Winchester disk drives, components produced in the millions in several countries. Throughout the lengthy process of review the applicant intervened repeatedly to keep the license under active consideration. But at no point was the company advised of any rationale for the concern that the product might be diverted and could contribute significantly to Soviet military efforts.

with reasonable predictability—that is, an exporter can count on obtaining approvals within a fairly consistent period of time. For other transactions, both West-West and West-East, the probabilities of a delayed response, of having an application returned without action, of receiving approval with conditions on the configuration of the product, and of apparent inconsistencies in the treatment of similar applications are much higher. In these circumstances the burden is on the exporter to take steps to prevent the process from becoming bogged down and to avert outcomes that effectively negate the sale or alienate foreign customers. Although there have been some successful efforts to computerize the license status process, many exporters continue to find it difficult to obtain sufficient information on the status, whereabouts, and prospects of license applications to coordinate production and shipment and to keep customers informed.

Firm Size Differences

The complexity, inefficiencies, and uncertainties of the licensing process suggest that the system creates its own scale economies and barriers to entry. Export controls are not designed to discriminate against small firms, but their operation adds to other difficulties small companies commonly experience in marketing internationally—difficulties in identifying markets, obtaining financing, and negotiating other hurdles to foreign trade.

There is no estimate of the amount of exports foregone because the perceived costs of export controls discourage firms from doing international business in controlled products. Nevertheless, the panel's survey data indicate that with regard to processing delays, inaction, conditional approvals—and other factors contributing to uncertainty—there are pronounced firm-size differences in the administration of national security controls.

Small-firm applications to Free World destinations take 25 percent longer on average than those of large-volume exporters. The processing time variance (longest processing times relative to average time) is 21 percent for large firms, 70 percent for medium-sized firms, and 150 percent for small firms. The likelihood of receiving a denial is two-and-one-half times greater for small exporters than for large ones; the probability of having an application returned without action is nearly three times greater; and the chances of having to modify the product or attach conditions to its use are also nearly three times greater.* The fact

---

*The comparisons are based on survey data summarized in Appendix C, Table C-8.

that large companies make much more extensive use of bulk export authorizations (such as distribution licenses) that obviate the need for prior approval of individual shipments simply compounds the differential. Complex regulatory schemes often have the unintended effect of discriminating against small enterprises. Export control administrators should take steps to minimize these disadvantages.

COMPETITIVE EFFECTS OF CONTROLS

The panel's survey respondents,* reflecting on their experience over the 12 months prior to May 1986, perceived the control system as frequently having significant adverse effects on their business:

- 52 percent reported lost sales primarily as a consequence of export controls;
- 26 percent had business deals turned down by Free World customers (in more than 212 separate instances) because of controls;
- 38 percent had existing customers actually express a preference to shift to non-U.S. sources of supply to avoid entanglement in U.S. controls; and
- more than half expected the number of such occurrences to increase over the next 2 years.

Before considering whether there is evidence of the magnitude of these effects, we need to review briefly the scope of coverage of the control system, a few of the analytical and practical difficulties of determining the magnitude of the trade impact, and the possible sources of adverse effects on U.S. competitiveness.

Scope of Coverage

Determining the value, size, and composition of the share of U.S. export trade affected by national security export controls is itself an elaborate and uncertain exercise. Nevertheless, a reasonable estimate is that in 1985 the United States exported $62 billion of dual use manufactured goods under the two most frequently used types of validated licenses—IVLs and distribution licenses.† Excluding military equipment,

---

*The sample of companies surveyed was oriented toward firms in the electronics (equipment and components), aircraft (airframes, engines, and parts), instrumentation, and machine tool sectors. The 170 respondents accounted for roughly $36 billion of foreign sales in 1985, or approximately 28 percent of estimated total U.S. high-technology sales.

†This estimate was derived from Commerce Department and survey data and is explained in detail in Appendix C.

controlled exports therefore constituted about 40 percent of total U.S. exports of manufactures in 1985 (more than one-half of manufactured exports to all destinations except Canada, for which no validated licenses are required) and were almost equivalent to the value of all high-technology exports (including exports to Canada, which are 12 percent of the total) as defined by the Department of Commerce (see Figure 5-1). Very likely, these shares have increased in recent years, but the data unfortunately do not permit historical comparisons.

As expected, the types of commodities that bear the brunt of controls—computers, aircraft and parts, instruments, electronic components, and communications equipment—are also the leading U.S. high-technology exports. But there are some curious anomalies. In the largest Control List category, electronic computing equipment (ECCN 1565), the Commerce Department approved roughly $26.1 billion in exports under IVLs alone; but the United States exported only $15 billion worth of computers in calendar year 1985. This discrepancy is attributable to several factors;[6] but most importantly it indicates that the Control List classification is at variance with the classification of trade data and even with common understandings. ECCN 1565 in particular encompasses a wide range of products that are licensed as computers because they contain a microprocessor but that are shipped under other product designations specified by the government for statistical purposes.

From a corporate perspective the control system's coverage also is very broad. Survey data in combination with Commerce Department information indicate that between 2,000 and 3,000 organizations apply for licenses each year.

But even these numbers greatly understate the amount of business activity reached by U.S. controls. The national security export control regime covers not only products and technology as they flow across U.S. borders but also a range of transactions by U.S. subsidiaries and foreign firms abroad. The latter include, for example, sales of products produced, manufactured, and distributed offshore by U.S. affiliates and sales of products manufactured by foreign companies incorporating U.S. components or produced with U.S. technology. The $6.4 billion worth of reexport approvals that were issued in 1985 are only the tip of the iceberg because many reexports are authorized at the time original IVLs are obtained and because the reexport authority of the distribution license is used much more extensively than are individual reexport authorizations. The value of data transfers under general license GTDR cannot be determined. Initially, the adverse competitive effects of the control system may show up only outside the United States, although eventually they will affect U.S. export trade.

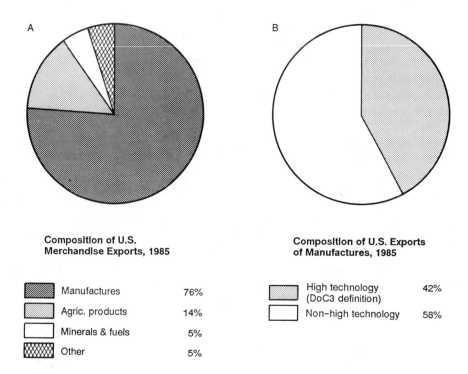

A

B

**Composition of U.S.
Merchandise Exports, 1985**

**Composition of U.S. Exports
of Manufactures, 1985**

Manufactures	76%	
Agric. products	14%	
Minerals & fuels	5%	
Other	5%	

High technology (DoC3 definition)	42%	
Non-high technology	58%	

FIGURE 5-1   Export coverage of U.S. national security export controls.

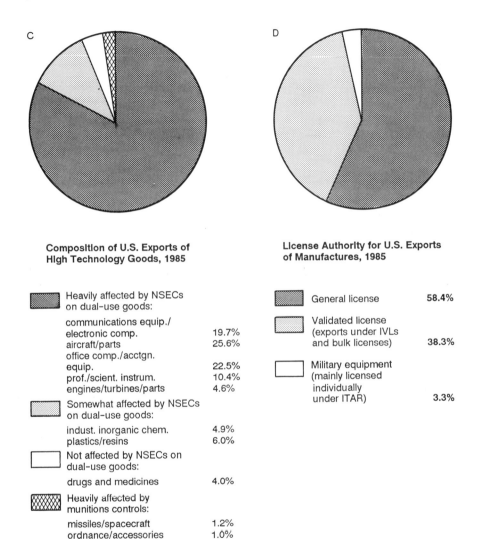

**Composition of U.S. Exports of
High Technology Goods, 1985**

Heavily affected by NSECs
on dual-use goods:

communications equip./ electronic comp.	19.7%
aircraft/parts	25.6%
office comp./acctgn. equip.	22.5%
prof./scient. instrum.	10.4%
engines/turbines/parts	4.6%

Somewhat affected by NSECs
on dual-use goods:

indust. inorganic chem.	4.9%
plastics/resins	6.0%

Not affected by NSECs on
dual-use goods:

drugs and medicines	4.0%

Heavily affected by
munitions controls:

missiles/spacecraft	1.2%
ordnance/accessories	1.0%

**License Authority for U.S. Exports
of Manufactures, 1985**

General license	**58.4%**
Validated license (exports under IVLs and bulk licenses)	**38.3%**
Military equipment (mainly licensed individually under ITAR)	**3.3%**

SOURCES: U.S. Department of Commerce; consultant reports.

FIGURE 5-1   *Continued.*

Lack of Economic Analysis

The complexity of international business operations is only one of the reasons that there has been no credible estimate of the economic cost of national security export controls.

To date the Department of Commerce, despite its trade promotion mandate, has undertaken no economic analysis of national security export controls. Affected exporters presumably are in the best position to know the extent of the administrative burden and lost sales resulting from controls, but they have great difficulty even estimating these costs. Sales personnel are not usually engaged exclusively in administering controls, and statistics on lost sales are not kept. Furthermore, customers rarely articulate the reasons for choosing one supplier over another, let alone assign relative weights to all of their considerations—price, specifications, quality, delivery time, and so forth. In the unusual circumstance in which controls are known with certainty to have been the sole or principal obstacle to a sale, disclosure of the circumstances poses some risk of harm to the company's future sales by raising questions about its reliability as a supplier. Finally, because of industry reluctance for commercial and legal reasons to disclose proprietary information to other firms, there is no mechanism to aggregate and analyze individual exporters' experience. For a variety of practical reasons, therefore, the business community's assertions regarding the costs of export controls are supported only by anecdotal evidence.

Like efforts to quantify the benefits side of the equation, any analysis of costs is hampered by certain inherent analytical problems. First, the continuity of national security export controls precludes examination in most instances of before-and-after effects on trade performance. In contrast, analysts have been able to estimate with some degree of confidence the economic effects of foreign policy trade sanctions that have a clearly delineated beginning and sometimes an end.[7] Second, the effects of export controls overlay and hence are difficult to isolate from a variety of other competitive factors such as exchange rates, general economic conditions, and specific sectoral conditions. Third, the licensing system cuts across a broad range of industries. Not only do the effects vary by sector, but they also vary over time and in how they are manifested—loss of sales, erosion of distribution networks, delays in shipments, and so forth. To capture *all* of these diffuse effects and distill them into a single number is a practical impossibility.

Notwithstanding these difficulties the panel commissioned an independent study to attempt a first-order approximation of those costs to the U.S. economy that are associated mainly with current features peculiar to the U.S. national security export control system. Using the assumptions

TABLE 5-1 Components of Economic Impact on the United States of National Security Export Controls, 1985 (in billions of dollars)[a]

Component	Loss ($ billion)
Lost West-West export sales	5.9
Lost West-East export sales	1.4
Administrative cost to firms	0.5
Reduced research and development spending	0.5
Value of licenses denied	0.5
Lost profits on foreign affiliate sales	0.5
TOTAL	9.3

[a] The methodology used to derive these estimates calculates the difference in lost sales (West-West and West-East), reduced R&D spending, the actual value of licenses denied, and the lost profits on foreign affiliate sales between the current control regime and a situation in which all CoCom countries administered the same control system.

SOURCE: Quick, Finan & Associates, Suite 340, 1020 19th Street, Washington, DC 20036.

described in Appendix D* and examining only the cost elements for which some data are available, this analysis estimated that the short-run direct costs of controls could be on the order of $9 billion annually. The study further estimated that this could in turn translate into an associated annual reduction in domestic employment of nearly 200,000 jobs (out of more than 2.6 million export-generated jobs in manufacturing). In addition, the application of a standard economic multiplier for the total reduction in the 1985 U.S. GNP associated with lost export sales (both West-East and West-West) and reduced investment in research and development would raise the associated annual loss in U.S. GNP to approximately $17 billion.

The panel notes that the estimated costs of U.S. national security export controls of approximately $9 billion would appear to be substantial in relation to total licensed U.S. trade (estimated in this study to be approximately $62 billion). Moreover, as can be seen in Table 5-1, these costs are estimated to be much greater for trade between the United States and other Free World countries than they are for trade between the United States and the Soviet bloc. Therefore, it is reasonable that a harmonized multilateral export control system could be more effective in the future in controlling technology flow to the East while simultaneously reducing impediments to West-West trade and yielding substantial economic benefits to the United States by reducing the costs of controls.

---

*The panel recognizes that the assumptions underlying such an exercise may be subject to debate. It has chosen nevertheless to present the results of the consultant's analysis as a frame of reference for appreciating the magnitude of the direct economic costs that may be associated with national security export controls.

It is important to emphasize that the panel did *not* base its findings or recommendations on these estimates of the direct economic costs of national security export controls. Rather, the panel's conclusions stand on their own. They are based on a broader range of noneconometric factors and on the outcome of the panel's own deliberations. Yet another reason why the panel did not base its judgments on these estimates is that they do not take account of such crucial considerations as the actual effectiveness of controls or their effects on cooperative relationships among the allies.

The methodology used to derive these estimates was based on a calculation of the difference between the current control regime and a situation in which all CoCom countries administered the same control system. The components of the direct cost estimate as derived in the analysis are presented in Table 5-1. The entire methodology, including an enumeration of certain known costs excluded from the calculation, is described in detail in Appendix D.

The remainder of this section examines more fully several aspects of the economic cost issue.

Sources and Extent of Disadvantage to U.S. Exporters

The control system poses major barriers to U.S. high-technology trade directly with the Soviet Union and Eastern Europe. For some U.S. industries (e.g., machine tools) and for some individual companies, Soviet bloc countries theoretically could represent significant markets, as they do for certain Western European sectors and firms with respect to West-East trade. Nevertheless, as the leader of the Western alliance the United States has been and for the foreseeable future is likely to be somewhat more restrictive than its allies. Moreover, structural features of the nonmarket economies, primarily their enforced self-sufficiency and limited ability to produce competitive goods for world markets, severely restrict their foreign exchange earnings and hence their imports. For what manufactured goods the Soviet bloc does import, the proximity of Western Europe and Japan and their greater use of Soviet energy and raw material exports make them more likely suppliers than the United States. In the unlikely event that the United States could capture the same share of Soviet bloc imports that it holds in total world manufactures trade (approximately 20 percent), U.S. exports would increase on the order of $3 billion to $4 billion. As described in Appendix D, a realistic estimate of U.S.-Soviet bloc trade loss attributable to export controls is not insignificant, but it is smaller than the range noted above.

Of much greater concern are the potential costs of export controls on U.S.-headquartered industrial firms engaged in West-West trade. These costs are a function of the significant differences in national treatment of internationally competitive suppliers of technology.

Among the disadvantages to U.S. exporters vis-à-vis *CoCom* country competitors are the following:

• In contrast to the time delays and high level of uncertainty characterizing U.S. individual (IVL) licensing, which conceivably discourage some producers from exporting altogether or from exporting certain products, other CoCom country licensing systems are characterized by rapid processing, prior consultation between exporters and licensing officials, and a high degree of predictability.

• For national security reasons the United States unilaterally controls some 27 categories of dual use products and technologies that are not included on the CoCom International List.[8] Among other CoCom members, only Canada and Germany maintain unilateral national security export controls, but these are limited to certain kinds of chemical products and nuclear items, respectively.

• The United States often requires foreign resellers to obtain a U.S. reexport authorization for U.S.-origin end products, U.S.-origin parts and components incorporated in foreign equipment, and even foreign products manufactured with U.S.-origin technology. No other CoCom member imposes reexport controls, and many do not use the other devices employed by the United States (e.g., denial lists and end-user and postshipment checks) to prevent the diversion of controlled goods from non-CoCom Western countries. (See Table 6-1.)

• In the past, U.S. bulk licenses, especially distribution licenses, have been *less* restrictive than some foreign licensing systems that rely even more heavily than does the United States on prior review and approval of individual transactions. Nevertheless, the U.S. distribution license procedure has recently become relatively more restrictive as these license holders and their foreign consignees have been required to establish internal control systems subject to U.S. government audit and as other CoCom members (Japan, France, and the United Kingdom) have adopted bulk export authorizations with less stringent conditions.

Among the disadvantages to U.S. exporters vis-à-vis *non-CoCom* country competitors are the following:

• In contrast to the elaborate system of U.S. controls, few non-CoCom countries (exceptions are Switzerland, Sweden, Austria, India, and Yugoslavia) maintain any national security controls on dual use exports.

• U.S. bilateral efforts to conclude control agreements with third countries disadvantage U.S. firms in relation to their competitors: in the short run by the use of license denials or delays as an instrument of negotiating leverage and in the long run in cases in which a country agrees to control only exports of U.S.-origin technology.

As the relative restrictiveness of U.S. controls becomes more apparent abroad, foreign customers are exploring alternative sources and some already have turned to non-U.S. suppliers. At the same time, U.S. firms are losing their relative competitive edge, not only in technological sophistication but also in price competitiveness, product quality, marketing, and service—factors that previously compensated for the negative competitive effect of export controls.

U.S. producers of medium- and lower-level technology products are most vulnerable because increasing numbers of non-U.S. sources, many of them with cost or other competitive advantages, exist for these items or for their essential components. Not only does the U.S. national security export control system weigh more heavily than the controls of other countries with increasingly competitive suppliers, but it also captures a great many lower-level items and treats them on a par with more advanced technology having greater military significance. Although the benefits of controls appear to be concentrated in a few technology areas, the costs are spread across a wide range of products of varying sophistication and strategic importance.

The panel developed two analyses that support the extensive anecdotal evidence acquired on its foreign visits and presented in briefings by exporters. The first analysis deals directly with the question of lost sales—in this case those resulting from the imposition of controls that have been in part unilateral. The second indicates that extraterritorial controls are having an adverse effect on the structure of business operations by which U.S. firms establish and maintain a competitive position in world markets.

The Case of Analytic Instruments

The category of analytic instruments provides a unique opportunity to isolate and measure the effects of U.S. unilateral export controls because of discrete regulatory changes in 1984 that affected products containing embedded microprocessors. In April 1984, following an extended public and internal government debate, the Department of Commerce announced decontrol of roughly one-half of the categories of instruments previously requiring a validated license. Eight months later, however, the department issued interpretations of new CoCom agreements redefining incorporated microprocessors and reimposing controls on many of the same instrumentation categories.

After adjusting for changes in exchange rates, price levels, and level of foreign industrial production, an analysis commissioned by the panel (see

Appendix C) indicates that when controls were relaxed early in 1984, U.S. analytic instrument exports increased (by the third quarter of 1984) roughly 7 percent over what they would have been without the change. Using the same assumptions and adjustments the analysis shows that when the relaxation was reversed late in 1984, exports (by the third quarter of 1985) were 12 percent below what they would have been if licensing requirements had not been reimposed. These fluctuations in trade reflect only the short-run observable effects probably attributable to unilateral export control. In the long term the on-off-on-again controls may erode the desire of foreign customers to purchase U.S. products. Also not reflected in the analysis are the effects these restrictions may have had on foreign transactions in similar instrumentation produced abroad with U.S. technology or containing U.S. components.

The Case of Foreign Consignees Under Distribution Licenses

In May 1985 the Commerce Department issued new regulations requiring distribution license holders and their foreign consignees to protect controlled items from diversion to the Soviet bloc by establishing internal control and recordkeeping systems subject to on-site inspection by agents of the license holder and the U.S. government.[9] For the vast majority of U.S. exporters and their affiliates holding distribution licenses, the flexibility of the license unquestionably outweighs the administrative and other perceived costs of the new restrictions. But the combination of increased administrative costs, foreign sensitivities to the extraterritorial application of U.S. law, and in the case of firms located in other CoCom countries the duplication of effort entailed in complying with domestic as well as U.S. export control regulations raises a concern that the rules discourage independent foreign companies from doing business with U.S. suppliers.

Surveyed in May 1986, only 1 month after the regulations became fully effective, distribution license holders responding (accounting for approximately 18 percent of the total number of licenses) reported the loss or removal of 32 percent of all the foreign consignees approved on their licenses—1,175 out of 3,686—in the previous 12 months since the regulations were issued. Business changes unrelated to the regulations, sales inactivity, and product decontrol actions were reported to account for one-half of these drop-outs; but the expense of compliance and consignees' refusal to comply accounted for 40 percent of the cases. More often than not, business is continuing with former foreign consignees under different licensing arrangements. Nevertheless, 28 licensees (25 percent of the sample) reported an immediate loss, albeit in the near term a small loss, of business as a result of the drop-outs. Companies also reported that under the new requirements it is becoming more difficult to recruit new consignees and that some consignees have reduced their orders although they remain on a distribution license.

Again, these findings represent only the short-run, observable effects of the regulations. Other evidence indicates that a number of foreign companies that chose not to terminate relationships with U.S. suppliers abruptly are now exploring alternative sources for the future.[10] A crucial stage in implementing the regulations is approaching as license holders and the Department of Commerce begin systematic auditing of foreign consignees. In the meantime the regulations have already brought about some erosion of the distribution networks of U.S. exporters, a marginal loss of business, and an increase in the volume of individual license applications.

TECHNICAL DATA CONTROLS

Some firms find it difficult to understand and apply the general license GTDR and validated license requirements for the export of technical data. There is substantial confusion regarding what transactions (i.e., oral communication with foreign nationals, visual inspection by foreign nationals within the United States, and application of knowledge abroad) are considered to be "exports"; there also is uncertainty as to what transfers are unrestricted (and thus eligible for general license GTDA) or require written assurances of nondisclosure by the recipients (under general license GTDR). Some firms argue that the requirements associated with the GTDR license inhibit internal corporate information flows without affording any more protection than customary corporate procedures for handling proprietary information.

Of greater concern to the panel, however, is the prospect of greatly expanded controls on technical data including data arising from research. There are at least three manifestations* of this emerging policy thrust.

---

*A fourth was announced just before the panel completed its deliberations. Under an October 1986 policy directive (a memorandum from the President's national security adviser, John M. Poindexter, on a "Policy for Protection of Sensitive, but Unclassified Information in Federal Government Telecommunications and Automated Systems for Immediate Implementation by All Federal Executive Branch Departments and Agencies," 29 October 1986), the National Security Council has instructed all federal departments and agencies to safeguard sensitive but unclassified information in government telecommunications and automated information systems. Although it is left to agency heads to identify "sensitive" information whose disclosure, loss, or destruction could damage national security or other government interests, the directive refers specifically to technological as well as other kinds of information. The directive does not, however, specify the means for protecting such information (for example, whether it is to be withheld from data bases such as the National Technical Information Service or, alternatively, whether access to such data bases is to be restricted); nor does it refer to penalties for unauthorized disclosure.

First, the Department of Defense is moving to place restrictions on unclassified technical data developed in DoD-sponsored research and falling within a category on the Militarily Critical Technologies List (MCTL). Although the export of such data always has been subject to the provisions of EAR and ITAR, domestic U.S. dissemination was unfettered. The current initiative relies on authority in the 1984 DoD Authorization Act to exempt such data from public disclosure through requests under the Freedom of Information Act.[11]

The panel does not question the authority of DoD to control technical data arising from militarily sensitive research projects it funds. Nevertheless, extending controls to unclassified technical data that relate to the wide range of technologies on the MCTL and allowing access to that data only by U.S. and foreign firms previously certified by the U.S. government would seriously encroach on the exchange of information in the technical community without necessarily enhancing national security.

Of particular concern is the impact of this new system on the communication of research through professional society meetings and publications. Communication fostered by scientific and engineering society activities has been crucial to the rapid advancement of commercial and military technology in the United States and thus to national security. Although Soviet access to this communication is of legitimate concern, the panel believes the risks are outweighed by the important role of open and rapid communication of ideas and findings, including conceptual dead-ends, in promoting innovation.

A second manifestation of efforts to expand controls on technical data concerns patent information. Serious constraints on the use of new knowledge to benefit U.S. commercial and military activities could result from the development by the Patent and Trademark Office, in consultation with the Department of Defense, of a new type of patent secrecy order.[12] (See also Chapter 4.) The order can be issued when a patent application contains unclassified technical data relating to inventions with military or space application. Although the patent would be withheld until the secrecy order was lifted, the data contained in the application could be disclosed to U.S. residents; the invention could be developed and marketed domestically; and the inventor could apply for patent protection in most European countries and Australia. Other foreign disclosure or marketing could occur only under a validated export license. Because the applicant would not be authorized to file for patent protection in most newly industrializing countries, marketing this invention could lead to legal pirating by enterprises in those countries.

Use of the MCTL or any other broad criteria as guidance could result in subjecting a considerable number of applications to such secrecy orders. The panel believes that extensive use of secrecy orders would undermine the benefits of the patent system, increase the duplication of R&D activities, and result in important innovations being withheld from commercial markets.

Third, the Department of Defense has culled from the MCTL a subset of critical dual use items with an eye to proposing that these technologies and the technical data associated with them be subject to validated licensing to Western destinations.[13] Of all the initiatives to restrict transfers of technical data, this is potentially the most troublesome because controls would not be limited to know-how or inventions derived from government-sponsored research and development or contained in patent applications but would apply regardless of the information's origin, form, and means of transfer—personal, print, or electronic.

Despite the problems associated with it, general license GTDR remains critical to the ability of many U.S. firms to conclude sales, explore international joint ventures, and transfer research results to foreign business partners. Requiring a validated license for data covered by broad categories of the MCTL would significantly alter the nature of communications within the Free World. Although the comprehensive operations license authorized in 1985 might limit the burden on large multinational firms, other companies with less well-established international operations would be adversely affected.

There is little doubt that unclassified but militarily sensitive technical information can be diverted from Western channels of communication; but there are enormous practical difficulties as well as political and economic risks in treating information in the same manner as tangible products. The flow of technical data within and among enterprises is essential to their operation. CoCom agreement to adopt similar restrictions is doubtful; some member governments lack legal authority to control intangible data. Finally, it is not clear that the benefits the Soviets derive from adapting, applying, diffusing, and improving upon unclassified technical data acquired from the West are substantial enough, relative to other means of obtaining technology, to warrant broad application of intrusive controls.

USE OF THE MILITARILY CRITICAL TECHNOLOGIES LIST

Regardless of the regulatory mechanism the panel is concerned by the prospective use of the Militarily Critical Technologies List as a de facto and possibly unilateral control list for technical data. It also considers unwise and unworkable the long-standing congressional mandate, renewed in the 1985 Export Administration Amendments Act, to integrate the MCTL with the U.S. Control List—except on a case-by-case basis in which CoCom negotiation and agreement precede the adoption of a new control by the United States.

As mandated in the Export Administration Act of 1979 and revised periodically by the Department of Defense, the complete MCTL is a classified document of 800 pages, including specifications and justifications. An abbreviated, unclassified version was published in October 1984. Updating has not changed its initial character. The MCTL is an extensive compilation of militarily useful technologies and equipment. It lacks prioritization and reflects the paucity of detailed information on near-term and long-term Soviet needs and capabilities. Further, the MCTL's development has not been disciplined by considerations of clarity, foreign availability, or enforceability, considerations that should be reflected if it is to be used as an operational control list accessible to licensing officers and exporters. The MCTL serves a useful but limited purpose as a reference document for developing control proposals and making informed licensing decisions. Explicit internal DoD guidance could enhance the latter role and dispel much of the confusion that surrounds the MCTL.

The Militarily Critical Technologies List was an attempt to embody general control criteria developed by a 1976 task force of the Defense Science Board under the chairmanship of J. Fred Bucy.[14] The Bucy task force implicitly faulted the traditional emphasis on controlling exports of products for neglecting the source of any nation's industrial capability and of the U.S. military advantage over the Soviet Union in particular—mastery of the know-how required to specify, design, build, test, maintain, and use sophisticated products. The Bucy task force instead proposed controls on critical design and manufacturing processes; essential manufacturing, inspection, and test equipment; and operation, application, and maintenance data accompanying products. Furthermore, the task force urged closer scrutiny of revolutionary rather than slowly evolving technologies and of active means of transfer—for example, turnkey factories, training, and ongoing technical exchanges—rather than routine sales of products.

The Bucy criteria have strong theoretical appeal but have proven extremely difficult to put into operation. They rely on distinctions—"critical," "revolutionary," "keystone"—on which opinions are widely variable and difficult to reconcile. As the panel's observations on technical data controls indicate, it is especially hard to define categories of know-how that need to and can be controlled, beyond proprietary protections but short of security classification, without disrupting routine and vital technical communication.

THE POLICY PROCESS AND THE BALANCING OF U.S. INTERESTS

The panel's findings underscore the need for a policymaking process that will continue to generate new information and weigh conflicting judgments. Economic and technological change in the West requires continuous balancing and rebalancing of diverse national stakes. Divided administrative responsibility, congressional oversight checks on administrative discretion, consultation with private industry, and negotiations with allies can ensure that some balancing of views and interests occurs in the evolution of export control policy. But these long-standing features of the policy process have limitations and drawbacks and are not up to the challenge of reconciling controls with the need to sustain a vigorous technological enterprise in an increasingly competitive international economy.

In many areas of economic and social regulation in the United States, federal statutes, executive orders, or judicial decisions directly require or indirectly encourage analysis of costs and benefits. This is not the case with export controls. Because they involve matters of foreign and military affairs, both national security and foreign policy export controls are exempt from the Administrative Procedures Act (5 U.S.C. 553), which provides for judicial review and for notice of and public comment on proposed regulations, and from Executive Order 12291, which mandates economic impact analysis of most domestic regulations.

To impose export controls for foreign policy purposes (or to maintain them after their automatic expiration after 1 year), however, the Export Administration Amendments Act of 1985 requires the President to determine that the adverse effects on U.S. export performance, the reputation of U.S. companies as reliable suppliers, and the welfare of companies, their employees, and communities will not exceed the foreign policy benefits. Furthermore, before applying foreign policy controls, the President first must have tried other means to influence the offending country's behavior. He also must have consulted with Congress, industry, and other countries so that he is in a position to certify to Congress that the actions he is considering are likely to achieve their objective, are enforceable, and are not likely to be undermined by the behavior of other countries. The General Accounting Office is directed to "second-guess" the President's judgments and to determine whether they meet the statutory criteria. None of these formal checks and balances, intended by Congress to contain the costs and ensure the effectiveness of the President's actions, applies to national security export controls. Nor has the bureaucratic structure served to produce analysis and debate.

Shared responsibility among agencies with diverse and often conflicting perspectives has been a chronic feature of export control policy and administration. The Export Administration Act assigns the Department of Commerce primary responsibility for the list of controlled dual use goods and technologies and for administering and enforcing the licensing system. The Department of State has the lead in negotiations with other countries, both CoCom and non-CoCom, to achieve cooperation on multilateral controls. The Department of Defense is charged with providing technical advice on the military significance of goods and technologies and the security risks of their transfer to proscribed countries. Finally, the Customs Service has primary responsibility for the enforcement of controls at points of exit and for investigations of diversions abroad.

Although this dispersion of authority has disadvantages, the panel believes that both the policy guidance and the division of labor set forth in the Export Administration Act are appropriate. It is not difficult to conceive of alternative arrangements, but none promises an ideal balance of the national interests in export controls. The deficiencies of the current arrangement, however, are threefold. First, there has been no regular policy guidance at the highest level of the U.S. government nor an effective means of reconciling differences among the agencies. Second, certain departments, notably Commerce and State, lack resources and assertiveness commensurate with their responsibilities. And third, recent changes within the departments have shifted export control responsibilities away from officials responsible for technology and trade development, resulting in a concentration of authority in administrative units with a narrower perspective.

The lack of an effective overarching mechanism has allowed a legitimate but limited view of military security to dominate without giving sufficient weight to the health of the economy as a crucial element of national security. The White House has intervened only intermittently and then to contain bureaucratic conflict rather than to give policy direction. The Senior Interagency Group on Technology Transfer has been a weak instrument of coordination and conflict resolution. It has not considered its responsibility to be that of balancing the requirements for enhancing U.S. competitiveness, maintaining the U.S. lead in military technology, and promoting cooperation with our major allies.

DoD's assertiveness on export control issues is not counterbalanced by the Departments of State and Commerce. On its foreign fact-finding missions, the panel was told repeatedly that the United States speaks with several voices on technology transfer policy to the consternation and frustration of foreign negotiators. By the same token, several recent DoD initiatives, notably on the review of foreign availability findings and of license applications to certain Free World countries, have had the effect of weakening the authority of the Commerce Department and the morale of its Export Administration personnel.

One unfortunate result of the imbalance is the lack of any effective mechanism for weeding out from the Control List those products and technologies that have ceased to be strategic or that have become so widely available that control for all practical purposes is impossible. The momentum is to add, not to delete, and the principal licensing agency, with a stake in keeping its task from becoming unmanageable, has been unable to slow it down.

A striking example is the failure of the Commerce Department's foreign availability program to yield the results intended by Congress when in 1979 and again in 1985 it mandated a procedure to eliminate one type of ineffective control—on items that the Soviet Union either can make itself or freely buy from uncontrolled sources. According to the statute, foreign availability exists when a non-CoCom-origin item of comparable quality is available to adversaries in quantities sufficient to satisfy their military needs so that U.S. exports of the item would not make a significant contribution to their military capabilities.

A newly created Office of Foreign Availability (OFA), with valuable technical assistance from defense, intelligence, and other agencies, has completed 44 investigations of the availability of items under control or proposed for control. Many of these studies have contributed needed discipline to the process by which new controls are conceived and developed. Of the 44 investigations, 20 were assessments of whether or not foreign availability should lead to the removal of existing national security export controls. Most of these assessments have languished in interagency review for periods as long as 8 months. Only two negative findings and three positive findings, the latter leading to preliminary decisions to decontrol automatic silicon wafer saws and mercury cadmium telluride uncooled array sensors and to modify specifications on floppy disks, have been published. One problem is that, although regulations specify expeditious Commerce Department evaluation of foreign availability claims, no constraints are imposed on the Defense Department's review of OFA findings. The review process is used as a means of delay. Further, DoD narrowly construes the foreign availability criteria to preclude decontrol in most cases. The panel believes that the meager results of this process mean that U.S. industry continues to bear unnecessary costs and the credibility of U.S. controls is further undermined.

Another recent change in the policy process is more subtle but no less consequential. In the current administration the bureaucratic balance of power has shifted toward security, intelligence, and law enforcement agencies and away from those entities responsible for technology development, trade, and international economic relations. In the Defense Department a new organization, the Defense Technology Security Administration, reporting to the under secretary of defense for policy, has assumed responsibility for technology transfer policy—responsibility that previously resided in the Office of the Under Secretary for Research and Engineering. In the State Department, security assistance officials have assumed the lead role formerly assigned to the Bureau of Economic Affairs. The Commerce Department has a statutory mandate to remove Export Administration from the International Trade Administration to stand on its own just below the Office of the Secretary.

These changes have contributed to a reinvigorated control system, a credible enforcement capability, better threat assessment, a more assertive diplomacy, and even improvements in license processing. The reorganization of Export Administration in the Department of Commerce and the appointment of a senior representative for strategic technology policy in the Office of the Under Secretary of State for Security Assistance, Science, and Technology are two recent positive efforts to upgrade the administrative capabilities of responsible agencies.

But there is a danger in isolating export control functions from trade and technology development responsibilities. The risk is that controls will become increasingly unrealistic and burdensome on U.S. competitiveness and innovation and that these adverse effects will not be acknowledged until they become obvious and possibly irreversible. The evidence of such effects is limited but sufficient to justify further adjustments in U.S. export control policy and administration.

NOTES

1. U.S. Department of Defense, *Soviet Acquisition of Militarily Significant Western Technology: An Update* (Intelligence Community white paper) (September 1985), Table 1, p. 6.
2. Ibid., p. 6.
3. U.S. General Accounting Office, *Export Licensing: Commerce-Defense Review of Applications to Certain Free World Countries* (Washington, D.C., September 1986).
4. U.S. Department of Defense, *Assessing the Effect of Technology Transfer on U.S./Western Security: A Defense Perspective* (February 1985).
5. Ibid., pp. 5-8.
6. For example, exporters may not use the full amount of license authorizations because sales are not completed or orders are reduced.
7. See, for example, U.S. Department of Commerce, *Foreign Policy Report to Congress, January 21, 1985, to January 20, 1986*; and Stanley D. Nollen, "Business Costs and Business Policy for Export Controls," *Journal of International Business Studies* 18, no. 1 (Spring 1987).
8. Congress has long pressed for the elimination of these unilateral controls either by decontrol or through CoCom agreement to adopt them as multilateral controls. Although many items have been removed over the years and others such as communications countermeasures equipment (ECCN 4516B) may be candidates for control under ITAR, a number of unilaterally controlled items appear to have little military significance and probably remain on the control list because of bureaucratic inertia.
9. 15 C.F.R. 373.
10. See "The Technology Gap: Western Countries Growing Apart?" (Speech by W. Dekker, president and chairman, N.V. Philips, at the Atlantic Institute for International

Affairs, Paris, December 5, 1985); and "Reagan Curbs Hit U.S. Electronics Sales Overseas," *Financial Times* (October 16, 1986).

11. 1984 Department of Defense Authorization Act, 10 U.S.C. 140c. See DoD Directive 5230.25, "Withholding of Unclassified Technical Data from Public Disclosure" (November 6, 1984).

12. *Federal Register* 51, no. 180, pp. 32938-32939.

13. U.S. Department of Defense, *Militarily Critical Technologies Program* (July 17, 1986), p. 21.

14. Defense Science Board Task Force on Export of U.S. Technology, *An Analysis of Export Control of U.S. Technology—A DoD Perspective* (February 4, 1976).

6

An Assessment of the Multilateral Export Control System

The rapid diffusion of technology and the globalization of production and marketing of high-technology products leave the United States little choice but to work to improve and bring additional Western countries into the system of multilateral export controls. The issue is how effective and reliable an instrument the system is or can be made to be—and what approach the United States should take in improving upon it.

By persuasion and pressure the United States has led its allies to agree to a broad set of controls on trade with the Soviet bloc. But U.S. policymakers have often acted outside the consensus, with or without multilateral consultation. The United States has imposed and maintained unilateral national security controls; foreign policy controls on the export to the Soviet Union of goods and technologies that have no military importance; and controls on reexports of U.S. products, parts, and components from CoCom countries. Some of these measures have posed few problems in alliance relations, but others have been major irritants.

The panel believes that the multilateral system is so essential to the effective denial or significant delay of strategic products and technology to the Soviet Union, and that restrictions on West-West trade and technology exchange are sufficiently harmful to U.S. economic and Western security interests, that the United States ought now to pursue the objective of developing a community of common controls in dual use technology among cooperating Western countries. This concept implies the construction of a common external "wall" of export controls to the East accompanied by a significant liberalization of controls within the

135

West. To be successful a community of common controls must in time include not only the industrialized allies but also a number of advanced or rapidly industrializing non-CoCom countries.

The panel recognizes that this objective will require major policy adjustments by both the United States and its major trading partners. Furthermore, there may be an incentive for one or more countries to remain outside the community as an island of unrestricted trading activity. This could only be prevented by strict community control of exports to the noncomplying country. Such contingencies need to be addressed in developing the community. Nevertheless, recent improvements in CoCom and moderately successful diplomatic initiatives with certain neutral European countries have made the concept of a community of common controls in dual use technology a realistic objective for U.S. export control policy.

This chapter considers the adjustments that have already been made in multilateral export controls and the obstacles to further progress. First, it addresses the state of the CoCom arrangement—its rejuvenation in recent years and its remaining deficiencies. Second, it considers the extent to which U.S. policies support or undermine international cooperation on national security export controls. Finally, it reviews the progress and pitfalls in securing the cooperation of leading countries that are not parties to CoCom.

PROGRESS IN COCOM

Since 1980 CoCom has attracted unprecedented attention at high political levels in member governments. In the wake of the Afghanistan invasion, the United States persuaded its CoCom partners to adopt a policy of allowing no exceptions for exports to the Soviet Union of items falling within the CoCom general embargo. The U.S. government not only has tightened its own strategic export controls but also has led a major effort to revitalize the multilateral system.* At the Ottawa summit of Western leaders in July 1981, President Reagan persuaded the allies to call the first ministerial-level meeting of CoCom in 25 years. The meeting took place in January 1982 and was followed by two other high-level meetings—in April 1983 and February 1985.

The 1982 ministerial meeting reaffirmed the strategic and political objectives of the organization; launched a comprehensive review of the

---

*Efforts by the Departments of Defense and State have led to: (1) important progress in CoCom list reviews, (2) the shift of emphasis from product control to technology control, and (3) improved administrative and technical support capabilities within the CoCom secretariat.

CoCom International List; called for national controls of "equal effectiveness," including measures to deal with the reexport of controlled equipment and technology from third countries; and urged improved administration and enforcement of CoCom controls. The 1983 meeting took place during the allies' confrontation over construction of the Siberian gas pipeline and focused on the details of what was by then a full agenda, as well as on the deficiencies of the CoCom establishment in Paris—inadequate staff, space, and equipment. The 1985 meeting ratified the outcome of the list review process; adopted a new procedure of continuous reviews; called attention to the diversion of goods in transit; approved expedited processing of exception requests for the People's Republic of China; and endorsed work on the means of dealing with the export of intangible technical know-how.

As a consequence of these agreements, CoCom members have tightened some of their licensing and enforcement procedures; admitted Spain to membership; upgraded Paris headquarters operations; launched a diplomatic effort to obtain the cooperation of nonmember countries; created a group of advisers with military expertise, most of them representing defense ministries; and added to the control list certain types of machine tools, dry docks, semiconductor manufacturing equipment, robotics, superalloy technology, telecommunications switching equipment, and software. Perhaps most importantly, a 10-year debate over the levels of computer hardware and associated technology that should be denied to the Soviet military was finally resolved by a compromise, removing lower-level computers from the International List.

In the panel's judgment the combination of a more up-to-date control list and the commitment of most member countries to adhere to it in trade with the Eastern bloc makes CoCom a reasonably effective, albeit imperfect, instrument of control on which the United States can rely with much greater confidence than the arrangement merited only a few years ago.

COCOM DEFICIENCIES

Intra-CoCom Differences

It is widely believed both in the United States and abroad that some CoCom nations are more assiduous than others in their adherence to CoCom restrictions against direct sales of militarily useful goods and technologies to the Soviet bloc. Goods that might not be sold if they were of U.S. origin may be approved for sale to the bloc by another CoCom country. Governments differ in their interpretations of the relevant technical parameters. In situations of uncertainty about whether or not equipment is controlled, U.S. firms tend to err on the side of caution by refusing to do business or by requesting an export approval; foreign firms are more likely to accept the order and ship the goods. This is particularly likely to occur in countries whose governments have not allocated adequate resources to enforcement of export controls and have not otherwise stressed the importance of compliance with export controls to their domestic producers.

Correcting such deficiencies and reconciling interpretations of the International List have been principal objectives of the United States— not only in CoCom negotiations but also in dealings with individual governments. Much remains to be accomplished, but the underlying allied consensus does enable the reconciliation of differences when a sound strategic rationale exists for items subject to control.

There are more serious differences among CoCom countries, with adverse consequences for both technology security and U.S. competitiveness, in the treatment of exports of CoCom-controlled items to other Western destinations that are potential points of diversion to the Eastern bloc.

With few exceptions,* all CoCom countries license the export of controlled dual use products to one another and to third countries as a precaution against diversion. A crucial control consideration in West-West trade generally is the reliability of customers. In conjunction with individual licenses,† therefore, various CoCom members employ several instruments, depending on the country destination, to ensure the reliability of consignees. These instruments include: (1) requiring from the recipient's government an import certificate (IC) and/or delivery verification (DV) statement usually pledging that the item will not be reexported to a proscribed country; (2) conducting a prelicense or postshipment investigation of the consignee (an "end-user check"); (3) demanding from the recipient (i.e., consignee) a declaration of the intended end use of the item or a letter of assurance against its reexport to a proscribed country; (4) maintaining a list of diverters or suspected diverters for use in screening original license applications; and (5) in the U.S. case alone, requiring that some reexports have the approval of the government of the country of origin.

Formal requirements and informal practice, however, vary consider-

---

*Canada, the United Kingdom, France, Germany, Japan, and the United States all issue bulk licenses restricted to West-West trade. Apart from the U.S. special license arrangements, the panel was able to acquire only incomplete information on the conditions for obtaining and using licenses under these systems.

†Validated licenses are not required for direct trade between the United States and Canada and vice versa.

ably from one CoCom country to another. Consequently, controls on International List items in West-West trade are inconsistently administered. For example, major CoCom partners have not been willing to maintain extraterritorial controls and do not cooperate in the enforcement of U.S. reexport restrictions. Few CoCom members conduct prelicense and end-use checks in the West or have formal mechanisms comparable to the U.S. Table of Denial Orders for denying export rights to known or suspected diverters. All CoCom members request import certificate and delivery verification documents from only a handful of nonmember countries (see Table 6-1). Because efforts to improve CoCom surveillance of exports to third countries have been only marginally successful, such surveillance remains the weakest link in the multilateral system.

The United States has been inclined to compensate for the weaknesses and differences in the CoCom system by "going it alone." The only plausible explanation for U.S. reexport controls on multilaterally controlled commodities exported to other CoCom member countries is that we do not have confidence that their control systems will reliably prevent diversion. The U.S. approach, however, is ineffective for two reasons. First, if direct controls by the host government do not adequately deter questionable sales, indirect controls asserted from a considerable distance are unlikely to be any more effective. Second, because the CoCom countries are not merely conduits of U.S. goods and technology but the source of equally sophisticated items of interest to the Soviet bloc, any policy that fails to address directly the weaknesses of CoCom is self-deluding. Thus, while there are problems with the CoCom system, it is the panel's view that there is no viable alternative to reliance on the multilateral approach to export control that CoCom represents. The United States should build on the widely shared perception of the Soviet threat and create incentives for governments and industry to cooperate in more vigorous and effective multilateral controls.

Scope of the International List

One of the impediments to more effective enforcement and cooperation, especially in terms of the control of exports to third countries, is the scope of the CoCom International List. As the panel confirmed in discussions with officials in Europe and Asia, many member countries believe the list far exceeds CoCom's grasp. Given finite resources, it is impractical to enforce sweeping controls. Overly broad coverage also reduces the credibility of the control system and encourages laxness on the part of public officials and industry. Curtailing the control list would have the further advantage of encouraging the cooperation of newly

TABLE 6-1 Comparison of CoCom Country Controls on Exports to Western Destinations

Country	License Required for Reexport from Another Country	Government-Issued Import Certificate or Equivalent Required	End-User Certificate Required	Prelicense and/or Postshipment Check of Consignees Conducted in Country of Destination	Exporters Required to Screen Transactions Against List of Denied Parties
United States	Yes	For exports to CoCom, Austria, Sweden, Yugoslavia, Switzerland, Singapore (except AEN, export to Canada, under distribution licenses, to governments)	Yes, in most cases	Yes	Yes
Canada	Only if more than 80 percent U.S. origin	For exports to CoCom, Austria, Finland, Hong Kong, Switzerland, Yugoslavia (except AEN, exports to United States, government agencies, spares)	Uncertain	No	No[a]
Federal Republic of Germany	No[b]	For exports to CoCom, Switzerland, Austria, Yugoslavia (except less than 20,000 DM)	Uncertain	No	No
France	No	For exports to CoCom, Austria, Finland, Sweden, Switzerland, Yugoslavia, Hong Kong	Uncertain	No	No
Japan	No	For exports to CoCom, Singapore, Malaysia, Switzerland, Sweden, Hong Kong, 6 other countries	Uncertain	No	No
United Kingdom	No	For exports to CoCom	Uncertain	No	No

[a] U.S.-published Table of Denial Orders used to screen applications.

[b] Requires letter authorization in some cases.

SOURCES: International Business-Government Counsellors report; panel foreign study missions.

industrializing countries that are becoming producers of lower-level controlled technology.

As a practical matter, CoCom may be able to control effectively only those commodities and technologies where only a few non-CoCom countries friendly to Western interests have developed indigenous capabilities. Although some non-CoCom countries have agreed to control reexports of CoCom country origin, they have for the most part refused to control indigenous goods and technologies that fall within CoCom control parameters. Thus, to maintain the effectiveness of its restrictions, CoCom is obliged to update continually its control parameters in accordance with the cooperation it has—or has not—obtained from relevant non-CoCom nations.

The CoCom List Review Process

Because of its investment in strategic technologies, its leadership role in the alliance, and its global security interests outside the alliance, the United States has typically advocated more extensive controls than its CoCom partners at every list review. The existence of a much larger export control bureaucracy in the United States may also account for the greater number of U.S. control proposals.

Individually and collectively, other CoCom members devote less effort to defining what controls are advisable and could be effective. As a result, many CoCom members take a reactive stance in the list review process, a stance often influenced by domestic commercial pressures. More thorough assessments by other major CoCom nations (Canada, France, Great Britain, Japan, and West Germany), comparable to those carried out by the United States, would contribute to the development of well-documented proposals for decontrol and to the evolution of a control list that is based on a solid consensus and equally supported and enforced by all members.

The CoCom rule of unanimity is an unnecessary obstacle to removing items from the CoCom list. Unanimous agreement to *add* items is essential; all members must agree on the wisdom of new controls. The requirement for unanimity to *remove* items from the list, however, undermines the credibility of the embargo. One objection may force the other CoCom members into giving lip service to controls that they no longer believe are tenable and that they may subsequently undermine through lax enforcement. A mechanism for implementing less-than-unanimous judgments favoring decontrol would have at least two positive effects: It would ameliorate the current situation in which there is, de facto, a lack of multilateral cooperation in controlling some items; and it would increase the effectiveness of the general embargo.

The capabilities being developed and acquired by competitive non-CoCom countries probably warrant even shorter list review cycles than those contemplated at the end of the 1985 round of CoCom discussions. To reduce the current 4-year cycle to, for example, 2 years would probably require a reduction in list coverage. This could be facilitated by adding a "sunset" provision, perhaps limited to administrative exception note items, that would cause these items to be removed automatically during the next regular CoCom list review unless their continued inclusion was rejustified and agreed upon.

The CoCom Exceptions Process

If an exporter wishes to ship goods or technologies on the International List to a Soviet bloc destination for civilian use, he must apply to his own government for permission. If national discretion authority does not apply, a government that is supportive of the sale must seek an exception at CoCom to the general embargo. CoCom approval of the exception request requires unanimous consent.

There are several problems with the exceptions process. The primary one is that member governments frequently interpret CoCom requirements or particular cases differently. For example, members may differ in their judgments about a product's technical characteristics and thus about the level of CoCom controls that apply to its export: whether it is eligible for shipment at national discretion, whether it should receive favorable CoCom consideration, or whether it requires full CoCom consideration and approval. Or members may disagree about the conditions under which an exception to the general embargo or favorable consideration may be granted. These conditions may be restrictions on the end use and end user or a requirement to substitute equipment with lower technical parameters for the item in the original application.

There is a widespread suspicion that members frequently object to other countries' exception applications or otherwise manipulate the exceptions process to benefit their own exporters. Individual members may adopt a more liberal interpretation of what constitutes a "safe" export and, in bringing such cases to CoCom as an exception request, create an impression that they seek a commercial edge. The fact that the United States has consistently submitted a majority of the requests for exceptions—formerly, for the Soviet Union, and more recently, for the People's Republic of China—is often interpreted abroad as an effort to get into the market first. In the United States it is taken as evidence of stricter U.S. adherence to multilateral controls. Especially on its visits to European and Asian countries, the panel sought evidence of U.S. use of the exceptions process for unfair commercial advantage. It found no evidence to support this allegation.

Another problematic feature of the exceptions process arises from member governments' needs for technical, end-use, end-user, and other commercial information to make informed judgments. Governments of the larger CoCom countries have sufficient in-house technical expertise, but governments of smaller nations often rely on industry advisers to assist in the evaluations. Even though the data are "sanitized" to protect proprietary information, such reviews by industry have fostered the suspicion that these governments may be seeking to promote commercial interests by providing their producers with access to valuable commercial intelligence.

The reliance of some member governments on private technical advice has been an argument for enlarging the role of defense ministries in national export control processes generally and in CoCom deliberations specifically. CoCom members have established a group of military experts representing the CoCom governments to consider the military relevance to the Soviet Union of particular Western technologies.* This organization meets independently of CoCom and reports its findings to the member governments. Another proposal is to strengthen the technical staff of CoCom so that smaller nations can participate in technical assessments without having to rely on industry assistance.

Finally, the CoCom exception decision process and the ability of member governments to weigh exception requests could be improved if CoCom established a "precedents file" containing exception decisions, commodity descriptions, and end-user information. Currently, these data are not computerized nor are they readily available for review by CoCom members.

Transparency of CoCom Decision Making

Most firms try to avoid the waste of time, money, and customer goodwill entailed in having a license application rejected. Difficult as it often is, especially for U.S. exporters, to discern the basis of national government export control decisions, the CoCom decision process and the criteria applied within it are even more obscure. This situation could be remedied if additional information on CoCom procedures and on commodities and end users approved or denied were made available. CoCom members could agree to submit appropriate information on approved and denied cases within a reasonable time (e.g., delayed 6 months) and sanitized in such a way that the information would not be useful for competitive

---

*See Joseph Fitchett, "West to Assess Exports With Military Use," *International Herald Tribune* (October 12-13, 1985).

purposes. The panel perceived a great deal of interest in such an arrangement during its overseas fact-finding missions.

U.S. POLICY AND INTERNATIONAL COOPERATION

Through foreign policy and economic cycles, the premise that Soviet acquisitions of leading Western dual use technologies represent a significant military threat has not been seriously challenged anywhere in the Western alliance. Although there have been lapses in attention and frequent disputes over the scope and means of control, there has not been a major international quarrel over principle. This consensus underlies the success of the current administration in revitalizing CoCom despite the fact that its initiatives coincided with a deep recession, a succession of trade disputes, and the uproar over the Siberian gas pipeline embargo.

The goal of U.S. policy should be to improve the multilateral control system to the point where removing controls from West-West trade is possible. However, the panel believes that there are two features of U.S. policy that impede progress toward this goal. One is the tendency to resort to foreign policy trade sanctions to penalize Soviet political behavior without clearly distinguishing them from strategic controls and without adequate consultation with our allies. The other is the use of extraterritorial controls that signal U.S. mistrust of our CoCom partners and offend their national sovereignty.

Foreign Policy Pressures on CoCom

CoCom is designed to restrict the flow of goods and technology to the Soviet bloc solely for national security reasons. This is reflected in the criteria used by CoCom for placing goods and technologies on the International List. However, U.S. foreign policy considerations, separate from the West-East military rivalry, have on occasion intruded on the CoCom process.

Particularly when dealing with the bloc nations, it is difficult to distinguish, clearly and consistently, measures that are aimed directly at the bloc's military strength from measures that are aimed at its economic growth and political adventurism. Obviously, a change in political orientation within the bloc can radically change the national security equation. For example, the radical changes in China's foreign and domestic economic policies since the Cultural Revolution have led to a far-reaching change in the West's perception of the national security risks entailed in selling sophisticated technology to the PRC. Nevertheless, the CoCom controls are intended to focus only on national security quite narrowly defined.

The United States has taken a much more expansive view of what types of goods and technology pose a military risk and has sought to use CoCom to punish Soviet behavior for essentially foreign policy reasons. Examples include the U.S. proposal after the invasion of Afghanistan to embargo turnkey projects amounting to more than $100 million and the U.S. initiative after the imposition of martial law in Poland to add oil and gas equipment and technology to the CoCom list. Such initiatives usually meet with allied resistance and may threaten the ability of CoCom to sustain the embargo of critical strategic items, even when undertaken after consultation with our CoCom partners. They are certainly damaging when taken abruptly and without prior discussion.

CoCom cannot function effectively without agreement on the national security criteria to be used in compiling and implementing the International List. There is nothing to prevent a member from using export policy to influence or express disapproval of another country's actions nor from trying to persuade its allies to join in a trade embargo. But such initiatives should not be presented as falling within the original CoCom mandate and should not be discussed or implemented within CoCom except after discussion and agreement in other venues such as NATO. Because controls based on foreign policy considerations are likely to produce dissension, it is wise to keep the CoCom process isolated from explicit foreign policy considerations.

Extraterritorial Controls

In some circumstances the United States attempts to exercise licensing control over reexports of U.S.-origin products from one foreign country to another. The objective of such controls is understandable: The United States seeks to ensure through the controls that products that were licensed for export from the United States to a particular foreign country do not find their way to proscribed destinations. In practice, however, the value of the controls is highly questionable.

First, the controls are premised on the assumption that the jurisdictional reach of the United States extends to actions by foreign citizens that are undertaken outside the territory of the United States.* Many other countries simply do not accept that U.S. authority has such an

---

*The acceptance of limits on the jurisdictional reach of the United States does not leave the United States without any power to deter diversion through reexport. If the U.S. license applicant makes false statements in the initial licensing application as to the intended destination of the product, then of course sanctions could be imposed on the applicant. Moreover, the United States could decline to approve licenses for further exports to a foreign recipient who has reexported products to a proscribed destination.

expansive reach. Indeed, some of our closest allies have legislation that is intended to block the United States' extraterritorial jurisdiction. The controls are thus premised on legal grounds that are questioned by those who are expected to comply.

Second, and perhaps as a consequence of doubts as to the legal justification of U.S. efforts to control reexports, foreign compliance with U.S. restrictions appears to be lax. The data examined by the panel suggest that foreign-owned businesses in CoCom countries often ignore the requirement to seek U.S. authorization to reexport, especially when the U.S. content (parts, components, or technology) of the goods is minimal or has lost its identity. This failure to observe U.S. requirements is not, of course, a vehicle of diversion when the host government controls exports in accordance with CoCom agreements.

Third, U.S. reexport controls impede progress toward a cooperative and unified system of controls among the allies. In every country visited by the panel on its European and Asian fact-finding missions, foreign businessmen and government officials expressed strong opposition to the U.S. system of reexport controls. The intensity of feeling is disproportionate to the burden that foreign companies currently bear, but the burden could become substantial if compliance were enforced.

Moreover, the grievance extends beyond questions of legal jurisdiction and potential cost. The explanation for this hostility is far more fundamental: Our reexport controls are seen as conflicting with widely accepted principles of international law and national sovereignty. Despite the existence of certain anecdotal evidence regarding their previous laxness in export control enforcement, our allies view current U.S. policy as reflecting mistrust as to whether CoCom partners or other countries that share our security concerns will adequately protect our common interest in preventing the diversion of sensitive products to the Soviet bloc.

The Political Costs of U.S. Policy

U.S. restrictions on West-West trade and technology transfer are becoming a significant irritant in allied relations. Especially in Western Europe, where U.S. export control policy has heightened prevalent feelings of technological and economic insecurity, the panel found that resentment against U.S. restrictions is surfacing in many quarters. As in the pipeline episode, the objections are mainly to the extraterritorial reach of U.S. law; but there is also concern about discrimination against friendly foreign nationals in access to U.S. research and suspicion regarding the terms of weapons cooperation agreements including those related to the Strategic Defense Initiative (SDI). As many Europeans see it, not only are they impeded in gaining access to the technology that would help Europe become competitive with the United States and Japan, but they are also hampered in their commercial applications of the technology (some of which they have helped to develop).

In 1985 the North Atlantic Assembly proposed a new European agency to promote European technological independence and to bargain with the United States on technology transfer issues. In a lengthy resolution adopted in February 1986, the European Parliament was even more critical of the "unilateral and especially indiscriminate proliferation" of U.S. technology controls, proposing that the Commission of the European Community consider seeking a European Court of Justice ruling on the compatibility of CoCom rules with provisions of the Treaty of Rome (which established the European Community). The resolution also advised European Economic Community member states to adopt legislation modeled on Great Britain's Protection of Trading Interests Act blocking the application of U.S. extraterritorial restrictions.

These statements reflect a mood that was forcefully conveyed to the panel on its European fact-finding mission by government officials, politicians, and private sector leaders alike. They raised the prospect of eroding trust and cooperation among the NATO allies.

The current friction over national security export controls should be viewed in the context of volatile but basically sound alliance relationships. National security export controls are only one of many prevailing irritants including traditional trade protection and subsidy issues, difficulties in coordinating macroeconomic policies, unilateral U.S. foreign policy controls, and obstacles (of which technology transfer policy is only one) to the creation of a two-way street in military equipment development and procurement. Moreover, West-West technology controls have not been an impediment to agreements to strengthen the multilateral export control system nor even to agreements on SDI collaboration. Fundamental differences over West-East strategic trade are likely to emerge only if there is a sharp divergence of perceptions regarding Soviet behavior under the new leadership and the prospects for West-East accommodation with the Gorbachev regime. So far no serious divergence has occurred.

The test of U.S. export control policy, however, is not the level of formal international cooperation that it engenders but the adequacy of the export control performance of the allies and other Western countries at both the governmental and private sector levels. The risk from the imposition of controls to which there are strong objections is that such controls will gradually undermine the credibility of the system and thus the degree of compliance with it. Maintaining and extending a web of unilateral West-West restrictions also may drive the development, application, and marketing of some technology to countries that are weaker links in the chain of controls.

NEGOTIATIONS WITH NON-COCOM FREE WORLD COUNTRIES

The Export Administration Act requires that the United States take "all feasible steps to initiate and conclude negotiations with appropriate foreign governments for the purpose of securing cooperation" in controlling exports and reexports of controlled goods and technology. Countries that agree to institute controls equivalent to those of CoCom shall be treated in the same manner as CoCom member countries with respect to U.S. licensing requirements (i.e., availability of the G-COM license for shipments of less-sensitive controlled items, availability of the proposed G-CEU license, and automatic licensing after 15 or 30 days).

Cooperation from countries that are not members of CoCom has become important to the success of the CoCom control efforts; it will be critical in the future as several third countries become significant markets for CoCom-controlled goods and develop indigenous products that fall within CoCom control parameters. As CoCom seeks to unify its controls on exports to the Soviet bloc, the threat of leakage of controlled products and technology through non-CoCom Free World countries grows. Approval for the shipment of controlled goods from CoCom to non-CoCom nations has come to be based in part on the nature of the commitments or controls these nations are willing to exercise to prevent reshipment of these items to proscribed destinations.

CoCom members have formally agreed to urge non-CoCom nations to establish and strengthen their controls vis-à-vis proscribed nations. CoCom's Subcommittee on Export Controls has reviewed the policies of some 20 non-CoCom third countries and grouped them according to their relationship to CoCom and the adequacy of their current controls. These groups include:

- nations sharing CoCom objectives such as New Zealand and Australia;
- nations sharing CoCom objectives but lacking adequate controls such as South Korea and South Africa;
- neutral nations that do not share CoCom objectives but apply some controls such as Sweden, Switzerland, Austria, and Ireland;
- nations that do not share CoCom objectives and apply few if any controls such as Singapore, Malaysia, and India;
- nations on which information is inadequate such as Hong Kong; and
- nations that have a special ideological attachment to proscribed nations.

The subcommittee also has set common objectives for member countries to guide their individual bilateral approaches to these nations. The

United States, for example, has proposed a number of objectives with respect to third country controls on exports to CoCom-proscribed nations. In the U.S. view, third countries should be asked to:

- assume responsibility for preventing reexports to the Soviet Union and the Warsaw Pact countries of imported CoCom-controlled items that do not have reexport authorization from the originating CoCom countries;
- monitor use of CoCom items in the Soviet Union and the Warsaw Pact countries after obtaining reexport approval;
- control the export to proscribed destinations of indigenously produced products that are functionally equivalent to CoCom-controlled items; and
- cooperate in enforcement measures.

If accepted, these conditions would amount to an adoption by third countries of the CoCom control list, both for imported and indigenously produced items, and of CoCom-like reexport and enforcement procedures for authorized exports.

Although important agreements to protect some CoCom- and U.S.-origin goods have been reached with a few countries, none of the agreements concluded to date comes close to meeting the comprehensive U.S. criteria. Agreements with the European neutrals include measures to implement controls on *selected categories* of CoCom-origin items and to coordinate these controls with the CoCom member country in which the controlled item originates. In most cases, indigenous products are not subject to such controls.

To date, negotiations with third countries have proceeded bilaterally. The United States has conducted discussions with a number of governments supported by occasional interventions by other CoCom members. To achieve effective control and to avoid placing U.S. exporters at a competitive disadvantage, it is important that these diplomatic efforts be closely coordinated in CoCom and that bilateral agreements concluded by the United States be followed as expeditiously as possible by agreements with other CoCom countries.

U.S. insistence on cooperation with U.S. reexport controls encourages neither coordination in CoCom nor the cooperation of third countries. An approach that does not create inducements for third country participation is unlikely to succeed with many governments, especially those of non-European, politically neutral countries. Raising the thresholds of CoCom-controlled products, extending favorable U.S. licensing terms to cooperating countries, and offering the prospect of a relaxation of U.S. reexport controls are the key inducements available to the United States in its efforts to extend the multilateral control system.

7

Findings and Key Judgments of the Panel

Based on the research initiatives and deliberations undertaken in pursuit of its charge, the panel reached unanimous agreement on a series of principal findings and key judgments. These are grouped below under seven major headings: (1) the practical basis for national security export controls; (2) considerations influencing national policy; (3) Soviet technology acquisition efforts in the West; (4) diffusion and transfer of technical capability; (5) foreign availability and foreign control of technology; (6) the effectiveness of multilateral procedures for national security export controls; and (7) administration of U.S. national security export control policies and procedures. These findings and judgments are reflected in turn in the recommendations that appear in the final chapter of this report.

THE PRACTICAL BASIS FOR NATIONAL SECURITY EXPORT CONTROLS

The fundamental objective of the national security export control regime maintained by CoCom is to deny—or at least to delay—the Soviet Union and its Warsaw Pact allies access to state-of-the-art Western technology that would permit them to narrow the existing gap in military systems. Yet, there are no well-defined criteria that can be used to determine whether a given technology will enhance significantly the Soviet military capability. For example, many technologies for which the military application is not self-evident can contribute to improving the quantity and quality of military goods. But many of these technologies also can be used for enhancing production in civilian sectors of the economy. Some observers see development of the civilian sector in the Soviet Union as offering long-run hope for ameliorating the Soviet threat to Western society. Others believe, however, that enhancing even civilian production will indirectly enhance Soviet military capability by relieving pressure on the general economy.

Such differing assumptions and viewpoints inevitably give rise to divergent judgments, divergent even on the extent to which a given technology can enhance *directly* the military capability of the Soviet Union and its allies. Without well-defined, agreed-upon criteria, it is conceptually impossible to draw a definitive line above which technology is critical—and below which it is not—either for military capability or for industrial productivity. But for an export control system to be operationally effective, such a line must be drawn—always recognizing that its location remains a matter of judgment. Determining the precise location of the line should be governed by the underlying objective of making the system effective in actually denying specific technology to the Soviet bloc. That in turn requires at a minimum a system that has the cooperation of all technologically advanced countries in the Free World and one that is comprehensible to the technologically advanced firms whose cooperation is essential to make the system work.

Thus, adopting, as a basis for national security export controls, the policy objective of constraining exports of Western technology that could have a significant impact on Soviet bloc military capabilities is problematic because it offers no precise identifiable threshold or definition of military criticality. Without more precision, policy implementation must depend on the world view of the decisionmaker. One individual might try to restrict only items destined directly for military systems; another might also want to restrict such items as numerically controlled production lines—no matter how benign the output—because manufacturing capability is important to military production. Yet another might want to restrict sales of subsidized grain because the Soviet resources freed in the process could be used to further military objectives. This conceptual vagueness can be surmounted in practice by establishing a definition that permits effective and practical implementation with our allies. In a practical sense this means restricting controls to technologies that are easily identified with military uses.

CONSIDERATIONS INFLUENCING NATIONAL POLICY

1. Technology Lead Is Vital to Western Security and Must Be Maintained

Western security depends on the maintenance of its technology lead in military systems over potential adversaries. This lead can be sustained only through a dual policy of promoting a vigorous domestic technological base and impeding the outward flow to the Warsaw Pact of technologies useful in military systems. Pursuit of this strategy is based on a recognition that maintaining the technology lead of the West depends on continued Western technological progress. Such progress in turn can be ensured only through active and full exchange of technical information, both among scientists and engineers within the United States and among the Western countries, and by maintaining healthy Western economies. The panel recognizes that, while continuing to out-innovate potential adversaries, it is also necessary for the United States and its allies to develop more rapid and efficient military R&D and procurement processes—as recommended in the recent report of the President's Blue Ribbon Commission on Defense Management (the Packard commission), *A Quest for Excellence: Final Report to the President.*

2. **Export Competitiveness Is Essential to the Health of the U.S. Domestic Economy**

Export markets have become increasingly vital to the U.S. domestic economy. Exports now represent a significant and growing percentage of total sales in a number of key industrial sectors (the portion of U.S. manufactured goods that were exported rose from 9 percent in 1960 to 25 percent in 1980 before declining to 18 percent in 1985); and they are especially critical to the success of high-technology enterprises (the high-technology sector accounted for 42 percent of manufactured exports in 1985). In some industries, remaining competitive in world markets is essential to maintaining their share of the domestic market because foreign competitors that dominate the international market may in some cases enjoy economies of scale not available to U.S. producers limited to domestic sales. Larger volumes of production result in lower average unit costs and also allow research and development expenditures to be amortized over a higher sales volume. Ultimately, these scale economies enable the transnational firm to develop superior products, reduce manufacturing costs, and gain worldwide market share. These realities are not yet fully reflected in the policies underlying current U.S. national security export controls.

3. **The Scope of Current U.S. National Security Export Controls Undermines Their Effectiveness**

U.S. national security export controls are not generally perceived as rational, credible, and predictable by many of the nations and commercial interests whose active cooperation is required for an effective system. The panel also concurs with this judgment. The scope of current U.S. national security export controls encompasses too many products and technologies to be administered effectively. In particular, the U.S. government has not provided a justification for the continued control of low-level technologies (e.g., some classes of memory chips) traded outside the Communist bloc, technologies that may be of marginal military significance and that in some cases are available worldwide with little or no restriction. The panel requested but did not receive information from the Department of Defense on the military significance of such technologies; it therefore was unable to evaluate the rationale for control of low-level items. However, during its two foreign fact-finding missions (see Appendix B), the panel *did* determine that many low-level products restricted by the United States are in fact available in other countries with little or no restriction.

4. **U.S. National Security Export Controls Impede the Export Sales of U.S. Companies**

National security export controls impede the ability of U.S. companies to compete in world markets. There is limited but specific evidence that export controls have negatively affected U.S. exporters in the following ways:

- export sales are lost because of delays in the licensing process or are foregone because of uncertainty as to whether a license will be approved;
- U.S. producers, especially small- to medium-sized firms, are deterred from exporting by the complexities and delays of the control regime; and
- foreign customers are discouraged from relying on U.S. suppliers due to uncertainties about future license approvals, follow-on service, spare parts and components, and possible reexport constraints, choosing instead to seek more dependable non-U.S. sources. Once changes in buying preferences occur, large investments of time and effort may be required to reverse them.

5. **Pragmatic Control Lists Must Be Technically Sound, Narrowly Focused, and Coordinated Multilaterally**

The control criteria developed in 1976 as part of the report of the Defense Science Board task force (i.e., the Bucy report), although theoretically sound, have not always proven useful to the implementation of national security export controls. After extensive deliberation the panel abandoned its efforts to develop an alternative approach. The considerations that must govern control decisions make it difficult to achieve a comprehensive solution within a simple set of criteria. In the panel's view, the preparation of the control lists must be a dynamic process that takes into account advice provided by technical advisory groups and that is constrained by the need to be clear, to focus control efforts more narrowly on fewer items, and to coordinate U.S. action more closely with that of our CoCom allies.

6. **The Extraterritorial Aspects of U.S. Controls Engender Mistrust and Weaken Allied Unity**

The cohesiveness of military alliances is important to Western security and depends on a high level of cooperation and coordination among the participating nations. Several elements of U.S. national security export controls, especially the requirement for reexport authorization, are having an increasingly corrosive effect on relations with the NATO allies and on the close bilateral relations that exist with Japan and certain other friendly countries. These controls are now viewed abroad as a signal of U.S. mistrust of the will and capacity of allies and other friendly countries to control the flow of sensitive technology to the Soviet bloc. This atmosphere of mistrust provides the Soviets with opportunities to take advantage of differences among the allies over export control issues—that is, to use this divisive issue as a "wedge" between the United States and its allies.

SOVIET TECHNOLOGY ACQUISITION EFFORTS IN THE WEST

1. **Available Evidence on Soviet Technology Acquisition Efforts Reinforces the Need for Effective Multilateral Export Controls**

The panel reviewed a substantial body of evidence—both classified and unclassified—that reveals a large and aggressive Soviet effort to target and acquire Western dual use technology through espionage, diversions, and to a lesser degree legitimate trade. There is limited but specific evidence on the means by which Soviet acquisitions are accomplished; there is also evidence to support the conclusion that such acquisitions have in some cases played an important role in upgrading or modernizing Soviet military systems. Effective, internationally coordinated export controls are necessary to counter the use of diversions and legitimate trade for such purposes. However, export controls are not a means for controlling espionage, which accounts for a high proportion of the successful and significant Soviet technology acquisition efforts. Thus, export controls must be viewed as one component in a more comprehensive program for controlling technology losses.

2. **Despite Systemic Difficulties, Soviet Technical Capabilities Have Successfully Supported the Military Objectives of the USSR**

The Soviet system does not enjoy the benefits derived from the robust commercial sector found in the West. This places the Soviets at a fundamental disadvantage vis-à-vis the West in the promotion of technological innovation. Nevertheless, the Soviets have demonstrated an effective technical capability to meet their military objectives, which has been achieved by prioritizing the allocation of resources and key people to military R&D projects and to programs devoted to the acquisition of foreign technology and its incorporation into military systems.

DIFFUSION AND TRANSFER OF TECHNICAL CAPABILITY

1. **Wide Global Diffusion of Advanced Technology Necessitates a Fully Multilateral Approach to Controls**

   Advanced technology has diffused widely throughout the industrialized countries and is becoming increasingly available in some of the more developed newly industrializing countries (NICs). As a result, U.S. control policies can no longer be based on the assumption that the United States holds a monopoly on nearly all dual use technologies essential to the most advanced weapons systems. The United States now must have the cooperation of other technologically advanced countries to succeed in blocking Soviet acquisition efforts. National security export control efforts cannot succeed unless two conditions are met: (1) there is an effective CoCom process in which the other major CoCom countries accept responsibility for regulating their exports (including reexports from their territory) of CoCom-controlled goods and technology to third countries; and (2) the more advanced NICs adopt CoCom-like standards for their own indigenous exports.

2. **Controls on the Employment of Foreign Nationals in the U.S. R&D Infrastructure Must Be Used Selectively and Sparingly**

   The movement of technical personnel between countries is another means of diffusing technology. Foreign nationals now play a significant role in U.S. domestic R&D activities as well as in the laboratories of U.S. foreign subsidiaries. Such individuals contribute significantly to U.S. technological innovation and hence promote the national interest. Efforts to use existing legislative authority to restrict technical exchanges and more specifically to limit the full participation of foreign citizens in the U.S. R&D community should therefore be used sparingly. It is particularly important that such efforts distinguish, as appropriate, between citizens of nations to whom exports are proscribed and those of all other nations. They should also reflect the varying levels of sensitivity of the specific facilities or activities in question. It would be especially damaging to

U.S. interests both at home and abroad if high-technology industries were prohibited from employing, in unclassified dual use areas, talented people from other countries. Similarly, in the panel's view, increased barriers based on citizenship to easy exchange among employees of multinational firms would be a major source of concern and could well slow the pace of U.S. technological innovation.

FOREIGN AVAILABILITY AND FOREIGN CONTROL OF TECHNOLOGY

1. The Congressional Mandate for Decontrol Based on Foreign Availability Is Not Being Fulfilled

The panel finds that the foreign availability provisions of the law are not being effectively implemented. The Export Administration Amendments Act of 1985 requires the Commerce Department to remove (i.e., decontrol) an item from the U.S. Control List once it has been determined to be available abroad beyond the control of CoCom and if it has been impossible, within a period of 18 months, to eliminate or restrict its foreign availability. Industry had expected that foreign availability determinations would open a number of markets that are currently inaccessible because of concerns about unwanted technology transfer. But in the 4 years that the Department of Commerce's Office of Foreign Availability and its predecessor have been in existence, there have been only 3 positive foreign availability findings (out of 20 assessments by the office) leading to preliminary decontrol decisions. Thus, as currently administered the foreign availability program has had virtually no impact on the objective of achieving decontrol.

The panel therefore finds that the lack of action on these foreign availability determinations is inconsistent with the provisions of the Export Administration Act of 1979, as amended. This may be attributable in some measure to the fact that no time constraints are specified in the legislation for the government processing of foreign availability claims (see the discussion in Chapter 5). Substantive disagreements between the Departments of Commerce and Defense, both over the evidence of and detailed criteria for foreign availability determinations and over the strategic importance of maintaining control over particular items, have thwarted decisive action. Although the Department of Defense has a legitimate role to play in providing technical input to the foreign availability process, it has acquired de facto veto authority over Commerce Department foreign availability determinations with which it does not agree—a role not prescribed within the provisions of the Export Administration Act.

In those cases in which foreign availability of U.S.-controlled items exists, U.S. industry is unfairly placed at a competitive disadvantage with respect to firms of other countries because U.S. sales are constrained by export controls, whereas its competitors' sales are not. During the often lengthy delays (as much as 2 years or longer in some cases) that occur while the U.S. government considers foreign availability petitions by industry, foreign sales may be hampered. This can lead to the erosion of competitive market advantages previously enjoyed by U.S. industry and in some cases to the permanent loss of markets.

2. Control of "Technological Commodities" Is Impractical

The control of goods for which the volume of manufacture is so large and the scope of marketing and usage so wide that they have become "technological commodities" (e.g., some classes of personal computers and memory chips) is not practical. The capability to develop and mass-produce products embodying advanced technologies is no longer unique to the CoCom countries—and will become even less so in the years to come—so that control at the source may not always be feasible. And even within CoCom the sheer volume and geographic distribution of daily commercial transactions and warehousing of such products make control efforts impracticable. Thus, given the volume in which technological commodities are produced and the growing number of entrepôt points that are unrestrained by the CoCom rules, decontrol to all Free World destinations is in some cases the only appropriate solution.

3. Bilateral Agreements with Free World Non-CoCom Countries Must Protect All CoCom-Origin Technology and Control Similar Indigenously Produced Goods

The United States, with the support of CoCom, has achieved some success in pursuing bilateral agreements with friendly non-CoCom countries as part of the CoCom "third country initiative," which is designed to obtain cooperation in protecting CoCom-controlled items. Although awarding "CoCom-like status" to cooperating countries is in principle a desirable approach, agreements that in practice restrict only the reexport of U.S.-origin goods and technology and do not restrict similar items produced indigenously or obtained from other CoCom sources unfairly disadvantage U.S. companies in international trade without achieving the intended export control objective. Unless these agreements with non-CoCom countries restrict the export of technology from all CoCom sources, as well as that produced indigenously by non-CoCom countries, they will not promote the effectiveness of the CoCom system.

4. **Other CoCom Countries Must Be More Vigilant in Preventing Diversions of Both CoCom and Indigenously Produced Technology**

   For the CoCom system to be effective, all CoCom countries must control the export of their indigenous technology with equal vigor. Currently, some members of CoCom could substantially improve their efforts to prevent diversions of CoCom-origin products and technology exported to third countries. Although compliance with U.S. reexport controls is not likely to become politically acceptable in most CoCom countries, some compromise solution must be reached. At a minimum, CoCom countries should be encouraged to undertake more rigorous enforcement of prelicense and postshipment checks and better screening of license applications against lists of known or suspected diverters.

5. **The Extraterritorial Reach of U.S. Controls Damages Allied Relations and Disadvantages U.S. Exporters**

   As the panel learned directly in its European and Asian study missions, the extraterritorial reach of U.S. reexport controls is anathema to most U.S. trading partners. Most foreign countries do not accept that the United States has jurisdiction over the actions of non-U.S. citizens outside the territory of the United States, and they view assertions of this jurisdiction as clear violations of their national sovereignty and of accepted principles of international law. Moreover, data from the Department of Commerce suggest that in fact compliance with U.S. reexport control requirements by foreign citizens is exceedingly poor. These controls are seen by our allies as reflecting mistrust of their capacity to further the West's common interest in preventing the diversion of sensitive products from their territory to the Soviet bloc.

   The panel finds that U.S. reexport controls work primarily to the disadvantage of U.S. companies because they provide incentives for foreign companies to seek non-U.S. sources of supply. Reexport controls typically present thorny legal issues, are ineffective, and have a corrosive effect on the Western alliance. In light of these facts, substantial alteration of U.S. reexport control policy is warranted.

EFFECTIVENESS OF THE MULTILATERAL PROCESS

1. **The United States Must Clearly Distinguish Foreign Policy Export Controls from National Security Export Controls**

   There is a substantial consensus—both domestic and international—on the need for more narrowly defined national security export controls. There is much less agreement on the appropriateness of trade restrictions for foreign policy reasons and even less on the specific foreign policy objectives that would warrant restrictions. To the extent that the United States fails to distinguish clearly between national security and foreign policy export control objectives, allied cooperation in the national security export control regime is undermined.

2. **The Impact of Controls on Advantageous Scientific Communication and Technology Transfer Within Western Alliances Must Be Minimized**
    Although it is essential for the United States to limit militarily significant transfers from allied countries to the Soviet bloc, continued open scientific communication and trade within the West are equally important to maintaining the Western lead over the Soviet Union in science and technology. Therefore, U.S. policy should have a twofold objective: to facilitate mutually advantageous scientific communication and technology transfer within its alliances and to limit militarily significant transfers from the allied countries to the Soviet bloc.

3. **The CoCom Countries Should Take Specific Steps to Bolster the Efficiency and Effectiveness of Multilateral Controls**
    The persistent efforts of the United States over the past 5 years to strengthen CoCom and improve its operational efficiency and effectiveness have produced positive results. Further efforts, however, will be required on the part of all participating countries to bring about greater harmonization of national policies and to work toward a more rational—and fully multilateral—system of national security export controls. Among the most important issues now facing CoCom are: (1) reduction in the overall scope of the International List to improve its credibility and facilitate its effective enforcement, (2) modification of the procedures employed for decontrolling items on the International List, and (3) greater transparency in CoCom decision making to reduce private sector uncertainty in international business decisions.

4. **The CoCom Process Would Benefit If All Country Delegations Had Balanced Economic and Defense Representation**
    The U.S. delegation to CoCom includes a significant contingent from the Department of Defense, but most other CoCom members are represented at CoCom meetings principally by their economic and trade ministries. The panel finds that a balance of economic and defense representation on all the CoCom delegations would enhance CoCom unity and the usefulness of the CoCom process, in part by helping to prioritize and resolve conflicts between competing economic and military objectives. On the other hand, the panel also

finds that the Department of State has failed to exercise leadership within the U.S. delegation to CoCom, sometimes permitting other agencies to overstep the bounds of their advisory role.

5. **Foreign Perceptions of U.S. Commercial Advantage Derived from Controls Impede Multilateral Cooperation**

There is a widely held view in Europe and the Far East that the United States uses its national security controls to afford commercial advantage to U.S. companies. Upon investigation, the panel found no substantive evidence to support this view. On the contrary, the evidence suggests that U.S. trade interests are harmed by these constraints. Nevertheless, the existence of such perceptions abroad makes it more difficult to gain effective multilateral cooperation on national security export controls.

6. **Unilateral Controls Are of Limited Efficacy and May Undermine Allied Cooperation**

The imposition by the United States of unilateral national security export controls for items of dual use technology can be justified only as a stopgap measure pending negotiations for the imposition of multilateral controls or in rare cases in which the United States determines that critical national security concerns are at stake and unilateral restrictions are required. It must be recognized, however, that except when used as a temporary measure until consensus can be achieved within CoCom, the application of unilateral U.S. export controls undermines the incentive of the allies to develop a sound basis for multilateral control. And it is only through multilateral regulation that an effective export control system can be achieved.

ADMINISTRATION OF U.S. NATIONAL SECURITY EXPORT CONTROL POLICIES AND PROCEDURES

1. **The Lack of High-Level Oversight and Direction Reduces the Effectiveness of U.S. Controls**

The management of national security export controls within the U.S. government involves a fundamental overlap of jurisdiction among the three principal line agencies: the Departments of Commerce, Defense, and State. The administrative structures established by the executive branch have not proven effective in resolving in a coherent and timely fashion the frequent policy differences that occur among these agencies on matters relating to national security export controls. The policy vacuum created by the lack of higher-level oversight and direction results in unclear and sometimes conflicting policies, long delays in reaching closure, uncertain lines of authority, and underutilization of information-sharing capacity.

2. **Unequal Effort by and Resources of the Three Principal Line Agencies Have Led to Conflict, Confusion, and Unbalanced Policy**

   The Department of Defense's determined efforts to reinvigorate the national security export control regime have been useful in raising the general level of awareness of the need for national security export controls among government agencies, high-technology industry, the governments of friendly countries, and world public opinion. But the aggressiveness with which these matters have been pursued also has had its costs. The exclusive DoD focus on tightening export controls without balanced input from other agencies concerning the possible economic and long-term national security consequences has resulted in a failure to bring the objectives of military security and economic vitality into balance. As a result, conflicts have arisen among the responsible agencies over the control and direction of U.S. export control policy; industry has been confused and alarmed by present and contemplated policy changes; and allies have become annoyed and in some cases have misunderstood the application and intent of U.S. policy.

   The increasingly active role of the Department of Defense in this area in recent years also has led to an imbalance in the distribution of government effort and resources with regard to the implementation of national security export controls. The Department of Defense has upgraded its capabilities by creating a new dedicated agency that is able to devote considerable manpower and financial resources to analytical activities and case review. Despite some recent reorganization, neither of the other two major concerned agencies—the Department of Commerce and the Department of State—has been able to implement equally effective measures to upgrade its human and technical capabilities and office automation. The result is a lack of balance in the interagency policy formulation process and an inefficient and unnecessarily slow licensing process.

3. **Shifts in Responsibility Within the Line Agencies May Preclude Broadly Informed and Balanced Policy Judgments**

   Reorganization initiatives in a number of the principal line agencies also have resulted in a shift of responsibility for managing export controls from organizations with expertise in technology development and international trade toward those whose principal and often only concern is technology control. A case in point is the Department of Defense, where the responsibility for export control decision making has been relocated from the Office of the Under

Secretary of Defense for Research and Engineering to the Office of the Under Secretary of Defense for Policy. Although there have been positive effects of this shift in responsibility, the loss of sustained technical input has been significant. The most important areas of technology (e.g., electronics) are changing rapidly, and their international character is extremely dynamic. Thus, the internal policy process within the line agencies responsible for national security export control matters must be capable of striking an adequate balance between the application of stricter controls and the promotion of trade and open scientific communication, all of which help foster the economic and technological strength upon which our defense ultimately rests.

4. **Current Licensing Requirements, Classification Procedures, and Proprietary Controls for Technical Data Are Both Appropriate and Adequate**

Although technical data that are not publicly available require a validated license for export to the Soviet bloc, data exports to other destinations for the most part are eligible for a general license. Thus, data that are not classified or otherwise subject to restrictions imposed by contractual undertakings with the government can be exported to Free World destinations. The need for the exchange of large volumes of data in international commerce and the desirability of wide-scale exchange of information among the international research community indicate that a strict system of control is neither feasible nor desirable. The costs of a comprehensive system of validated licenses would be enormous, and even if such a system were supported, it would be doubtful whether effective control could practically be achieved.

Although national security and corporate interests may not always be coincident, substantial national security protection is afforded by the fact that data proprietary to U.S. corporations, including militarily significant data, are carefully controlled already for commercial reasons. The fact remains, however, that much nonnuclear information is developed entirely under private auspices and therefore cannot be controlled by the government except through a secrecy order imposed by the Commerce Department's Patent and Trademark Office. Other government efforts to restrict the dissemination of privately developed information have been futile and at times counterproductive.

5. **Controls on Unclassified DoD Technical Data Have a Chilling Effect on the U.S. R&D Community and Should Be Imposed Sparingly**

The Department of Defense Authorization Act (DAA) of 1984 permits DoD to impose restrictions on domestic dissemination or export of DoD-funded or DoD-generated technical data whose export would otherwise require a validated license under EAR or ITAR. Such restrictions have the effect of creating de facto a new category of unclassified but restricted information;* this is a new, more comprehensive restriction on technical data both within the United States and abroad. As a result, these restrictions also have had a "chilling effect" on some professional scientific and engineering societies that have elected voluntarily to close certain sessions or in a few cases entire meetings to foreign nationals—including those from CoCom and other friendly countries (except by special prior arrangement)—in anticipation of possible conflict with DAA provisions. It is the panel's judgment that broader controls on technical data are not warranted by the demonstrable national security benefits and that the system of security classification has been and remains the most appropriate mechanism for restricting access to technical information considered critical to the security of military equipment and systems. In those circumstances, however, in which *unclassified* technical data arising from DoD-funded research have particular military significance, the selective use of restrictions on data dissemination may be appropriate. In such cases the controls should be built upon contractual agreements.

6. The Congressional Mandate for Integrating the MCTL into the Commerce Department Control List Practically Cannot Be Accomplished

In the 6 years since its first release on a classified basis, the Militarily Critical Technologies List has been used inappropriately as a control list, and its annual revision has resulted in a voluminous itemization of many important technologies without apparent prioritization. Because the Departments of Defense and Commerce maintain fundamentally different objectives in their list development exercises—the former to identify those technologies with military significance and the latter to identify items subject to licensing—the congressionally mandated task of integrating the MCTL into the Commerce Department's Control List cannot practically be accomplished.

7. The Complexity of U.S. Export Control Policies and Procedures, Such as the Export Administration Regulations, Discourages Compliance

The complexity of U.S. national security export controls discourages compliance, especially by foreign firms and small- to

---

*This mandate is further expanded by the recent directive of the President's national security adviser authorizing all agencies of the federal government to create a new restricted category of information known as "sensitive."

medium-sized U.S. companies. One obvious example are the Export Administration Regulations, which currently amount to nearly 600 pages of rules and procedures. This document could be reduced and simplified substantially—and made more "user friendly." There also is no effective means whereby a small or new exporter—or a foreign firm—can get an advisory opinion quickly from the government on any aspect of export controls—for example, which control category a given product falls under or even whether an item is subject to export controls at all.

8. **There Is a Need for High-Level Industry Input in the Formulation of National Security Export Control Policy**

   There is a need for an effective mechanism within the government to provide meaningful input from the private sector on the formulation of a coordinated national security export control policy. Such a group must be constituted at sufficiently high corporate levels to reflect major industry concerns, and it must be able to have an impact on the actual policy process. This might be accomplished through a variety of mechanisms, including the President's Export Council. Currently, however, the council does not have significant influence at senior policy levels of the government.

9. **Voluntary Cooperation from U.S. Industry Is Important to the Enforcement of Export Controls**

   Voluntary cooperation by U.S. industry, particularly companies with overseas subsidiaries, and other commercial entities is important to the effective enforcement of export controls, especially in the identification of violations. U.S. companies frequently have knowledge otherwise unavailable to the government of possible violations by other firms. Some degree of positive feedback from government agencies on the usefulness of information provided by industry would help to ensure continuing active cooperation.

10. **Adequate Information to Evaluate the Impact of National Security Export Controls Is Not Maintained by the U.S. Government**

    This study has revealed serious shortcomings in both the quality and quantity of information maintained and analyzed by the U.S. government on the coverage, operation, and domestic and global impacts of national security export controls. The Department of Commerce, for example, has not used its own data bases to measure the effectiveness of its licensing activities or the impact of national security export controls on firms of different sizes and on different industrial sectors. There also appear to be serious statistical discontinuities between the licensing application data maintained by the Department of Commerce and the trade data recorded by the Bureau of the Census. As a result the government currently has no accurate means of tabulating the value of shipments made under export licenses or of sorting dollar values of exports according to type of license. It will continue to be difficult for policymakers to arrive at more informed and balanced judgments as to the advisability of controls in the absence of this type of information. The panel notes that the Department of Commerce already is required under the terms of the Export Administration Amendments Act of 1985 to report annually to the Congress on the impact of national security export controls. Such reporting, however, has so far failed to produce the data necessary to measure actual impacts on the U.S. economy or on specific industrial sectors.

11. A Comprehensive Cost/Benefit Analysis of Controls Currently Is Infeasible

Despite some initial attempts to assess the competitive effects of national security export controls, a *comprehensive* empirical analysis of the costs and benefits of controls currently is precluded by the lack of data, by the complexity of the system, and by a variety of qualitative judgments that must enter into an evaluation. Most affected industries have not maintained data on the economic costs of controls, although some are now beginning to do so. Likewise, comparable methodological and data problems are encountered in attempts to assess the military significance of specific controlled items or the potential savings to the defense budget of continuing to control them.

The process of international technology transfer requires constant monitoring and periodic modification as conditions warrant to maintain the proper balance between promotion of national economic vitality and protection of military security. Failure to do so can result in frequent and unpredictable changes in policies and procedures (i.e., controls). In the late 1970s the U.S. government reacted to mounting evidence of Soviet bloc technology acquisition efforts and to the emergence of new sources of militarily significant dual use technology by largely revamping and revitalizing the U.S. and CoCom national security export control systems.

There is little doubt that, without the heightened attention to these issues initiated in the early years of the current administration by DoD, the problem of Western technology diversion to the Soviet Union would by now be considerably worse. But the panel is concerned that this policy "correction," as useful and needed as it was, should not now overshoot the mark. Although the new, more stringent controls may restrain the flow of militarily significant technology to the Warsaw Pact countries, this success is likely to be achieved at an unacceptably high price in terms of economic vitality and allied cohesiveness.

The panel wishes, therefore, to reiterate its concern about the continuing lack of balance within the policy process for national security export controls regarding the representation of technical, national security, economic, and domestic and international political interests. Equilibrium among these interests, supported by adequate data, standards of measurement, and reliable intelligence information, should be developed and maintained within each agency, among agencies of the U.S. government, and among countries participating in CoCom.

In the final chapter of this report, the panel sets forth a series of recommendations for changes in the existing national security export control regime. These changes are designed to bring better balance to the development and management of our future course of action on this important national and international matter.

8

Recommendations of the Panel

PREAMBLE

National security export controls should seek to preserve and enhance the technology lead and military capabilities of the West while minimizing the constraints on the economic vitality of the United States, its allies, and other nations friendly to Western interests. In today's global trade environment, U.S. economic vitality can be maintained only by ensuring that the nation's products remain competitive—in terms of quality, price, and availability—with the best that other nations can offer. Trade promotes economic and technological strength, which is vital to Western military strength. Thus, maintaining the vigor and productivity of the U.S. technological base is fundamental not only to the continued economic vitality of the West but also to its military security. National security export controls also represent an important, albeit secondary, means of maintaining military security by impeding the flow of those goods and technologies deemed militarily important to the Soviet Union and its Warsaw Pact allies.

The panel's recommendations therefore are directed toward enabling the United States and its allies to maintain a balanced and effective export control regime. The recommendations are offered within the context of what the panel considers appropriate national policy objectives. *It should be the policy of the United States*:

1. to promote the economic vitality of Free World countries,
2. to maintain and invigorate the domestic technological base, and

167

3. to cooperate with its allies to impede the Soviet Union and other Warsaw Pact countries in their efforts to acquire Western technology that can be used directly or indirectly to enhance their military capability.

RECOMMENDATIONS

Within the context of the declaratory policy set forth above, the panel makes two basic recommendations, together with a series of corollary prescriptions.

I. STRENGTHEN THE COCOM MECHANISM

The panel recommends that the United States take the lead in further strengthening the CoCom mechanism so that it can function as the linchpin for a fully multilateral national security export control regime for dual use technologies. Under current and prospective global circumstances, such a multinational system is essential to achieve maximum export control effectiveness without impairing Western economic vitality. To strengthen the current system of multilateral controls will require greater harmonization of the current U.S. approach and that of our technologically advanced allies through closer consultation and through the adoption of policies that promote cooperation. The two most immediate objectives are: (1) to limit the coverage of the U.S. Control List and the CoCom International List to those items whose acquisition would significantly enhance Soviet bloc military capabilities and that are feasible to control, and (2) to obtain agreement on a common approach to reexports of CoCom-origin items.

The United States should strive to create a community of common controls on dual use technology—that is, a set of trade relationships unimpeded by national security restrictions—among those Free World nations that share an expressed willingness to adhere to common or equivalent export control restraints on the transfer of strategic and controllable goods and technologies to the Soviet Union and its Warsaw Pact allies. While recognizing that there are certain systemic deficiencies in the existing national security export control regime that will require sustained effort to overcome, there remain a number of initiatives that can be undertaken to advance this objective.

Accordingly, the panel recommends the following changes in U.S. policy:

1. Control Only CoCom-Proscribed Items

As a general policy the United States should seek to control only the export of CoCom-proscribed items, and then only when they are destined for a proscribed country or for a non-CoCom country that has not entered into an agreement* to protect items controlled by CoCom.

2. Within CoCom, Seek Controls on Exports to Third Countries

With respect to CoCom, the United States should:

- Negotiate agreements with member countries† regarding control of their exports and reexports from their territory to third (i.e., Free World non-Cocom) countries, thereby obviating the need for U.S. reexport authorization. These control agreements might involve a variety of mechanisms appropriate to national policies and legal practices, including the use of import certification/delivery verification procedures, end-user checks, export denial lists, and so on. Such agreements should stipulate that participating countries share and act on information regarding potential diverters.

- For almost all goods, eliminate the requirement to obtain validated licenses and reexport authorizations for exports to those trading partners with which the United States has reached agreement on the control of exports to third countries. Validated licenses should be required only for exports of extremely sensitive high-level technology (e.g., supercomputers). Reliance should be placed on cooperating foreign governments to prevent diversions from their own territory. There also should be a provision for reinstituting validated licensing requirements for CoCom countries that subsequently fail to implement and enforce national security export controls on trade with non-CoCom Free World countries.

- For those CoCom countries unwilling to agree to or unable to implement controls on exports to third countries, retain the present system of validated licenses and reexport authorization while continuing to pursue adequate control arrangements.

3. Negotiate Comprehensive Understandings with Third Countries

With respect to non-CoCom Free World countries, the United States should:

- In coordination with other key members of CoCom, negotiate *comprehensive* understandings—or equally effective informal arrangements deemed acceptable by the U.S. Department of State— that specify controls on the export of all CoCom-proscribed goods and technology (including those produced indigenously) to the

---

*Such an agreement might be implemented either through a formal memorandum of understanding or an informal arrangement that achieves the same result.

†It may be most feasible to begin this process initially with such key members of CoCom as Japan, France, the Federal Republic of Germany, and the United Kingdom.

Warsaw Pact countries and to other noncooperating third countries. A graduated scheme of incentives should be developed for third countries that agree to less than comprehensive controls.

- Accord full "CoCom-like" treatment (meaning that exporters to those countries should not be required to seek validated licenses or reexport authorization) for exports to those third countries that have agreed to comprehensive arrangements, or that have been judged by the State Department to maintain equivalent standards, as soon as these countries can demonstrate their ability and willingness to enforce export controls. Such a commitment to enforcement should include formal or informal sharing of information on possible diverters.
- Continue existing licensing requirements, as appropriate to their Commerce Department country group classification, for exports to third countries that are unwilling or unable to enter into comprehensive understandings or informal arrangements.

4. **Remove Items Whose Control Is No Longer Feasible**

   Regardless of the rate of progress on CoCom and third country negotiations, the United States should actively seek to remove from both the U.S. Control List and the CoCom International List items whose control is no longer feasible or necessary. This would include goods and technologies:

   - for which there is demonstrated foreign availability from any country that has not agreed to adhere to export controls and for which this availability has not been eliminated within a reasonable period of time through negotiated agreements (see Item II.4 on pp. 175–176); or
   - for which control at the source is not practicable, that enter into world trade channels through multiple entrepôt points, and that are manufactured and shipped in volumes so large they have in effect become "technological commodities" (e.g., certain computer memory chips and some personal computers).

5. **Maintain Unilateral Controls Only on a Temporary Basis or for Limited, Unique National Security Circumstances**

   Regardless of the rate of progress on CoCom and third country negotiations, the United States should eliminate the use of unilateral national security export controls *except* in those circumstances in which active efforts are under way to negotiate multilateral controls within and outside of CoCom—in which case unilateral controls could be maintained on a temporary basis—*or* in those situations in which unique national security circumstances warrant the imposition of such controls for limited periods of time. Where a decision has been taken to impose or maintain unilateral national security export controls, such restrictions should be subject to a 3-year "sunset provision" requiring their periodic rejustification.

The panel wishes to emphasize that the phrase "unique national security circumstances" does not justify retaining present U.S. unilateral controls. Rather, it recommends that controls be established on a multilateral basis and that, in cases in which the United States or another CoCom member country cannot achieve unanimity on the need to control a particular item, no unilateral controls should be imposed. In rare cases the United States or another CoCom country may believe that critical national security concerns are at stake and may wish to reserve the right to establish a unilateral restriction on their domestic industry. This exception should be used sparingly.

For these few exceptions, it would be useful for CoCom countries to report their exports of new, uncontrolled items going to the Soviet bloc. Such reporting would over time better inform CoCom on the advisability of establishing controls on the proposed item and better inform U.S. and other CoCom policymakers on the effectiveness of the unilateral control. The panel recommends that the United States explore within CoCom the feasibility of developing a practical reporting system for this category of items.

6. **Eliminate Reexport Authorization Requirements in Countries Participating in a Community of Common Export Controls on Dual Use Technology**

To further the objective of developing a community of common controls on dual use technology among cooperating countries of the Free World and to encourage international cooperation and trust, the United States should eliminate any requirement that a buyer seek authorization for a reexport that is subject to CoCom or "CoCom-like" controls by the country of initial export. Reliance should be placed instead on foreign governments that participate in CoCom or that have agreed (formally or informally) to impose "CoCom-like" controls on exports to prevent diversions from their territory.

7. **Maintain Current Control Procedures on the Transfer Within CoCom of Sensitive Information, Technical Data, and Know-How**

The United States should continue to rely on current security classification procedures and the protection afforded by general license GTDR and individual proprietary interests to control the transfer within CoCom of information, technical data, and know-how that are considered to be militarily sensitive. This approach is based on the recognition that the benefits of additional controls on technical data are outweighed by the potential damage of such restrictions to international business operations and R&D activities in the West. The attempt to exercise broader control of technical data is likely to prove unnecessarily restrictive to all such international cooperative ventures.

8. Reduce the Scope of the CoCom List and Modify CoCom Decision-Making Policies and Procedures

There are a number of steps the United States—together with its CoCom allies—should take to improve the efficiency and effectiveness of the multilateral process. The most important step is to reduce the overall scope of the CoCom International List to improve its credibility and enforcement. List credibility also would be improved by the imposition of a 4-year "sunset provision" that would cause lower-level CoCom items to be removed automatically from the list—unless their inclusion can be rejustified—when they come up for periodic review. The panel further recommends that the general procedure for decontrolling International List items be modified—decontrol should no longer require unanimity—to improve the effectiveness of multilateral enforcement.

To ensure balanced consideration of economic and military factors, the panel also supports greater participation by defense officials of the allied countries, as initiated through the establishment of the CoCom military experts group, in the multilateral decision-making process. Finally, the panel recommends that the uncertainties industry often associates with CoCom decision making be reduced through greater transparency. This could be accomplished by encouraging member governments to provide industry with appropriately sanitized and delayed information regarding approval and denial precedents.

9. Maintain a Clear Separation Between National Security and Foreign Policy Export Controls

Existing statutory authority describes separate systems and procedures for the control of exports for foreign policy versus national security reasons. Therefore, the U.S. government should maintain the clearest possible separation between the unilateral control of exports for political—that is, *foreign policy*—purposes and the system of multilateral controls that are maintained for national security purposes. Although examination of the system of foreign policy export controls was beyond the scope of this study, the panel notes that many of our CoCom allies continue to disagree profoundly with some U.S. foreign policy export controls. If not effectively isolated, such controls can have a corrosive effect on the resolve of the CoCom allies to cooperate in the implementation of national security export controls.

II. ACCORD GREATER IMPORTANCE IN U.S. NATIONAL SECURITY EXPORT CONTROL DECISIONS TO MAINTAINING U.S. TECHNOLOGICAL STRENGTH, ECONOMIC VITALITY, AND ALLIED UNITY

The panel recommends that executive branch decisions concerning national security export controls accord greater importance than they currently do to maintaining U.S. technological strength, economic vigor, and allied unity. Ultimately, an effective multilateral national security export control regime can be established only through the commitment and support of the President and Congress. Nevertheless, the decision-making and advisory mechanisms of the executive branch also must be constituted and tasked appropriately to facilitate the effective implementation of the policy approach proposed above.

As a general policy the United States should strive to achieve clarity, simplicity, and consistency in its national security export control procedures, as well as in the multilateral CoCom structure, and to obtain broader consensus on the need for national security export controls among the Free World nations that use and/or produce dual use technology. To achieve this goal, the United States should design policies and procedures that emphasize efficiency and effectiveness over comprehensiveness. Over the long term, U.S. national security export control policies also should remain flexible to political and economic changes in the world situation.

Toward these ends, the panel recommends the following specific changes in U.S. policy and procedures.

1. Balance the Protection of Military Security with the Promotion of National Economic Vitality Through Affirmative Policy Direction

The President should require that the National Security Council (NSC) implement the *existing* policy mandate—as set forth in the Export Administration Act of 1979, as amended—which calls both for the protection of military security and for the promotion of national economic interests. Currently, because of insufficient attention and leadership from above, the existing policy mechanisms either are not being used or are producing results that fail to take adequate account of important national interests. This problem can be ameliorated by providing *regular*, affirmative policy direction to the responsible line agencies.

Accordingly, NSC should take steps to fulfill its responsibility on national security export control matters by providing the necessary balanced policy guidance. The secretaries of commerce and treasury should participate in NSC meetings at which export control matters are to be addressed. Moreover, as a matter of urgency, NSC should be staffed properly to deal with these matters and a senior NSC staff member should be given responsibility for bringing representatives of conflicting agencies together to resolve policy differences. Although NSC can assume such responsibility without legislation, the panel further recommends that Congress consider whether the National Security Act of 1947 (as amended) ought to be modified to reflect the growing importance of international trade as a fundamental element of U.S. national security.

2. Provide Sufficient Resources and Authority to the Departments of Commerce and State to Allow Them to Fulfill Their Roles in the Export Control Process

To establish a more balanced policymaking process within the federal government, the Departments of Commerce and State should be allocated sufficient resources dedicated to the implementation of national security controls. In particular, the Department of Commerce should upgrade significantly the capacity and sophistication of its automated systems and the quality of its in-house technical and analytical expertise. The Export Administration Act specifies that the Department of Commerce has primary responsibility for export licensing policy and procedures. In the case of national security export controls, Commerce has lost much of that leadership role because of its ineffective performance in the past and must now establish the organization, competence, and drive to merit regaining that role.

It is also essential that the Department of State vigorously fulfill its traditional role of ensuring that the U.S. government speaks with a single, coherent voice when dealing with foreign governments and foreign firms on national security export control matters. Another State Department responsibility should be to work to reduce conflicts within the ranks of CoCom, conflicts that stem in part from differences among the respective national delegations over how to prioritize conflicting economic and military objectives. Although the United States has had some modest success in encouraging allied defense officials to participate in the CoCom process, it is essential that State Department officials now play a more assertive leadership role in the U.S. CoCom delegation so as to create a balanced representation of U.S. economic and defense interests.

3. **Restore Technical Judgment and Overall Balance to the National Security Export Licensing Process**

The locus of responsibility and decision making within the Department of Defense has shifted from the office responsible for research and engineering to the office responsible for policy. This shift has resulted in greater attention to extant deficiencies of the CoCom process and increased efforts to stem the leakage of technology to the Soviet bloc. Although the pursuit of these policy objectives has led to the resolution or improvement of a number of long-standing problems, there has been at the same time a significant reduction in the weight accorded to technical factors and a resultant imbalance in the policy process. It should now be the goal (1) to establish greater balance within DoD between its technical and policy elements and (2) to reduce the DoD role in detailed license review as parallel steps are taken within the Department of Commerce to strengthen its capability to implement national security export control licensing procedures. The role of the policy side of DoD on export control issues should focus on the broader goal of maintaining the strategic balance and the contribution of technology to military systems.

4. **Implement the Decontrol Procedures Required by Law When Foreign Availability Is Found to Exist**

The lack of action by the federal government on foreign availability determinations is contrary to the statutory language expressed in the Export Administration Act of 1979, as amended. This is due in part to the fact that no specific time lines for the completion of foreign availability determinations are specified in the legislation. Moreover, apart from the broad statutory criteria, there is still no generally accepted definition of foreign availability. Serious effort should be devoted to developing an interagency consensus on such a definition and reasonable deadlines for decisions.

The Department of Defense has overstepped its legitimate statutory role of providing technical input to foreign availability determinations and has exercised de facto veto authority by delaying the review of such determinations. The result of this situation has been that, in 4 years, the Departments of Commerce and Defense have been able to reach preliminary agreement on the decontrol of only 3 items (out of more than 20 foreign availability assessments). At the very least the Export Administration Act should impose specific and equal time constraints on *all* responsible agencies. Because the process for determining foreign availability is not now functioning effectively, there is a need for effective remedial action by both the executive and legislative branches.

5. **Withdraw the Statutory Requirement to Integrate the MCTL into the Commerce Department's Control List**

    Congress should withdraw the statutory requirement to integrate the Militarily Critical Technologies List (MCTL) into the U.S. Control List. The fundamentally different nature and functions of the two lists—the former an exhaustive list of all technologies with military utility and the latter a specific list of items requiring an export license—make this goal unattainable. The Department of Defense should develop guidance for use of the MCTL as a reference document within DoD and as a basis for developing proposals to CoCom.

6. **Provide Effective, Two-Way Communication at the Highest Levels Between Government and the Private Sector**

    A mechanism should be established (or upgraded) to provide effective, two-way communication between the highest levels of government and of the private sector on the formulation and implementation of coordinated national policies that balance military security and national economic vitality. One such group already exists: the President's Export Council (PEC) and its Subcommittee on Export Controls. However, its advice currently is not receiving appropriate attention at senior policy levels within the government. The panel recommends, therefore, that senior policy staff of the Executive Office of the President meet periodically with the PEC (or with other respected representatives of the private sector) and inform the President of their concerns regarding national security export controls. It may be necessary, however, for Congress to establish a mechanism to ensure appropriate consideration of industrial concerns in the formulation of national security export control policy.

7. **Develop Reliable Data Regarding the Operation and Impact of U.S. National Security Export Controls**

    This study has revealed serious shortcomings in both the quality and quantity of information maintained and analyzed by the U.S. government on the operation of national security export controls and their domestic and international impacts. The panel recommends, therefore, that the Department of Commerce be instructed by Congress to develop and analyze such data and that the department be given sufficient resources to carry out these tasks.

8. Make More Systematic Use of Intelligence Evidence on Current and Anticipated Soviet Acquisition Efforts

The Intelligence Community should structure its efforts with regard to West-East technology transfer so as to anticipate future Soviet technology acquisition efforts. The line agencies of the U.S. government, for their part, should strive to make more systematic use of existing intelligence resources for modifying the composition of the U.S. Control List, proposing changes to the CoCom International List, and reviewing sensitive individual export licensing cases. In addition, the Intelligence Community should increase its efforts to sanitize and declassify "finished" intelligence products to provide a more informed public understanding of the technology transfer problem.

CODA

The panel notes in conclusion that there is a need for national security export controls and that current statutory authority recognizes the necessity to accommodate *both* military security and economic vitality. But the recent performance of the U.S. government on this matter has not been satisfactory—and will be increasingly less so because of prevailing trends in international trade and technology diffusion—because it has tended to focus on tightening controls while giving little attention to their effectiveness and costs. Although most of the necessary mechanisms appear to be in place, the U.S. policy process for national security export controls continues to lack proper direction and affirmative leadership at the highest level. As a result, the executive branch has failed to implement the existing provisions of law in a coherent and effective manner, which has in turn created uncertainty, confusion, and criticism both at home and abroad. In the absence of appropriate corrective measures, these continuing problems will exact ever-higher tolls—on both Western economic vitality and innovative capacity and on the military security of the United States and its allies.

Appendixes

A

COSEPUP Charge to the Panel

The purpose of the Panel on the Impact of National Security Controls on International Technology Transfer is to seek strategies to regulate the international transfer of technology through industrial channels in such a manner as to balance the national objectives of national security, economic vitality, scientific and technological advance, and commercial, educational, and personal freedom. In pursuit of this objective, the panel shall:

(1) Examine the international environment in technology to provide insight into:
   a. the problems of regulating the availability of "dual-use" technologies;
   b. the international competitive status of these technologies and range of practices to promote their use both in CoCom and non-CoCom countries;
   c. the problems in extending controls on the international exchange of data;
   d. the role of technology transfer and the interdependence among industrialized countries of the Free World in the development and application of technology; and
   e. the role of foreign nationals in developing and applying "sensitive" industrial technology of U.S. origin.

(2) Assess the control problem for the Free World industrialized countries. Examine what is being lost through commercial chan-

181

nels, how, and to whom—in order to provide a basis for establishing priorities among alternative control measures. Consider the nature and extent of the Soviet effort to acquire technology from the West and the actual capacity of the Warsaw Pact to absorb and utilize such technology within their military systems.

(3) Assess the effectiveness of the current control scheme employed by the member states of CoCom and, in particular, investigate the views of and constraints on the non-U.S. members of CoCom.

(4) Review and assess the impacts on industry of current export control policies and proposed regulatory changes, including multinational companies, U.S.-based exporting companies, and nonexporting companies.

(5) Examine the current assignment of policymaking responsibilities on export control matters within the U.S. government and among the CoCom countries. Consider the practicability and desirability of new mechanisms or approaches to balance the military, commercial, scientific, and educational interests affected by export control decisions.

(6) Consider alternative approaches to the technology transfer problem, including a possible emphasis on alternative strategies that maintain the technology lead. Make recommendations, as appropriate, for the adoption of new approaches by private industry, the U.S. government, and by industries and governments in other countries.

B

Panel Foreign Fact-Finding Mission Reports

During the first quarter of 1986, delegations of panel members and staff traveled on two fact-finding missions to six Western European countries (the United Kingdom, Belgium, France, Austria, the Federal Republic of Germany, and Sweden) and to five Asian countries (Japan, Korea, Hong Kong, Malaysia, and Singapore). The stated objectives of these missions were to seek the views of government officials, industrial leaders, academics, and others regarding: (1) the U.S. national security export control regime, (2) the indigenous export control policies and procedures of each country, and (3) various means for improving the effectiveness of the Western control effort.

At each stop on a particular mission's itinerary, the delegation received a briefing from the appropriate country team at the U.S. embassy. At the request of the panel, embassy control officers, who accompanied the delegation to some of its meetings with government officials, generally were not present for meetings with private industry. All meetings were considered unofficial and "off the record," and delegation members provided assurances that nothing in the panel's report would be attributed to specific individuals.

The two major sections of this report, one concerning the European mission and the other the Asian mission, are based on the detailed trip notes prepared by the members of the particular delegations (panel members and staff) and on the tapes of debriefing meetings held en route. Each section is, in turn, divided: first, into a summary of the most significant generic policy issues that emerged from discussions through-

183

out the trip; and second, into a brief presentation of the special characteristics of and problems with the export control policies and procedures
of each country.

EUROPEAN MISSION*

Generic Policy Issues

UNDERLYING ASSUMPTIONS

During the course of their visits to the United Kingdom, Belgium,
France, Austria, the Federal Republic of Germany, and Sweden, the
various delegations identified a number of common assumptions that form
the basis of European views on national security export controls. Although there was, of course, some degree of variation, the following
points represent the foundations of European thinking:

1. The panel found support for the basic premise of U.S. national security
export controls: namely, that truly strategic products, processes, and technical data should be denied to the Soviet Union and the other Warsaw Pact
countries. The principal difference between the European position and
that of the United States involved *what* should be considered truly critical.

2. Europeans expressed a related concern that overly broad restrictions could neutralize whatever might be achieved, through the effective
use of trade, to encourage political and social change within the Soviet
Union and to enable Eastern European nations to distance themselves
somewhat from Moscow.

3. Europeans also reiterated their view of trade as a right—as distinguished from the U.S. view of trade as a privilege. This view has led, in
turn, to a presumption in favor of exports (rather than the reverse). It is
possible, however, that this view may be driven as much by reaction to
the aggressive U.S. pressure for export controls as by fundamental
philosophical positions.

4. European concerns about export controls focused primarily on the
impact of controls on West-West trade. Europeans considered West-East
trade to be far less problematic due, in part, to the impact of the French
Farewell papers and a certain cynicism about the commercial (if not the
scientific) importance of the East.

---

*The delegation to the United Kingdom was headed by John McLucas and included panel
members Tom Christiansen and Ruth Greenstein and staff members Mitchel Wallerstein and
Stephen Gould. Richard Cooper led the delegation to Belgium, France, and Austria; the
remaining members were the same as that to the United Kingdom. The panel delegation to
the Federal Republic of Germany and Sweden was led by G. William Miller; once again, the
remaining members were the same.

5. A number of individuals pointed out that the entire Western control effort can work only if the relationship is built on trust. U.S. efforts to impose restrictions on West-West trade with the CoCom countries send precisely the wrong signal; that is, they have the effect of destroying the element of trust in the relationship.

COLLATERAL IMPLICATIONS OF CONTROLS

The delegations consistently heard a number of views, stemming from the assumptions stated above, that illustrate important collateral aspects of the control effort.

1. The panel groups were reminded frequently of the apparent discontinuity between U.S. policy on technology sharing for weapons cooperation and coproduction, including the Strategic Defense Initiative (SDI), and the thrust of West-West controls. The implication drawn was that the two DoD policies frequently conflict with one another in ways that are damaging to the NATO alliance.

2. The continuing tension between scientific cooperation and protectionism was noted. It was suggested that, in an era of constrained budgets, it is unrealistic to expect the European nations to be anxious to cooperate on expensive joint science and technology undertakings if they are denied full access to the information produced. This is especially true for fields in which the United States is not preeminent.

3. The sentiment was expressed that continued discrimination against nationals of CoCom countries (e.g., in terms of access to university research or sessions of professional society meetings) is likely to lead to a further deterioration in the level of trust and goodwill within CoCom.

4. There is a continuing concern in those countries in which SDI research has been discussed actively that such research will result in a one-way flow of technology to the United States—both for commercial and military applications—and that the Europeans might even lose the right of access to information they themselves had produced.

SCOPE OF CONTROLS

The Europeans generally agreed that the current control regime includes too many items to be practical, from the point of view of either administration or enforcement, and that current list review procedures are biased toward adding rather than deleting items. This perception of bias is reinforced by their view that the United States tends to place items on the CoCom agenda with little or no prior notice and then to demand immediate action. They further suggested that an overly broad set of controls undermines the legitimacy of the process if countries perceive that items of only limited national security importance are controlled. As a result, items approved for export at the national discretion level may receive minimal review in most European countries. If this judgment is accurate, the practical implication is that U.S. exporters are handicapped—both when selling items that are controlled at the national discretion level as well as when selling items that are unilaterally controlled by the United States—without a commensurate benefit to national security.

Another frequently noted issue relating to the scope of controls was the failure of the current control regime to take account of foreign availability. It was suggested that, particularly for some of the "low-end" technology controlled either unilaterally by the United States or multilaterally through CoCom, export restrictions were virtually futile because of the extensive availability of the technology in question. Most Europeans did favor the notion of a common approach to those so-called "third countries" (i.e., non-CoCom, Free World countries) that might represent alternative sources—or points of reexport—for controlled items. But they also emphasized that, in most cases, reexport controls are not the answer, particularly for widely available technologies that are considered to be virtual commodities by many countries.

Controls and Commercial Advantage

Many Europeans, in a number of the countries visited by the delegations, expressed the view that somehow the United States had designed its controls to confer commercial advantage on American companies. (Perhaps the most frequently cited example was the recent change in the U.S. policy toward the People's Republic of China.) At the panel's request, some vague anecdotal information was presented to back up such claims, but a cause-and-effect relationship was never substantiated. Most interlocutors reacted with bemusement to panel members' suggestions that U.S. industry felt that *it* actually was more severely disadvantaged by the control regime. Nevertheless, the feeling in Europe was very real (and is probably increasing) that some substantial part of U.S. national security export controls are a "smokescreen" for the protection and promotion of American commercial interests.

National Security Versus Foreign Policy Controls

The delegations encountered a substantial degree of confusion throughout Europe concerning the distinction between the application of export controls for foreign policy purposes versus controls for national security reasons. It was made abundantly clear in a number of meetings, particularly those held with government officials, that the U.S. attempt to impose controls on pipeline equipment after the invasion of Afghanistan—and European resistance to that initiative—has been a factor in all subsequent control efforts. It was difficult, at times, to determine the depth of the professed European uncertainty about the circumstances in which export controls are justified on the basis of foreign policy or to assess whether such doubts were part of a more general antipathy toward economic embargoes. (It is worth noting that the delegation traveled to Europe shortly after the imposition of U.S. economic sanctions on Libya.) The net effect, however, is that the CoCom countries often suspect that the United States attempts to justify, or perhaps mask, its foreign policy initiatives by invoking the mantle of national security. Europeans contend that, if this suspicion is accurate, such attempts have the effect of seriously diluting the consensus within CoCom on truly important national security matters.

EXTRATERRITORIALITY

Yet another area in which Europeans see a clash of foreign policy and national security motivations is the U.S. effort to extend the reach of its law to other countries through the imposition of reexport controls. U.S. demands to permit the inspection, investigation, and audit of firms on another nation's soil frequently appeared as another manifestation of the same issue. For the British, in particular, all forms of extraterritoriality constituted matters of high principle and were generally considered to be anathema. Elsewhere in Europe, opposition to U.S. reexport controls was based on a combination of ideological and practical considerations. Even in countries in which ideological opposition to extraterritoriality was muted, there seemed to be a general belief that such an extension of one nation's law to another was probably counter to established international norms. Outside CoCom, reexport controls were criticized primarily because of practical problems in their implementation.

CoCom VIEWS/POLICIES

There seemed to be widespread agreement among the countries the delegations visited on the value and importance of CoCom, which was viewed as substantially more effective and efficient than it was 5 years ago. Furthermore, most interlocutors felt that CoCom should be strengthened so that the United States could rely on its restrictions and procedures as an alternative to the unilateral imposition of reexport controls. Panel members frequently encountered concerns regarding the establishment of a military subcommittee to CoCom; many Europeans contended that such an action would reinforce the existing bias toward increasing the scope of controls.

Among CoCom member countries, there was considerable resentment about the way in which the United States handled the changes in its policy toward the People's Republic of China (PRC). The belief was fairly widespread that the United States deliberately failed to consult with its allies on the proposed change in order to give U.S. companies an advantage in the China trade. Moreover, there was a general perception that the United States is inconsistent in the positions it has taken within CoCom, appearing to delay the applications of other countries while promoting U.S. interests. It was pointed out also that the United States is the single largest requester of exceptions to the CoCom International List of controlled dual use items. Overall, the twin issues of confidence and trust were paramount in the minds of the Europeans: They saw U.S. unilateral and extraterritorial initiatives as seriously damaging to the spirit of cooperation that must exist for CoCom to be effective as an informal, nontreaty arrangement.

During the course of the trip, the delegations heard and discussed a variety of proposals to improve the operational effectiveness of CoCom. Among the most prominent (and viable) were the following:

• *Transparency*—For better understanding of the CoCom decision process, provide industry with sanitized information about specific CoCom license approvals and denials in a reasonably prompt manner (e.g., within 6 months) but enough delayed that the information would not be useful in specific deals by competitors.

• *"Sunset provision"*—Consider adding a provision, at least for administrative exception note items, that would cause these items to be removed automatically from the CoCom International List after a set period of time (e.g., 4 years) unless their continued inclusion were rejustified.

• *Two-tier system*—Recognize explicitly that there is a natural division within CoCom in terms of the commitment of different countries to treat and enforce export control policies and "reward" compliant countries with the removal of reexport requirements.

• *Treaty*—Formalize the CoCom arrangement as an international treaty to require all participating nations to deal with national security export controls on a multilateral basis.

VIEWS ON U.S. POLICIES AND PROCEDURES

Europeans recognized clearly that little progress would be achieved with respect to increased rationalization of CoCom or any other related issue without the agreement, or at least the acquiescence, of the United States. But government and industry people also reported substantial confusion and consternation with existing U.S. policies and procedures. The issues below were the most frequently cited.

1. *Speed and rationality of the licensing process*—The most universal concern indicated by European companies was the length of time required to obtain a validated export license and the apparent impenetrability of the Commerce Department licensing process. The claim was made that there is virtually no "institutional memory"; as a result, each case is considered de novo—even if it involves precisely the same technology licensed previously. The delegations also heard of multiple examples of licensing decisions sent back to Europe by surface mail, thereby wasting weeks in the process, simply because a clerk failed to recognize that the applicant was located outside the continental United States.

2. *Reexport controls*—This was probably the issue of second greatest concern due to the onerous and confusing nature of the requirements and the issues of national sovereignty raised by the extension of U.S. law to other countries. A good deal of support was registered for the idea that reexport control regulations must and should take account of a "de minimis" requirement; that is, when the percentage or dollar value of U.S. componentry in an item falls below a certain level, the shipment becomes exempt from licensing requirements.

3. *Distribution license regulations*—Bulk licensing regulations were judged to be confusing, and great resistance was expressed to both company and Department of Commerce audit requirements.

4. *Technical data controls*—There is growing concern in Europe about possible revisions to the technical data controls specified in the Export Administration Regulations and the impact such revisions would have on the capacity of U.S. and European firms to discuss future commercial relationships.

5. *DoD "15-country list"*—Great resentment was expressed over what was seen as the singling out of European countries on the list of non-Communist destinations for which DoD has review authority.

6. *Embassy expertise*—A common criticism concerned the level of competence of U.S. embassy personnel in regard to the technical details of export control regulations. Many European companies reported that they have felt obliged either to open their own Washington or New York office or to retain a law firm to represent them on U.S. licensing matters.

DIVERSIONS

There was universal agreement throughout the countries visited by the delegations that the diversion of licensed products to nonapproved end

users was undesirable. As might be expected, diversions were a particularly sensitive issue in the two non-CoCom countries, Sweden and
Austria; but West German officials also reacted somewhat defensively to
charges that the Federal Republic of Germany served as a point of
diversion to the German Democratic Republic (East Germany). In both
Sweden and Austria, the delegation heard evidence of efforts to modify
the system to detect and deter diversions. It also was apparent, however,
that there were limits to what the non-CoCom countries were prepared or
able, under existing laws, to do to stop reexport operations—especially
since none of the other CoCom countries currently impose reexport
licensing requirements.

GOODS IN TRANSIT

A problem similar to that of diversions exists with respect to goods
transiting a country under bond. The CoCom countries in principle
indicated a willingness to enter bonded customs zones to open shipments
when evidence of possible illegalities was presented; they emphasized,
however, that most governments had neither sufficient staff for nor great
interest in embarking on such "fishing expeditions." Furthermore, in
some countries, including the Federal Republic of Germany, there are
legal limitations on the handling of goods in transit. Other deterrents to
investigative action include the central importance of trade and, in the
case of Austria and Sweden, their neutral status, all of which make these
countries reluctant to take any action that might impede commerce.

ENFORCEMENT

The delegations were struck by the wide variety of governmental
approaches to export enforcement. Some of the countries handle the
matter strictly through customs, while others deal with it through their
ministries of trade. The overall impression the panel members gained,
particularly from discussions with U.S. embassy officials, was that the
quality of the enforcement effort is uneven. In general, the British,
French, and Germans take enforcement seriously and cooperate with
U.S. customs agents (albeit on an informal basis). Other CoCom countries are viewed, even within the European context, as being far more
lax in their efforts—to the point where there may occasionally be
violations of agreed-upon CoCom proscriptions. Enforcement in the
non-CoCom countries is especially delicate, given that these nations are
under no specific obligation to stop goods that have left the country of
origin. Often, the United States or some other originating CoCom country
can do no more than ask the host government to delay the forward

movement of a shipment while some legal means is found to stop a potential diversion.

EUROPEAN INDUSTRY VIEWS

U.S. foreign policy controls continue to be of great concern to European industry; furthermore, such controls tend to raise the specter of U.S. industry as an unreliable trading partner. U.S. unilateral national security export controls (both in terms of original exports and reexports) raise economic concerns—uncertainty, delay, hassle, special procedures—all of which add up to additional cost. Industry representatives with whom the delegations spoke indicated that obtaining a U.S. license approval within a month or two was unusual and that 6-month delays were frequent. There also was widespread disgust with the inefficiency of the system: Europeans cited lost applications; the high number of unexplained or "silly" license applications returned without action, for example, because of the absence of a street address for a firm in a rural Third World area; technically incompetent questions; and delays caused by the use of surface mail.

None of the company representatives with whom delegation members talked could disaggregate all the factors that now militate against buying from U.S. firms. However, among those most frequently cited were the following: (1) the possibility of additional U.S. embargoes, (2) the additional cost of dealing with U.S. controls, (3) the nuisance value of complying with a myriad of U.S. procedures, and (4) the recent strength of the U.S. dollar. Company after company made it a point to discuss their efforts to identify—and, where possible, design around—U.S. parts and components. Most indicated a substantial reluctance to disrupt long-established supply relationships. But it was evident that, once the link to U.S. suppliers is broken and new trade relationships are established (e.g., with the Japanese or others), it becomes extremely difficult for U.S. companies to recapture their share of the market.

NON-CoCom-COUNTRY ISSUES

In the countries visited by the panel delegations, some distinction was made between the European non-CoCom countries and those in the rest of the world. Because Switzerland, Austria, and Sweden have recently instituted CoCom-like policies and procedures, Europeans frequently expressed the view that these nations do not now represent the same degree of problem as that posed by the rapidly industrializing countries of the Far East, such as Korea, Taiwan, Singapore, or Malaysia. There was general agreement that diversions and foreign availability from the so-called "third countries" (non-CoCom, Free World) were serious—and growing—problems; there also was agreement that CoCom needs to develop a common approach to these countries and that reexport controls are probably not the answer. Some hope was expressed for the current CoCom "third country initiative."

"Running Faster"

Although it was not discussed at length, several interlocutors volunteered that the answer to Soviet efforts to steal, divert, or purchase Western technology was simply to continue to "run faster" technologically. Some even suggested that the realization of the West's intent to stay ahead was the only thing that eventually would prod the Soviets toward meaningful disarmament negotiations.

U.S. Export Control Regime Modifications

Because almost all the countries visited (except the United Kingdom) consider the U.S. control regime to be a given, the majority of suggestions for improvement focused on how the current system could be made to work better.

• Abandon reexport controls on exports to other CoCom countries. (It was noted that the new G-COM license works only for lower-level goods and that a broad distribution license is not available for all users.)
• Provide some form of general or bulk license (a so-called "gold card") for well-established firms that are considered responsible, whether or not they are consignees of a U.S. distribution license.
• Establish a European office that could provide, either directly or by computer link with Washington, knowledgeable export control advice to European firms, thereby minimizing the delays inherent in the licensing process.
• Reduce the reach of the CoCom control list. (Little guidance was offered, however, as to how this should be accomplished.)
• Increase the "transparency" of the system by providing, in a reasonably prompt fashion, sanitized information about specific CoCom licensing decisions.

Country Summaries

The United Kingdom

Among the CoCom countries, the United Kingdom maintains an export control posture that is probably closest to the U.S. view of the Soviet threat and the need to control the flow of sensitive technology and products to the Warsaw Pact countries. It is partially (but certainly not exclusively) for this reason that the British are so offended by what they see as a lack of trust by the United States. They find this particularly irksome in view of the efforts they have made over the past 2 years to tighten their system.

By far, the overriding issue in the minds of U.K. government officials and industrial leaders is extraterritoriality. This is for them both a matter of high principle and immediate practicality. They object in principle to the extension of U.S. law and regulations to Great Britain, and they object in practical terms to the additional delay and paperwork necessary to obtain a license and/or submit to an internal audit. There is a strong feeling in the United Kingdom, especially in the high-tech community, that extraterritoriality represents a lack of trust in the British and their control regime. Moreover, there is a feeling that the United States lacks a sense of proportion, often seeking to treat relatively inconsequential parts and components the same way as major end items. As a result, U.S. credibility is undermined, and cooperation within CoCom suffers.

A widespread British view maintains that the U.S. control regime—and, indeed, U.S. behavior within CoCom—is designed to work to the advantage of U.S. companies. (The change in U.S. policy on exports to the PRC was mentioned frequently.) There also is a general residue of ill will created by a series of discrete events, including the pipeline foreign policy embargo, grain sales, and the so-called "IBM letter" that was circulated within the United Kingdom; these will not soon be forgotten.

Despite these problem issues, there still appears to be an opportunity for the United States to redeem itself in the eyes of the British—but that opportunity may be limited. The delegation heard strongly from both government and industry about a conscious effort under way in the United Kingdom to use non-U.S. sources wherever possible or to produce the needed technology indigenously. Moreover, panel members were reminded that, officially at least, the European Economic Community will eliminate all trade barriers in the early 1990s—an action that will greatly complicate U.S. export problems if the United States continues to proceed unilaterally. In the final analysis, the British would like to see a system that is based on trust and that relies firmly on coordinated, multilateral action.

BELGIUM

The panel delegation's meetings with Belgian government and industry officials were of limited duration. It was apparent, however, that, given the degree of U.S. penetration within their economy, the Belgians will do little to depart from the accepted line on controlling exports to the Soviet bloc. Like many of the smaller CoCom members, Belgium faces a particular problem in reaching informed judgments on cases brought before the multilateral forum. There are, as a result, some circumstances in which the government must consult with Belgian industry to formulate its position.

The Belgians expressed uneasiness regarding U.S. reexport controls, particularly the audit requirements under the distribution license. Nevertheless, they seem resigned to accommodating U.S. controls, although they prefer that the audits be kept strictly as internal company matters. They also expressed the idea that the United States manipulates CoCom for its own ends; the PRC export policy change again was cited. The Belgians, aware of their position as a lesser member of CoCom, would like steps taken to ensure a "level playing field." Yet, they also want CoCom to remain small and informal.

The North Atlantic Treaty Organization

Part of the time spent by the delegation in Brussels was devoted to meetings with the U.S. delegation to NATO and representatives of the North Atlantic Assembly, a nongovernmental group that meets in parallel with NATO. The U.S. NATO delegation emphasized a clear separation of responsibilities between NATO and CoCom; the former is responsible for armaments cooperation and production and for security within the Atlantic alliance, and the latter is responsible solely for the control of trade to proscribed destinations. There is apparently little, if any, communication between the two organizations, which is indicative of the somewhat paradoxical policy adopted by DoD, which advocates increased cooperation within NATO on arms coproduction, standardization, and so on, but also seeks to restrict access to the most sensitive U.S. technology.

Within the NATO context, the final decision on whether or not to share a particular technology and enter into coproduction may rest on domestic considerations, primarily the impact on jobs within the domestic economy. Whatever the reason(s), the inhibitions on technology sharing have direct costs both in military and economic terms—for example, higher R&D costs, slower technological advancement, redundancy, and so forth.

The Commission of the European Economic Community

While in Brussels, the delegation met with senior officials of the European Commission, the administrative body of the European Economic Community (EEC). These officials reported that the pipeline restrictions imposed by the United States were a "rude jolt" to several European Community member countries and probably have colored their view of all subsequent export control efforts. The restrictions have, for one thing, stimulated the search for non-U.S. sources of supply—sources that would not be subject to interruption. Here again, the "trust issue" emerged, with the feeling expressed that U.S. efforts to impose extraterritoriality are offensive and degrading and imply nonequality of treatment.

The commission is, of course, mindful of the fact that the EEC is to become integrated by 1991. This suggests the need for a common approach to export controls within Europe, an approach in which controlled items might be traded freely within the EEC countries (and, by inference, within CoCom). Such a communalization of the issue is problematic, however, because Ireland, which is a member of EEC, currently is not a member of CoCom.

The European Parliament

Although the delegation did not actually visit members of the European Parliament, some of its recent deliberations deserve mention. In early 1986, the parliament adopted a resolution* calling on the EEC to investigate whether the 1985 amendments to the Export Administration Act eliminated the conflict between U.S. reexport licensing requirements and the requirements of the Treaty of Rome, which mandate unconstrained movement of goods within EEC countries. The resolution further stated that, if it is determined that the conflict continues to exist, the commission is to take action to bring the matter before the European Court of Justice for settlement.

The resolution went on to criticize U.S. technology transfer limits, claiming that U.S. restrictions—particularly those that involve extraterritoriality—go far beyond those agreed to in CoCom and that they are ineffective in any case. The resolution also recommended the development of an independent European technological capability that would rival that of the United States.

France

The delegation to France received the definite impression that French views on the national security export control issue changed rather dramatically in 1981. In that year, the government obtained through its

---

*As reported in *Aviation Week and Space Technology* (March 17, 1986).

intelligence services the 1979 and 1980 editions of the Soviet Western technology "shopping list," the so-called Farewell papers. As a result of the revelations in these papers, the French government assigned ongoing responsibility for these matters within the General Secretariat for National Defense (the equivalent of the U.S. National Security Council). Its mandate includes gathering evidence and examining cases of fraud or evasion of controls; analyzing and warning the government of pending changes in CoCom or the regulations of other countries; and evaluating Soviet military/scientific capabilities, especially their efforts in new technologies.

The French have a relatively tight system of export controls on indigenous technology, although reexport approval by the government is not required. The system relies on end use certification. If and when it is discovered that a foreign consignee has violated the end-use statement, the firm is denied the right to make future purchases. The French now are in the process of establishing their own distribution license system, which will, unlike the U.S. system, handle *imports* as well as exports. French foreign consignees operating under U.S. distribution license requirements also will have to qualify for the French license, and the system will permit the French government to perform audits on behalf of the U.S. government. This is important because the French, like the British, take a generally dim view of U.S. extraterritorial provisions.

Although the French are concerned about the appearance of accepting U.S. extraterritoriality, they are generally far more pragmatic in their approach than the British. They also are pragmatic with regard to CoCom; they feel that it has increased in effectiveness in recent years, and they see little to be gained from altering its status (e.g., making it a formal treaty organization or even acknowledging the existence of a "two-tiered" CoCom). There also is sensitivity in France to the growing problem of technology available from third countries, including those in Europe.

French industry in general also takes a pragmatic approach both toward CoCom and toward the U.S. export control regime. Because of the Farewell papers, French industry is now probably "overcareful" about exports to the Warsaw Pact. Nevertheless, the view was expressed that there is an excessive amount of unnecessary paperwork associated with U.S. reexport licenses and that, in any case, licenses should not be required for companies from CoCom countries. Both the French government and French industry recognize that, in order to maintain their world position, they must continue to develop and export new technology. There is great concern about how export controls will affect this effort.

THE EUROPEAN SPACE AGENCY

While in Paris, the delegation made a brief visit to the headquarters of the European Space Agency (ESA). ESA officials pointed out that the origins of ESA are in the scientific community and that it still retains characteristics associated with the relatively open exchange of information. These officials stated their opinion that the U.S. government is sometimes unreasonable in its technology transfer policies. They offered the example of a European subcontractor who provided technical data to a U.S. prime contractor, who was then denied permission by the U.S. government to license the information for transfer back to Europe.

There also was a feeling among those interviewed that some U.S. controls exist more to protect commercial interests in rapidly developing fields, such as supercomputers, than to support legitimate national security aims. Nevertheless, it was indicated that controls, although a nuisance, currently do not present an insurmountable problem. For ESA in particular, however, there may continue to be problems associated with cooperation on the space station due to the fact that two ESA member countries, Ireland and Sweden, are not part of CoCom.

THE FEDERAL REPUBLIC OF GERMANY

The West Germans, like the French, take a generally pragmatic view of both the U.S. national security export control regime and the need for multilateral export controls. If anything, the West Germans are even more tolerant of U.S. extraterritoriality provisions than are the French, which may derive in some degree from the special U.S.-West German postwar relationship. On the other hand, government officials and industry leaders in West Germany are becoming increasingly concerned about the time delays and costs associated with reexport licensing.

The situation is complicated, of course, by West Germany's relationship with its Communist "other half." In talks with the panel delegation, West German government officials acknowledged that an export to East Germany is more or less tantamount to a transfer directly to the Soviet Union. Trade with East Germany is limited to control such transfers; nevertheless, it is of considerable political importance. In general, however, West German customs officials and the Ministry of Trade have been diligent in pursuing active diverters.

The delegation also was told that liberal elements within the West German government would like to increase trade with the East and are concerned about the extent of controls over major high-technology exports. It was pointed out repeatedly that, unlike the United States,

West Germany must trade to survive (one-third of its GNP is derived from exports). Further, "transit trade" (see the earlier section on "Goods in Transit") is very important in Europe due to the geographic proximity of the countries and the nature of the EEC agreement. Controlling transit trade is an especially difficult aspect of the West German export control problem.

West Germany currently maintains few restrictions on exports to third countries such as Brazil (with which it has a large volume of trade); many people with whom the delegation spoke felt that this aspect of West German policy must be addressed in the near future. There also was concern about the implications of German involvement in SDI—namely, whether technology developed in West Germany might get "sucked in" by the SDI program and become inaccessible for commercial exploitation.

The West Germans fully support the CoCom process and favor increased transparency, streamlined lists, and better definitions of exactly what is controlled. However, there was some suspicion that certain countries (read: the United States) try to railroad through controls in CoCom without permitting time for adequate response by other members. Some interlocutors felt that an informal, two-tiered CoCom arrangement already exists de facto.

AUSTRIA

The fundamental message conveyed to the panel delegation visiting Austria (one of the non-CoCom countries of Western Europe) was that the only way the nation can remain master of its own destiny is by maintaining its status of permanent neutrality. This can only be accomplished if its economy remains stable, which in turn depends on its ability to trade (exports account for 35 percent of Austrian GNP). Austrian interlocutors emphasized that in Austria trade is a right and not a privilege (as it is in the United States). Moreover, because of Austria's neutral status, it is politically impossible for it to accept the CoCom control lists in toto. Although Austria does not share the U.S. view of the need for export controls, it respects the right of the United States to determine what is in its national security interests.

At the end of 1984, the Austrian government adopted a new, "autonomous" export control policy and appropriate implementing legislation, which is now being carried out. This new system essentially mimics the extant controls of the country of origin for a particular shipment; whatever restrictions are imposed there (including reexport licensing requirements) also are imposed in Austria.

Given its geopolitical situation, Austria continues to have significant problems both with respect to diversions and to goods in transit. In part due to Austria's neutral status and also to its long history as a trading nation, its customs officials have difficulty with the idea of seizing shipments moving through bonded customs zones. The officials indicated, however, that they can act if something is mislabeled, although they do not have the manpower to find "needles in the haystack" unless they are tipped off in advance. A revised U.S.-Austrian customs agreement was signed recently and is now being implemented.

Sweden

Like Austria, Sweden carefully guards its neutral status. Yet, Swedish attitudes toward export controls have been changing rapidly over the past few years, driven in large measure by the publicity surrounding some of the major diversion cases (c.g., the VAX 11/780 computers). It is important to point out that export control problems in Sweden generally are not related to illegal or questionable activities by the major Swedish manufacturers; the problems involve the so-called "techno-bandits," diverters who set up companies in Sweden solely for the purpose of reexporting proscribed technology to the Warsaw Pact countries. Part of the difficulty Sweden has encountered in trying to stop diverters stems from the fact that it has few applicable laws on the books.

In 1982 the Swedes set up a system (under their Defense Material Administration) to issue end-use certificates and conduct prelicense checks of facilities (as well as follow-up visits every 12 months) whenever there was to be an import of sensitive U.S.-origin computers or computer-related technology. Recently, the Swedes announced additional regulations designed to make it more difficult for diverters to use Sweden for their operations. In all their efforts, however, the Swedes must tread a narrow line to maintain their neutral status; they are under continuing criticism by the Soviets for "catering" to the United States on export control matters.

Officials in Swedish industry and the Swedish government made it clear that, although they do not like the extraterritorial provisions of the U.S. export control regime—particularly reexport licensing—they comply with them and will continue to do so. At the same time, industry representatives indicated an active interest in designing around U.S. components wherever possible, although they also admitted that the United States is simply too important an export market to abandon. Sweden also is consulting closely with the other two major non-CoCom neutral countries, Austria and Switzerland, and is determined to maintain control policies that are roughly analogous to what the other two are doing with respect to the U.S. control regime and the other CoCom countries.

ANECDOTAL COMMENTS OF EUROPEAN INTERLOCUTORS*

United Kingdom

- *There's an increasing tendency for U.K. firms to non-U.S. source parts and components to avoid present and future complications with U.S. export controls of any kind, not just national security.*

- *U.S. reexport controls are very long and difficult to follow. . . .The time required for U.S. reexport approvals can also be very long.*

- *Apprehension about the scope of U.S. extraterritorial controls has caused (_____) to develop their own internal sources of some critical components and in other cases to seek non-U.S. suppliers.*

- *Recipient countries (e.g., U.K.) are looking for alternative sources (e.g., Japan) as a result of U.S. extraterritorial controls. Where no alternative sources exist, European companies are asking the European Economic Community to set up research projects with the goal of eliminating dependence on U.S. products. Whenever the U.S. imposes additional unilateral controls, companies look for non-U.S. sources.*

- *(_____) is using a computer to draw up a list of U.S. components in order to seek alternate suppliers.*

- *(_____) has teamed up with two other European companies to eliminate dependence on U.S. sources.*

- *The backlash against U.S. export controls has not become overt. However, the resentment is steadily building and could become problematic.*

Belgium

- *Difficulties with the U.S. reexport licensing process prompt foreign firms to buy non-U.S.*

- *Extensive time delays are often compounded by erroneous clerical assumptions within the U.S. government. Such misconceptions are most difficult to deal with when the Pentagon becomes involved in the review process, whether in the West-East cases or in those West-West transactions now subject to DoD review. Difficulties are also encountered with U.S. unilateral controls and supplying U.S. licensed spare and replacement parts/subassemblies for use in controlled and noncontrolled foreign products.*

---

* To maintain confidentiality, identifying nomenclature has been deleted.

France

- *To avoid the extraterritorial reach of U.S. export/reexport controls, some French companies may be trying to avoid the use of U.S.-origin parts and components in favor of non-U.S. sources.*

- *(_____) believes that they are penalized vis-à-vis American firms because the U.S. might approve an export of an AEN-level item while (_____) would have to apply for a reexport license. There is also a cost in delays in terms of technology exports and legal fees in the U.S. It is unacceptable that (_____) must seek approval to reexport from France to West Germany or Italy. U.S. approval may take up to 6 months.*

Austria

- *We need a source of reliable information and a source of necessary papers (i.e., forms and applications) in Europe to assist Europeans to follow U.S. regulations.*

- *Keeping track of U.S.-origin parts and components in Austrian products and filing the appropriate reexport requests is very burdensome on Austrian firms. It takes an inordinate amount of time and effort, and receiving decisions from the U.S. is a lengthy process. As a result, non-U.S. sources are being actively sought. It's highly doubtful that the time and effort expended on reexports is worth it.*

- *Austrian manufacturers, not certain that U.S. approvals will be forthcoming, often look for alternate, non-U.S. sources of supply so they won't be caught unprepared.*

Federal Republic of Germany

- *The U.S. Department of Commerce uses surface mail to issue approvals, and send RWAs [notices of licenses "returned without action"] even though (_____) uses airmail—this adds weeks to the process.*

- *Although buying non-U.S. parts, components, and other products has its difficulties, some West German firms are beginning to explore this approach since it would insulate them from potential, capricious U.S. interference in their freedom. This also applies to West German firms with U.S. subsidiaries.*

- *Small- and medium-sized West German firms who are or who wish to become foreign consignees under the U.S. distribution license are just now seriously looking into the requirements of the U.S. internal control guidelines. They are very concerned since the requirements are quite complex, and they wonder how they can possibly carry them out.*

- *U.S export licensing controls extended to Western countries are difficult to cope with—long, unexpected, unforeseeable delays are characteristic. In addition and particularly annoying are U.S. reexport controls. To avoid these, some West German firms seek to avoid U.S. suppliers, a clearly uneconomic move.*

- *There is evidence that the Soviets are rejecting offers for non-U.S. equipment containing major critical U.S. parts or components. This is on the basis that the U.S. reexport authorizations will not be granted, or, if granted, service or the supply of U.S. origin spare parts and/or replacement parts may be curtailed sometime in the future.*

- *(_____) questioned if it was worthwhile to have some research on West German products performed in the U.S. since this might result in the application of U.S. export/reexport controls.*

- *(_____) wanted to exhibit at a Moscow trade fair, but they could not determine whether they would be granted a license for the equipment. So they went with a non-U.S. supplier.*

- *(_____) said the company's European activities submitted 625 U.S. reexport requests in 1985, most from customers. Three to four weeks were required on the average to obtain a decision, although ten weeks were required for some (surface mail was not involved in either direction). Of the 625, 53 were returned without action, usually requiring further information.*

Sweden

- *U.S. reexport controls pose a major problem. For many years, they [Swedish firms] have avoided difficulties by specifying a certain amount of reexport in the major individually validated licenses. . . .Recently, however, the approvals have had riders deleting some countries. This requires time-consuming and separate applications and may lead them to consider non-U.S. sourcing.*

- *(_____) would like to establish some engine manufacturing facilities in the U.S. This would benefit both countries. However, there's a reluctance to become involved because many of these activities would become enmeshed in the U.S. export controls.*

- *(_____) has real problems figuring out U.S. Control List classifications. The Department of Commerce returns applications by surface mail! (_____) does not have same problems with European companies and they are definitely looking for non-U.S. sources.*

- *(_____) have not been denied licenses but have experienced long delays. The process takes too long.*

- *(_____) has a major problem with low-level bureaucratic delays and foul-ups in the U.S. Commerce Department, including occasional lost submissions.*

- *Smaller Swedish firms have a difficult time with export and reexport controls. They have little knowledge and experience a difficult time of getting information from foreign suppliers.*

ASIAN MISSION*

General Issues

COUNTRY CAPABILITIES

The remarkable economic strides of the Pacific Rim countries and the deterioration of the U.S. trade position vis-à-vis these countries have fostered an impression that the Asian newly industrializing countries (NICs) are on the same development path as Japan and will become formidable competitors in high technology as well as basic industries. In fact, the differences are as striking as the similarities.

Abundant capital and technical manpower ensure that Japan will continue to be the United States' major rival virtually across the board in high-technology industries and will assume world leadership in a growing number of specific technologies, primarily commercial but also military. Acknowledgment of this reality is implicit in several recent U.S. initiatives—efforts to gain access to the results of Japanese government-sponsored R&D, an agreement to acquire selected military technologies, an agreement to control the sales and use of supercomputers, and stepped-up monitoring of Japanese developments by teams of U.S. experts. What is less apparent is that the United States will soon find itself in the unusual position of identifying foreign technologies as candidates for CoCom control in advance of their domestic development or acquisition by the United States in military systems.

Korea's technological capabilities are concentrated in a handful of large, diversified, export-oriented conglomerates that together account for more than 40 percent of Korean GNP. A few of these companies are already producing, in volume, some CoCom-controlled commodities (e.g., high-density memory chips and 16-bit microcomputers) and are committed to acquiring more advanced electronics capabilities (e.g., fiber optics, robotics, machine tools, new materials, chemicals, and biotechnology). These highly leveraged companies are not deterred from these new ventures by cyclical downturns in world markets. Indeed, over the short term, they appear unconcerned about returns on world markets.

Nevertheless, there are several clear vulnerabilities in the Korean economy: a degree of duplication of effort that is unsustainable by the

---

*The delegation to Japan was chaired by Lew Allen and included panel members John McLucas and Richard Meserve; staff members were Mitchel Wallerstein and Stephen Merrill. The Korean delegation was led by John McLucas; accompanying him were panel member Leif Olsen and Mitchel Wallerstein and Stephen Merrill. The delegations to Hong Kong, Singapore, and Malaysia were led by John McLucas; the remaining members were the same as those for the Korean trip.

small domestic market, dependence on foreign (mainly U.S. and Japanese) technology and/or critical components (16-bit microprocessors), growing protectionism among the industrialized countries, a large external debt ($47 billion) and potential political instability, and a shortage of highly trained resident scientists and engineers. The latter is more a constraint on innovation than on the development of highly productive manufacturing capacity. Japanese industrialists agree that Korea and Taiwan, probably alone among the Asian NICs, are able to absorb and replicate sophisticated production processes. Conscious of the boomerang effect (in steel, shipbuilding, and now automobiles), the Japanese are growing more reluctant to transfer advanced technology to the Koreans and regard American firms' openness to high-technology joint ventures with Korean companies as shortsighted.

Hong Kong has almost no indigenous high technology. Roughly 60 multinational companies, most of them American, employ 35,000 people in the assembly of electronic components and the manufacture of some finished products. These companies export to their home markets for final processing and/or sales. Upwards of 1,000 firms under domestic Chinese management employ 60,000 people in the manufacture of consumer goods or low-technology components (circuit boards and capacitors) or in the servicing of other companies. These capital-poor, labor-intensive operations have experienced real difficulties in the recent electronics recession. The three or four exceptions to this pattern—firms engaged in higher-technology, capital-intensive activities (e.g., wafer fabrication)—are closely linked to the PRC. It is generally agreed that their product is of poor quality. They have had little success in marketing locally or worldwide and are experiencing difficulty obtaining financing. PRC aspirations for these companies to become commercially viable are considered unrealistic.

In recent years the Singapore government has made a big push to shift the economy into higher value-added, more capital-intensive manufacturing to differentiate Singapore from its neighboring low-wage competitors. More money is going into research, into programs to encourage automation, and into a "science park." Foreign investment, especially if it entails R&D activity, is welcomed. Nevertheless, until recently a policy of rapid wage increases and high forced savings (to finance the social security system) has driven up business costs and exacerbated the current economic crisis—2 or 3 years of negative or negligible growth following two decades of 8 percent annual growth—attributable also to the slump in shipbuilding, petroleum refining, and other key sectors. Singapore has been pricing itself out of the assembly business, so far without securing a firm foothold in higher-technology manufacturing.

In Malaysia, a policy of inducements for foreigners to set up manufacturing operations in nine designated free trade zones has resulted in a bifurcated economy. Although Malaysia is one of the world's largest exporters of semiconductors, these are exclusively the product of American, Japanese, and a few European companies that import materials and export assembled components to home or third markets. Their main contribution to the domestic economy is the employment of a semiskilled, overwhelmingly female but diminishing (on account of automation) work force. As a general rule, American multinationals provide more opportunities for local managers and engineers than do other foreign-owned companies. The government's current strategy is to encourage diversification—domestic production of integrated circuit materials and manufacture of finished consumer electronics—in the hope that these activities will spill over into the domestic economy. In a more ambitious step, the government has created MIMOS, the Malaysian Institute of Microelectronic Systems, to design chips for specialized commercial applications. NEC, the Japanese firm, has contributed $1 million to MIMOS. Despite its high-level political support, however, and the enthusiasm of its staff, observers are skeptical that the venture will be successful.

ROLE OF FOREIGN TECHNOLOGY

Japan, historically, has been an importer of technology. That balance has now shifted, but the Japanese continue to place a premium on acquiring the latest U.S. developments. The NICs are acutely aware that their progress will continue to depend on licensing or copying Western technology for some time to come. National policies to encourage technology imports vary widely. Korea places many conditions on foreign investment; Malaysia offers generous tax and other concessions.

Governments and businesses in Asia generally professed a strong preference for American over Japanese technology and investment for a variety of reasons: historical antipathy to the Japanese, continuing belief in the superiority of U.S. technology, Japanese reluctance to transfer technology, the closed Japanese management system, and the reclusiveness of Japanese resident managers. Nevertheless, such prejudices appear not to have gotten in the way of government and private decisions, and many representatives of American firms fear that they are losing ground to the Japanese on both exports and direct investment opportunities, largely because "Japanese companies plan for the long term."

PERCEPTIONS OF THE SOVIET UNION

Generally speaking, the five countries visited by the delegations view the Soviet Union as a political adversary and a potential military threat;

but these perceptions are highly colored by local and regional concerns— for example, the Soviets' support of North Korea and Vietnam, their occupation of the northern Japanese islands, the downing of KAL 007, and so forth. Few of the public or private officials the delegations spoke with shared the U.S. preoccupation with the global military balance of power or the belief that the West's technological lead is critical *and* threatened. Because the Japanese exposure is mainly to technology in the Soviet civilian sector, the prevailing view is that Japan and the United States possess a commanding (5- to 20-year) lead (especially in computers, software, and telecommunications) that is widening rather than narrowing.

PERCEPTIONS OF THE PEOPLE'S REPUBLIC OF CHINA

With the exception of Hong Kong, whose future is tied to the mainland, Asians are ambivalent about China and suspect that U.S. liberalization of technology trade with the PRC has proceeded too far and too fast. Their reservations reflect not a perceived military or other external threat but two somewhat contradictory concerns—worries about future Chinese competition and doubts about the stability of China's internal political and economic course. For the time being, the latter are predominant. Even the Koreans are willing to do business with China, albeit indirectly and in nonstrategic goods. (Korean exports to the PRC, mainly through Hong Kong, amount to nearly $1 billion annually.) Koreans are concerned about the reflow of dual use technology with military application from China and the Soviet Union to North Korea and about Chinese and Soviet behavior in the event of a North Korean move against the South; but they do not expect the Chinese to encourage the North to take significant risks. Japan and the NICs are not counting on the Chinese to maintain their liberalization and modernization drives without occasional sharp deviations and setbacks. China's current shortage of foreign exchange has reduced expectations everywhere, but especially in Japan.

Export Control Issues

FOREIGN AVAILABILITY/DOMESTIC CAPABILITY

The delegations were struck continually throughout their study mission by the widespread availability of "low-end" technology ostensibly controlled by CoCom. In every country visited, they determined either through direct observation or reliable reporting that microelectronics products and computers with sophistication at least equalling that controlled at the administrative exception note (AEN) level by CoCom were available for sale over the counter. In some cases, these products were of CoCom origin, while in others they were either domestic copies or "no-name" generic technology.

Looking beyond the current situation, the delegations were afforded the opportunity to tour a number of R&D and production facilities in most of the countries. One could not help but be impressed by the singleness of purpose with which the goal of high-technology development is being pursued in areas such as fiber optics, memory chips, and so on. It was not difficult, on this basis, to arrive at a view that, whereas the current control problem involves (with the obvious exception of Japan) foreign availability of CoCom-origin technology, the day is not far off when many of the East Asian NICs will be able to develop and produce technology rivaling that on CoCom's International List.

DIVERSIONS

Direct transfers of locally produced dual use technologies from the five countries to the Soviet bloc occur, but they appear—at least currently—to represent only a minimal problem. Japan adheres closely to formal CoCom restrictions and maintains tight visa controls and close surveillance of bloc visitors. The Japanese repeatedly asserted that their insularity and habits of loyalty to group, employer, and country are effective deterrents to illegal activities. The sale a few years ago of a floating drydock that the Soviets used to repair warships was an embarrassment "that will not be repeated." The few Soviet students in Japan are studying language. Japan has virtually no scientific exchanges with bloc countries. There are several small- and medium-sized trading firms, so-called "friendly companies," that do extensive business with the Soviets, but these are well known and presumably watched fairly closely. A potentially bigger loophole is the absence thus far of a Japanese espionage statute, another legacy of the postwar antimilitaristic sentiment.

There is no official Soviet presence in South Korea, internal security is tight, and Koreans conduct negligible direct trade with the Soviets. The first and last factors apply also to Hong Kong. Needless to say, however, there is a large PRC presence in Hong Kong, and trade relations, communications, and travel are extensive and increasing. Most of the known or suspected cases of illegal diversions to the mainland apparently involve relatively low-technology, widely available products.

The delegations all heard from many sources in the countries they visited that numerous opportunities exist in the Far East for diversion of controlled products to the Soviet bloc through third countries, given the absence of all but minimal controls on reexports and goods in transit.

Government officials and foreign business representatives displayed a natural tendency to point the finger elsewhere—the Japanese and Koreans to Hong Kong and Singapore, the residents of Hong Kong to Singapore and Indonesia, and the Singaporeans to India. Because the delegations received little specific information on documented or suspected cases, they had little basis on which to judge the magnitude or locus of the problem, let alone to compare it to the situation in Europe. Nevertheless, based on their overall assessment of the situation, the delegations found it reasonable to conclude that diverters can and do ship through the freewheeling, high-volume ports of Singapore and, to a lesser extent, Hong Kong, with virtual impunity. This would be particularly true with respect to goods originating in CoCom countries *other* than the United States, which do not impose reexport control requirements.

ENFORCEMENT

Recently, Japan successfully prosecuted its first two cases of export control violations. Penalties were minimal—small fines and/or brief suspension of exporting privileges—but the actions, regarded as symbolically important, received favorable press and public reaction. Given the "loss of face" for the companies (and individual executives) involved, these penalties may be more severe within the cultural context than they would at first appear. Previously, when the United States reported suspected diversions to the government of Japan, there was rarely an official response. It is assumed that investigations ensued and violators were dealt with, if only by reprimand, but the government took no public action. The Ministry of International Trade and Industry has authority to require postshipment reports and to conduct on-site inspections but has used it sparingly, if at all.

Hong Kong trade officials emphasized their limited capability to monitor shipments through the harbor. The customs agency has 14 full-time investigators and 300 officers engaged part-time in spot checks. Hong Kong Department of Trade officials indicated that they have power under the terms of a "direction order," which requires that the item in question cannot move farther than Hong Kong without the permission of the original exporter. To date, no such direction orders have been imposed on goods in transit, nor, apparently, has the U.S. government requested such action. Although U.S. consular officials consider Hong Kong authorities fully cooperative, both sides complain that they spend far too much of their time chasing after low-level, widely available products intended for the PRC.

Singapore officials emphasized that the task of closely monitoring trade through the port would greatly exceed their resources. Surprisingly, in view of concerns about the extent of diversions through Singapore, the responsible U.S. Customs attaché is stationed in Bangkok, from which he covers three countries (Malaysia, Thailand, and Singapore). The Singaporeans claim that they have a system—the import certificate/ delivery verification (IC/DV) system, which is discussed elsewhere in this volume—by which items can be tracked through Singapore. However, despite persistent questioning of various interlocutors, the panel delegation could find no evidence that any system was in operation that could spot, much less prevent, diversions.

Enforcement has not yet become an issue in Malaysia, primarily due to the fact that the movement of all CoCom- level technology is controlled directly by the multinational corporations operating in the country's free trade zones.

ATTITUDES TOWARD COCOM

Japanese and Hong Kong spokesmen expressed general support for CoCom but offered the following observations.

• The scope of the CoCom dual use list is too broad, encompassing items of marginal strategic significance that are available from a variety of sources with minimal or no controls (e.g., personal computers and commodity semiconductors). Efforts to control the uncontrollable detract from the effectiveness of controls in various ways—diverting resources from review and enforcement activities focused on the truly critical technologies, undermining support for the system within CoCom countries, and discouraging the cooperation of non-CoCom countries that are beginning to produce products at the low-technology end of the control spectrum.

• Compliance is uneven. The Japanese suggested that some European members interpret the agreements to suit their commercial interests. Although not alleged to be in violation of CoCom agreements, the greater willingness of U.S. companies to transfer technology abroad in the interest of short-term returns is viewed as undermining the effectiveness of controls.

• The lack of accountability is troublesome but represents the price of avoiding divisive political controversy in some CoCom countries. It may be feasible, however, to institute an appeals mechanism for cases that are turned down under the rule of unanimity.

• In the eyes of Hong Kong officials, the relaxing of controls on China while retaining its proscribed status will not be tenable for long. They urge the removal of China from the CoCom control regime. The proliferating economic ties between Hong Kong and the PRC may force the issue well before the 1997 political transfer, for it will become increasingly difficult to treat Hong Kong as a CoCom territory while maintaining China's modified proscribed status.

VIEWS ON U.S. POLICIES

To the extent that Asians distinguish at all between CoCom and U.S. controls, they made the following comments.

Export Licensing   The administration of U.S. licensing has delayed but not prevented access to U.S. technology and products. For exports to non-CoCom Asian countries, 3-month delays are considered common *and* unreasonable. Peripheral and component suppliers to Japanese systems houses reported delays of up to 3 months for imports under individual validated licenses (IVLs), but major Japanese firms cited much shorter periods (3 to 4 weeks) for approval.

A number of additional dimensions of the U.S. export licensing system also were identified as problematic. The current lack of a "de minimis" provision in the current reexport control regulations—a provision that allows shipment without a reexport license when the percentage of U.S. componentry in a product falls below a stated threshold—is viewed as a serious disadvantage. Many examples were cited of the problem of the "$2 U.S. microchip in a $20,000 machine," which meant that the entire product had to receive a U.S. reexport license. A second problem cited was the current requirement that exporters who do not hold a distribution license must go through the entire licensing procedure each time the identical technology was exported under an IVL, with no apparent institutional memory of previous case processing or rulings.

Investment   A number of Japanese expressed greater concern about other U.S. national security restrictions, especially those on the participation of foreign nationals in scientific conferences and on foreign investment in U.S. companies performing military-sponsored R&D. Japanese equity investments have been blocked or withdrawn in four or five recent instances involving U.S. ceramics, materials, and communication satellite firms; and these cases have received wide publicity in Japan. Where military R&D is not involved or is insulated from foreign management control, however, the Japanese have not experienced any difficulty in dealing with U.S. subsidiaries and partners.

Mixed Motives   As in Europe, there is a strong suspicion in Asia that the U.S. government mixes security, foreign policy, and commercial motives in formulating and administering national security export controls; but the only example cited was the manner in which the United States liberalized technology trade with the PRC. It is assumed that U.S. companies had forewarning and thus a competitive advantage.

Technical Data   Because Japan, Korea, and other Asian countries all prize their access to U.S. technology, any expansion of U.S. controls on West-West transfers of technical data would have serious political repercussions. Notwithstanding MITI's licensing of technical data, Japanese businessmen insisted that proprietary controls are adequate. They anticipate serious problems with U.S. subsidiaries and partners, as well as endless arguments about reexport controls on technology of mixed national origin, if the United States revises its policy. They indicated that technology flow in both directions would be curtailed. Elsewhere in Asia, tightened restrictions on technical data would be interpreted as evidence of a U.S. shift toward protectionism.

Extraterritoriality   The Japanese consider U.S. extraterritorial (reexport) controls to be a violation of international law. They also complain about the fact that, technically, if a Japanese company makes an engineering change in a U.S. system in which there is technology under license, it is obligated to report the change to the Department of Commerce; this requirement is considered anathema. The Koreans suspect that the United States delays reexport approvals on dual use and military items to help U.S. firms usurp sales. Nevertheless, the behavior of both countries is pragmatic. They dislike U.S. reexport requirements and refuse any official cooperation, but they do not block voluntary compliance. Above all, they have no intention of imitating the United States. It would be extremely difficult, according to several Japanese, for their government to take any steps that would be harmful to trade with third countries. Consignees (other than U.S. subsidiaries) under U.S. distribution licenses had only recently become aware of the new requirements for internal control programs and U.S. government audits. They suggested that the effects on U.S. business would become apparent only when U.S. officials begin to conduct the audits.

COMMERCIAL VERSUS MILITARY TECHNOLOGY

Asian countries with military forces and domestic arms industries acknowledge the concept of dual use technology, but in practice they draw a sharp distinction between commercial and military technology, defining the latter as narrowly as possible to limit the impact of either domestic or U.S. restrictions on arms sales. In Japan, the virtual ban on military exports and the political sensitivity of national defense generally has led to a rigid segregation of military and commercial activities even within the companies engaged in both. (The delegation was told by one firm that even the president of the company must make special arrangements to visit the military side of the operation.)

Korea is a modest arms exporter but is dependent on U.S. weapons technology, not to mention the goodwill of the United States. The Korean Ministry of National Defense maintains its own controls on military exports, including requiring assurances against reexports, and accepts U.S. reexport restrictions, although there have been differences over Korean arms shipments to some Middle East countries. (The delegation, in turn, received sharp questioning from the Koreans on the recent diversion of Hughes helicopters through West Germany to North Korea.) Similarly, Singapore is amenable to U.S. reexport controls on military items, although it has been diversifying its sources of military technology. All of these countries, on the other hand, are reluctant to impede commercial exports they consider vital to their economic growth. A Korean source suggested a related reason for this double standard: "In dual use technology trade, it is a buyer's market; but in arms sales, it is a seller's market."

Third Country Initiative

Singapore, Korea, and Malaysia are among the approximately 30 countries targeted by CoCom for negotiations intended to lead to agreements to control exports in a manner comparable to CoCom arrangements. CoCom members have split up the list with a view to concluding a series of bilateral memoranda of understanding (MOUs) that will become the basis of similar agreements between each CoCom member and each third country. The United States has taken the initiative with all three Asian countries. The panel delegations were not privy to the terms of the proposed MOU, but they were assured that the agreement would be comprehensive (i.e., covering all CoCom-level technology regardless of origin) and would be endorsed by the other CoCom partners.

During the delegation's visit to Singapore, an article appeared, not coincidentally, in the Singapore *Business Times*. Among the points noted were the following.

• Control of exports is one of a number of trade issues (intellectual property rights, generalized system of preferences, textiles) on which the United States is taking an increasingly protectionist line vis-à-vis the NICs but refusing to accept trade-offs.

• U.S. treatment of export licenses to Singapore—as if the country were a significant diverter—is unjustified and offensive. The United

States has not offered any incentives, by way of more favorable treatment, if Singapore agrees to the MOU.

• The MOU covers items that Singapore and other NICs are just beginning to produce, that are available from many other sources without controls, or that have not been shown to represent a significant security risk if the Soviets acquire them.

• The United States is asking Singapore to undertake commitments that it cannot fulfill because of limited manpower and authority to monitor transshipments through the port of Singapore.

• The draft MOU presented to Singapore is broader than those the United States has accepted in other cases (e.g., India, which has agreed to control only U.S.-origin technology).

• Acceptance of the MOU in its present form would disadvantage Singapore in relation to its competitors.

The delegations explored this set of issues with officials in other countries the panel visited. In most cases, the delegation met with incomprehension when it asserted that national security export controls are separated from other trade policy issues in U.S. thinking and bureaucratic responsibility. The Japanese, on the whole, understand that the two are not at all closely linked.

VIEWS AND PRACTICES OF U.S. BUSINESSES

U.S. company representatives are concerned about Japanese competition in Asia and NIC competition in the U.S. market, but few perceive U.S. export controls to be a major competitive handicap—as distinct from a significant administrative cost, source of bafflement, and considerable nuisance. Nevertheless, several companies reported lost sales as a result of delayed licenses (especially to China and India), citing examples of deals with government agencies whose spending authority expired before a transaction could be consummated. One source claimed that delays on licenses to India, pending India's signature on an MOU, had cost U.S. exporters hundreds of millions of dollars and created an opportunity for a Norwegian firm to capture a large share of the Indian computer market and to establish a joint venture with the Indian government. Several companies were especially critical of reexport authorization requirements that apply to foreign products with minimal U.S. content and of regulations that sometimes restrict the supply of spare parts and servicing but not the sale of the original equipment. It was the consensus that the distribution license greatly facilitates original sales and reexports but that the new conditions attached to it—for example, audit requirements—may well discourage its use.

Not surprisingly, small firms and distributors reported many more problems than large multinational corporations. Many conceded that, with a bit of ingenuity, it is relatively easy for U.S. or foreign competitors, not to mention would-be diverters, to circumvent controls. A number of company representatives speculated about the likely impact of export controls on some of the business practices now being introduced in the Far East. Specific mention was made of two factors: (1) the difficulty of maintaining "just-in-time" delivery procedures (a policy adhered to to avoid large inventory requirements) if there are delays in licensing—especially when the Japanese *can* deliver on time; and (2) the growing use of "drop shipments" (wherein goods are purchased for delivery elsewhere), which may well be problematic for some destinations under current licensing procedures.

Country Summaries

JAPAN

Despite the fact that Japan is a member of CoCom, there are certain difficulties inherent in dealing with Japan on technology transfer matters. For one thing, Japan approaches the problem from a different cultural and governmental perspective. To be found violating government regulations is a severe "loss of face" for a Japanese company and is simply not done. Moreover, Japanese company representatives work closely with their government counterparts. As a result, export license applications are rarely submitted if they are not virtually certain to be approved.

The Japanese constantly reiterate their strict adherence to the CoCom lists. Although this is apparently true, there is some definite question of "the letter" versus "the spirit" of enforcement. There is no evidence that the Japanese ever have been engaged in shipping CoCom-proscribed technology directly to the Warsaw Pact countries. On the other hand, Japan has enormous markets in Hong Kong, Singapore, and elsewhere, and it makes little or no attempt to determine whether there is reexport through these destinations and, if so, to whom.

Diversions that are undertaken by Japanese companies occur largely through the so-called "friendly trading companies." There are no estimates available of the scope or seriousness of these activities. The Japanese have, until recently, been extremely reluctant to prosecute such cases, but the tide of public opinion appears to have changed. As a result, the government of Japan recently prosecuted a company in public for the first time. The more common practice is for MITI to call in the president of a company for "administrative guidance." This, too, is considered a loss of face for the individual in question.

MITI officials described the principal features of the Japanese control system they administer.

• MITI annually processes about 400,000 individual license applications for exports of CoCom-listed items to all destinations. Applications must be accompanied by an import certificate issued by the government of the importing country. Exports to Communist countries (1 percent) are reviewed by the newly established Office of Security Export Control (11 staff members). All other applications are processed by MITI's industrial bureaus and regional offices (350 to 450 people are involved). The system is not automated. Other agencies have no formal role and are rarely consulted. The average turnaround time on bloc applications is 2 months; on Free World applications, 2 to 3 days. Exporters frequently consult with MITI before submitting applications; in the case of exports to proscribed destinations, they are strongly advised to do so. Denials, as a result, are extremely rare.

• Transfers of technical data relating to the design, manufacture, or use of items on the CoCom list are separately licensed for security, not economic, reasons. There is a separate list of controlled technologies. The exporter must identify all types of technology referred to in the sales contract. No import certificate is required.

• A bulk licensing procedure was introduced in 1985. Coverage is limited to CoCom country parties with which the exporter has a continuing contractual relationship, but there are no product exclusions and consignees are not checked. Approximately 120 such licenses were granted in the first year. They must be renewed annually.

• Aside from the IC/DV procedure, there are few controls on reexports of Japanese products. No end-use statement is required except from consignees in proscribed countries, no end-use or postshipment check is made, no denial list is maintained (insofar as could be ascertained), no use is made of the U.S. Table of Denial Orders, and there is no requirement for Japanese government approval of a reexport.

• The Ministry of Foreign Affairs conducts bilateral and multilateral negotiations and represents Japan at CoCom. MITI shares enforcement authority with but also supervises customs operations (part of the Ministry of Finance). The National Police Agency conducts criminal investigations.

In the view of the government of Japan, CoCom has been functioning well. The principal defect government officials see with CoCom has been its inability to do something about the third country problem. Although Japan is willing to cooperate in a multilateral initiative, it believes that progress is more likely through bilateral initiatives (which it is supporting). The maintenance of exports is unquestioningly vital to the health of the Japanese economy, but it was reiterated that trade with the Soviet Union could never be normalized until the "northern territorial issues" were settled.

KOREA

Korea maintains no formal export controls other than on military equipment. The Koreans find no need for export controls because they produce nothing of a dual use nature that is militarily sensitive. Furthermore, they are constantly aware of the omnipresent threat from the North and that it would be inimical to their own interests to have militarily sensitive technologies find their way there. Nevertheless, it is clear that Korea is now capable of producing memory chips and entire computer systems that are at or near the lower threshold of CoCom-controlled items.

The Koreans are pushing hard and successfully to join the developed country "club" and, more specifically, to catch the Japanese. As this goal becomes more and more a reality, export controls will become increasingly necessary. There was some indication that Korea might be willing to join CoCom—if for no other reason than the prestige of being recognized as a developed country. Over the near term, efforts will have to be initiated soon by the United States to negotiate an MOU with the Korean government.

HONG KONG

The situation in the Crown Colony of Hong Kong presents a fascinating study in contradictions. The vitality of the city is due in large measure to the fact that the People's Republic of China has needed an entrepôt since the days of the Communist revolution. Hong Kong's natural port also has served as a convenient, geographically central location from which to break up shipments for reexport in smaller lots to a variety of Pacific destinations. Import/export trade is the complete preoccupation and lifeblood of the city; without it, the economy would wither and die.

At the same time, Hong Kong now anticipates the fundamental changes that will commence with the shift of governance in 1997. It is not clear to anyone what the future holds for this model of capitalist entrepreneurial spirit after the PRC takes control. The delegation was struck, however, by how little concern it detected. There seems to be general confidence that the PRC needs Hong Kong.

In the meantime, as a British territory, Hong Kong adheres to CoCom requirements and procedures. Licenses for exports to *other* than proscribed destinations are processed locally by the Hong Kong Trade Department in consultation with technical specialists, although there is no provision for denial of such applications. Applications for the Soviet bloc and China are submitted to the U.K. Department of Trade and Industry, which also handles submissions to CoCom. The number of applications referred to this department has increased from 239 in 1983 to 457 in 1985. Hong Kong Trade Department officials insist that they have no authority to require an import certificate from the government of a nonproscribed recipient country.

Under Hong Kong law, goods passing through the colony that are transferred from one vessel to another for onward movement are considered *transshipments*; they must be registered as an import and licensed as an export. *Goods in transit*, on the other hand, are those that remain on the same ship or are transferred temporarily to a bonded warehouse before being returned to the same ship; they are considered to be neither imports nor exports and therefore are not scrutinized. Finally, goods brought into Hong Kong that remain for a period of time, often after being broken up into smaller lots, are considered *reexports* and are subject to licensing.

The delegation heard substantial anecdotal evidence from U.S. company representatives operating in Hong Kong. There was little or no suggestion that there was active diversion trade directly to the Warsaw Pact countries. Most of the discussion focused around the competition (primarily with the Japanese) for the PRC market. It was suggested that everyone bends the CoCom rules to some extent to avoid losing sales, but it was felt that the Japanese are particularly lax, both with respect to the PRC and with respect to other East Asian NICs. Mention was also made of the fact that, beginning in February 1986, the PRC Ministry of Foreign Economic Relations and Trade will issue end-use certificates for 27 product categories. This procedure is supposed to facilitate a higher volume of trade with the CoCom countries, but businessmen fear that it now will result in additional bureaucratic delays in China being factored on top of licensing delays at CoCom.

Singapore

Like Hong Kong, Singapore "trades to live." It is the only country in the world whose exports are three times its gross domestic product. There is no interest in Singapore in facilitating the movement of high technology to the Soviet bloc, but Singaporeans *are* interested in maintaining the free flow of trade, which is their lifeline. There are approximately 400 ships per month through the Singapore harbor, about 10 percent of which arefrom the Soviet Union or other Eastern bloc countries. There is a small Soviet and East European presence in Singapore, but its expansion is not actively encouraged, either by the public or private sectors.

The government of Singapore currently exercises no control over exports other than munitions and explosives, although trade officials insist that they routinely issue import certificates for imports from CoCom countries. In fact, representatives of the government claimed that there was an IC/DV system in place, a system capable of monitoring the movement of goods through Singapore and on to the next destination. Additional delegation queries, however, revealed that the system is largely mythical; companies rarely, if ever, apply, and the government does not require enforcement. And representatives of many U.S. firms in Singapore were unaware that import certificates were either issued or required by the U.S. government.

Even more than Hong Kong, Singapore is an archetypical free trade port. There is little doubt that diversions are occurring with regularity through Singapore to the Soviet bloc. As noted earlier, the United States has been increasing pressure on the government of Singapore to sign an MOU, but the Singaporeans so far have resisted.

MALAYSIA

Malaysia is not a "typical" newly industrializing country. For one thing, more than 50 percent of the population are from immigrant families who place a high value on education. As a result, the population is highly literate. In 1979, Malaysia "turned east," focusing on the United States, and there are now reportedly more than 25,000 Malaysian students in this country learning engineering, computer science, and business administration. At the same time, Malaysia's economy is deeply dependent on multinational enterprises, which operate with virtually complete freedom out of nine free trade zones.

Although Malaysia controls imports and exports to Israel and South Africa, it maintains no formal export controls for reasons of national security. It does not, for example, control semiconductor exports (although it is the world's largest assembler of semiconductors) or the machines that make semiconductors. So far, the government of Malaysia has not focused on the problem of export control or diversion. But, given the rate at which the Malaysians are attempting to develop high-technology industry (especially in the microelectronics area), that day may not be too far off.

ANECDOTAL COMMENTS OF ASIAN INTERLOCUTORS*

Japan

- (_____) *is making no effort to non-U.S. source.*

- (_____) *encountered delays on U.S. export approvals of six months to a year.*

- *Most Japanese businesses do not reexport U.S. products/components.*

- *National security controls inhibit Japanese access to technology and might reduce investment in the United States.*

- (_____) *anticipates serious problems with U.S. subsidiaries and partners, and endless arguments about reexport controls on technology of mixed origin, if the U.S. revises its policy on technical data. Technology flow in both directions would be curtailed.*

- *The U.S. Commerce Department should put together a readable summary of U.S. regulations in Japanese for use in Japan.*

- *CoCom should have some sort of appeals or grievance process.*

- *U.S. embassies are not well enough informed to help exporters with questions about U.S. regulations.*

Korea

- *There is a "huge technology gap" between Korea and Japan and the U.S. Korea will have to rely on imported technology for at least 20 years.*

- *Controls on the transfer of U.S. technology are seen as an attempt by the U.S. to maintain a competitive edge.*

- *There is no point in controlling exports to Hong Kong and Singapore because goods are too widely available there.*

- (_____) *had a difficult time obtaining an export license for laser technology from the U.S. They eventually chose to buy from a German company to avoid U.S. export regulations due to the delays they had encountered. Each time they wished to import the item they encountered a 2- to 3-month delay for essentially the same product and the same application.*

- *A license was required for a voice-recognition system, even though it is widely available in toys.*

Hong Kong

- *If there are difficulties in dealing with U.S. companies due to technology transfer, it may cause the venture firm to look to other sources.*

---

* To maintain confidentiality, identifying nomenclature has been deleted.

- *DoD has blocked the sale of ruggedized computers out of Hong Kong for use in coal mines because such computers are controlled by ITAR; however, versions of this equipment from European and Japanese sources are already present in the PRC.*

- *The PRC is requiring a clause in licenses with U.S. companies that says that, if a device is not delivered within 9 months, the contract will be cancelled.*

- *(_____) had a contract to provide equipment to a new hotel in PRC. The contract was delayed by a license application, and a Japanese company went to the hotel and said that they could provide the equipment immediately. (_____) lost the contract.*

- *U.S. trade is hurt by controls. There are many cases of the PRC buying from Japan or France to get what they want.*

Singapore

- *Singapore is experiencing increasing delays in obtaining U.S. products, in part because it is one of the countries reviewed by DoD. If these delays continue, it will turn increasingly to Europe and Japan.*

- *(_____) is looking to buy chips from Japan for silicon processing due to problems of getting technology out of the U.S.*

- *Licenses for machine tools with computer and numerically controlled devices were very hard to get; a "ton of forms" had to be filled out a year in advance. Japanese companies promised to deliver the spare parts with no delay, and so the company wound up buying the U.S. machine and Japanese electronic components.*

- *(_____) estimates that they lost $8.6 million of business due to export controls to India and China. One license was applied for in early 1984 and not granted until October 1985. Another sale was lost because, by the time the license was approved, the PRC ministry had lost its funding authority.*

- *Distribution license holders can promise delivery within 30 days while IVLs require 90 days minimum. Since acquiring a DL requires a solid sales record in a country, new or expanding companies are at a real disadvantage since they must use IVLs.*

- *The American Business Council conducted a survey of its membership last year on the loss of business due to controls. They found no evidence of loss at that time but they found growing concern about opportunity cost.*

Malaysia

- *Exports are extremely important to Malaysia. Any actions that impede this process would be viewed with extreme disfavor.*

C

Operation and Effects of U.S. Export Licensing for National Security Purposes

STEPHEN A. MERRILL
Senior Staff Consultant

INTRODUCTION

Determining the economic effects of U.S. national security export controls requires a detailed understanding of how technology trade is conducted, how U.S. controls operate, how they compare with the control systems of other countries, and how controls interact with relative prices, productivity, product quality, and other factors to affect international competitiveness.

In administering controls, government officials and private practitioners acquire knowledge of or an intuitive feel for only certain pieces of this complex puzzle. For purposes of analysis, large pieces are missing altogether and must be assembled from many sources—public and private, domestic and foreign. The magnitude of the task is illustrated by the lack of data on essential elements of the analysis.

Volume and Structure of Affected Trade

The U.S. control system not only affects direct exports from the United States but also reaches sales of U.S. affiliates and foreign firms where these involve resale of U.S. products or original sales of foreign products incorporating U.S. components or technology. Apart from aggregate figures on the number and value of individual export license applications and approvals, detailed information on the amount and composition of business affected is not readily available. Trade data on exports and

221

foreign sales are reported for industrial categories that correspond only roughly to those on the list of controlled commodities.

Operation of U.S. Controls

An elaborate set of procedures is required of all companies that export controlled products and data; but the scope and mechanics of corporate compliance vary with the commodities being exported, their origins and destinations, and, especially, the type of validated license employed. In addition to licenses for individual exports and reexports (individual validated licenses, or IVLs), the Department of Commerce issues bulk licenses (distribution, service supply, and project licenses) permitting multiple transactions in controlled products and services with approved customers in Free World countries over a limited period of time. Substantially more information is available on the processing and use of IVLs, although even those data are incomplete and in some respects misleading because they do not include actual shipments and relate only to the government's handling of license applications. Virtually no information is available on distribution licenses, the most widely used bulk export authorization.

U.S. Versus Foreign Control Systems

If U.S. export controls were identical to those of other Western countries with competitive suppliers, their economic costs would be confined to the costs of compliance and of proscribed trade. The effects on relative competitiveness would be negligible. In fact, U.S. controls exceed those of other members of the Coordinating Committee on Multilateral Export Controls (CoCom) in their complexity, product coverage, and extraterritorial reach. Moreover, the U.S. export licensing process appears to be less efficient and predictable. Together, these differences make it likely that U.S. firms bear competitive as well as administrative costs in complying with export controls; but there are large areas of uncertainty. One uncertainty is precisely how national control systems vary, not only in formal requirements but, more importantly, in practice. Information even on the former is spotty. Another major uncertainty is how foreign purchasers perceive, weigh, and act on the differences in control systems when choosing among suppliers. Evidence on this score has been strictly anecdotal.

Export Controls Vis-à-Vis Other Competitive Factors

U.S. export controls may have a net negative competitive effect, but their impact may be relatively slight if U.S. firms are able to offer more advanced technology, lower prices, or better service support than their foreign competitors. The effects of the control system cannot be viewed in isolation from exchange rates, relative productivity, comparative quality, and other competitive factors. No analysis has attempted the difficult task of disentangling these effects at a particular point in time, let alone attempted to forecast their variation and interaction over time.

To begin to fill in these gaps, the National Academy complex's Panel on the Impact of National Security Controls on International Technology Transfer commissioned several studies, of which two are summarized in this appendix. They are (1) Quick, Finan & Associates, Inc., "Analysis of the Effects of U.S. National Security Controls on U.S.-Headquartered Industrial Firms,"* and (2) Stephen A. Merrill, "International Business Under the Distribution License."†

These studies deal in varying degrees with the issues described above. First, an effort was made to determine the value and composition of U.S. foreign sales of manufactured goods affected by national security export controls. This analysis included direct exports and sales by U.S. affiliates. With the exception of the relatively few reexports for which they seek separate U.S. authorization, the analysis did not include independent foreign companies' sales of products with some U.S.-controlled content, on which data are not available.

Second, the administration of export controls, from government and private perspectives, received considerable attention. Most of it focused on the processing of individual validated licenses and individual reexport authorizations because delays and uncertainty in the handling of IVLs have long been considered to be significant problems, especially for smaller U.S. exporters.

Third, the studies attempted to ascertain how U.S. companies and, indirectly, foreign firms view the relative coverage, stringency, and efficiency of the control systems of the major Western industrialized countries. A separate consultant study,‡ which appears in the companion volume of this report, represents the first published comparison of the major features of the control systems of five CoCom and two non-CoCom countries. The findings generally support the private sector perceptions described below.

---

*A report in two volumes submitted to the panel August 25, 1986, by Quick, Finan & Associates, 1020 Nineteenth Street, N.W., Suite 340, Washington, DC 20036. Principal investigators were William F. Finan and Karen M. Sandberg.

†A report submitted to the panel September 1986 by Stephen A. Merrill, independent consultant, 148 Eleventh Street, S.E., Washington, DC 20003. Both reports are available for a nominal fee from the National Academy of Sciences.

‡"A Study of Foreign Country Export Control Systems," prepared for the National Academy of Sciences by International Business-Government Counsellors, Inc., October 1986.

Finally, the two studies attempted to determine the administrative costs to U.S. businesses of complying with U.S. export controls and, in two separate contexts, to estimate the magnitude of the competitive effects of these controls. In both cases, discrete actions by the U.S. government to relax existing controls or to impose new controls permit quantitative analysis of the effects of controls on the operations of U.S. companies. In one instance, it was possible to link regulatory changes to changes in the level of U.S. exports in a particular product group after accounting for the effects of fluctuations in exchange rates, foreign industrial production levels, and prices. A preliminary estimate of the aggregate economic costs associated with certain features of the U.S. export control system is described in Appendix D.

DATA SOURCES AND LIMITATIONS

The Quick, Finan & Associates and Merrill studies rely on data from four principal sources—U.S. government trade and foreign investment data, the Commerce Department export licensing data bank,* surveys of U.S.-based companies affected by national security export controls, and interviews with corporate officers responsible for compliance. The major components of the studies are summarized below.

Commerce Department Data Bank

1. A sample of 500 cases was drawn at random from 3,613 individual validated licenses approved between April 15 and April 30, 1986. The approvals represented 85 percent of the 4,259 cases for which processing was completed in the 2-week period. Data collected on each case in the sample included processing time, destination country, U.S. Control List number (ECCN), value of shipment, and company size (based on number of employees, determined independently).

2. A random sample of 200 cases returned without action (RWAd) was drawn from the total of 20,675 RWAs during calendar year 1985. Repeat RWAs are included in the sample, which was taken prior to a change in Commerce Department procedures intended to reduce the number of and turnaround time for RWAs. The data collected were the same as those for the sample of approved licenses.

---

*The panel obtained access to the data bank for its consultants under a "national interest" exception to the nondisclosure provision, Section 12(c), of the Export Administration Act of 1979. Protection of the confidentiality of business information is a strict condition of such access.

3. A sample of 761 reexport authorization applications was drawn from all requests originating in five Western countries during the first quarter of 1986 and in a sixth Western country during 2 months of that quarter—a total of 1,894 cases. In addition to value, ECCN, and country of destination, the data collected included the country of origin and whether the applicant was a U.S. or foreign company.

4. A sample of 1,617 cases (approvals, denials, and RWAs) was drawn from the total number of IVL cases (approximately 3,200) for which processing was completed during the week of June 2, 1986. Commerce Department licensing officers examined each case in the sample to determine, regardless of the actual destination, whether the proposed export was (1) within the CoCom administrative exception note (AEN) limits and thus eligible for export to the Soviet bloc without referral to or approval by CoCom; (2) above the AEN limits but within the China "green zone" limits and thus eligible for export to the People's Republic of China without CoCom concurrence; (3) above the green zone limits but eligible for export to approved Western affiliates, distributors, and end users under a distribution license; or (4) ineligible for export under a distribution license, thus requiring an IVL to all destinations. As stated, these categories are mutually exclusive; but they represent progressively higher levels of military sensitivity or criticality, as determined for administrative purposes in U.S. government deliberations and CoCom negotiations.* Additional information collected on each case included the ECCN, destination country, value, and processing time.

Survey Questionnaires

1. With the cooperation of 10 industrial trade associations, a questionnaire prepared by Quick, Finan & Associates was mailed to U.S.-based member firms in the aerospace, machine tool, electronics, medical equipment, robotics and automated manufacturing, and instrumentation industries. Because of multiple association memberships, many firms received two or more questionnaires. The 170 respondents were estimated to account for about one-third to one-half of U.S. aerospace, electronics, instrument, and machine tool exports in 1985. The questionnaire focused primarily on experience in the use of IVLs.

2. With the assistance of the Commerce Department, a separate questionnaire prepared by Stephen Merrill was mailed to all recent and current holders of distribution licenses. One hundred seven (107) compa-

---

*In theory, items of greater military sensitivity are subjected to closer scrutiny by one or more agencies of the U.S. government and, if destined for the Eastern bloc or China, by CoCom.

nies or corporate divisions holding a total of 116 licenses responded with general information on their distribution license activities and detailed information on one or more licenses. The responses represent 18 percent of the estimated 650 distribution licenses outstanding between the first quarter of 1985 and the second quarter of 1986.* Only 10 companies responded to both surveys. The characteristics of distribution license holders in both samples were similar except that respondents to the Merrill survey included relatively fewer very large firms and none in the aerospace industry. Of course, neither survey sample can be considered to be representative of the total population of U.S. exporting firms.

Interviews

Follow-up interviews were conducted with several survey respondents who indicated a willingness to confirm, clarify, or elaborate on their written answers. The companies participating in the interviews were of various sizes and in diverse industrial sectors.

In reviewing the findings described below, the reader should bear in mind several limitations of the analysis. First, no attempt was made to assess directly either the effectiveness or the benefits of export controls in preventing or delaying technology transfers to the Soviet bloc. Indeed, it is not possible to determine from the data collected the extent to which U.S. firms are complying with controls, although it is possible to reach some judgments about the relative degree of compliance with U.S. reexport controls by U.S. and foreign firms.†

Second, because all but a few survey respondents were active or recent users of validated export licenses, the data derived do not yield any estimate of the extent to which the costs, complexities, or uncertainties of the licensing system deter companies from exporting controlled items.‡

---

*In its FY1984 Export Administration Annual Report to Congress, the Department of Commerce reported 780 outstanding distribution licenses. As late as May 1986, when the questionnaire was mailed, the department's mailing list contained a number of duplications, companies that were no longer active license users, and one-time applicants that had not received a distribution license. The estimate of 650 active distribution license holders is that of Commerce Department licensing officials.

†In interviews, several firms suggested that stepped-up enforcement activities, especially the Customs Service's Operation Exodus, account for a large share of the recent increase in individual license applications—about 70 percent since 1981. Compliance with reexport controls is discussed below.

‡Interviews were conducted with a few small company survey respondents that did not report any licensing activity. They indicated that the system's complexity has a deterrent effect but that the magnitude is uncertain. For many small and medium-sized firms that deal in controlled products within the Free World, the control system apparently discourages marketing to Eastern bloc countries even of products that do not require validated licenses.

On the other hand, the surveys were designed to elicit information on the experiences of companies of different sizes.*

Third, with the exception of a few U.S.-based affiliates of foreign-owned companies, foreign firms were neither surveyed nor interviewed. Evidence of their views and behavior with respect to U.S. export controls was obtained indirectly, from the U.S. companies with which they have done business.

Fourth, the data collected relate primarily to U.S. exports and affiliate sales of manufactured goods. Controlled transactions involving services or transfers of technical data not directly related to product sales were not examined in detail.

Fifth, an effort was made to distinguish national security export controls from controls for foreign policy, nuclear nonproliferation, short supply, and other purposes; but it is not always possible to isolate data on national security controls. The IVL samples obtained from the Department of Commerce, for example, contain a small proportion of foreign policy cases. Similarly, survey respondents may in some cases have included information on transactions controlled for other than national security reasons. The distribution license, for example, is available for items to countries subject to nuclear nonproliferation controls.

Finally, the data were collected for periods ranging from a few weeks to several months between 1984 and 1986 during which administrative and regulatory changes were being implemented. From one point of view the analysis represents a snapshot of conditions in flux. From another perspective, however, the studies capture many of the regulatory changes instituted since the late 1970s as part of a general policy of strengthening export controls and improving some aspects of their administration and enforcement. Unfortunately, there are no historical data with which to compare current and past experience of the operation and effects of the control system.

COVERAGE OF NATIONAL SECURITY EXPORT CONTROLS

The segment of U.S. trade covered by national security export controls must be broken down by type of transaction (i.e., export or other foreign sale), type of license, commodity group, and destination to give an accurate picture of the scope and incidence of controls. The narrow objective of preventing or delaying Soviet acquisitions of products and know-how with significant military value tends to obscure the fact that

---

*Depending on available data, various measures of firm size were used in the analysis— number of domestic employees, annual domestic sales, and annual foreign sales. Where data are reported below by size of firm, the measure is described.

controls affect a large share of U.S. international business, primarily with Western countries.

Exports

The Quick, Finan & Associates and Merrill studies first attempted to determine the aggregate value of direct U.S. exports of manufactured goods under validated licenses. Commerce Department data in combination with survey data indicate that the total in 1985 was on the order of $62 billion, or nearly 40 percent of all U.S. exports of manufactures. The total comprised the following:

1. *Exports under individual validated licenses.* In FY1985,* the Commerce Department issued licenses for approximately $50 billion of manufactured goods. Included in this figure was approximately $6.4 billion in reexport authorizations. In briefing the panel, Commerce Department officials estimated that about 85 percent of the value of approved individual licenses is actually shipped. The Quick, Finan survey elicited an identical estimate, which did not vary by firm size. Furthermore, although the $50 billion of approved licenses does not include military equipment licensed under the International Traffic in Arms Regulations (ITAR), it does include a small percentage—probably as little as 1 percent—of items controlled for foreign policy reasons. Thus, the value of national security controlled, dual use manufactures exported from the United States under IVLs in FY1985 was approximately $36 billion.

2. *Exports under distribution licenses.* Respondents to the distribution license survey reported that in calendar year 1985 they exported nearly $3.7 billion in manufactured goods under 109 licenses, representing 17 percent of the estimated 650 distribution licenses outstanding in 1985. Large companies holding distribution licenses may have been underrepresented in the sample. In that case the estimate of $22 billion in exports under such licenses in 1985 is conservative. This figure is significantly higher than a recent Commerce Department estimate (of $12 to $15 billion) that was derived from a sample of 1985 shipper's export declarations submitted to the Bureau of the Census. The latter sample excluded export documentation filed electronically, typically by large exporters. The distribution license is not available for the most sensitive dual use products, for munitions, or for items restricted to particular countries for foreign policy reasons; but it is available for items controlled for nuclear nonproliferation reasons, some of which may be included in the estimate.

---

*Department of Commerce licensing data are reported on a fiscal year basis. Survey responses were on a calendar year basis, as are U.S. government trade data.

TABLE C-1   U.S. Exports of Manufactures Under
Validated National Security Export Licenses in 1985
(in billions of dollars)

Exports under individual licenses	36
Exports under distribution licenses	22
Exports under other bulk licenses (project, service supply)	4
TOTAL	62

SOURCES: Commerce Department license data; Quick, Finan and
Merrill surveys of U.S.-based firms.

3. *Exports under other bulk licenses.* Survey respondents reported that
their 1985 shipments of goods under service supply and project licenses
did not exceed 1 to 2 percent of their total exports. The value of all 1985
exports of manufactures under these types of bulk licenses was approximately $4 billion. (See Table C-1.)

U.S. Affiliate Sales

U.S. business activity affected by national security export controls is
not limited to direct exports from the United States but extends to sales
of licensable commodities by U.S. corporate affiliates abroad. It is impossible to determine precisely the value of affiliate sales under validated U.S.
export licenses, but it is possible to derive rough approximations.

In 1982 affiliate sales were nearly 30 percent of the worldwide sales of
U.S. companies; and in five industries heavily affected by export controls, affiliate sales were about one-fourth of parent company sales ($77
billion of $309 billion).* Survey respondents who fell mainly into these
five industrial categories reported that 60 percent of their 1985 foreign
sales (exports *and* affiliate sales) were under validated licenses.

Because of the reexport authority the distribution license accords
approved foreign consignees, U.S. multinational companies rely heavily
on the distribution license to cover the activities of affiliates. The Merrill
survey obtained estimates of the value of affiliates' 1985 sales under this
type of bulk license. For a sample of 112 licenses, the figure was
approximately $3.8 billion and for all distribution license holders was
probably on the order of $22 billion—or roughly equal to the value of
direct U.S. exports under distribution licenses.

---

*See U.S. Department of Commerce, Bureau of Economic Analysis, *U.S. Direct
Investment Abroad: 1982 Benchmark Survey Data* (Washington, D.C.: Government Printing
Office, December 1985), p. 16. The industry categories were office equipment, other
machinery, electrical equipment, other transportation equipment, and instruments.

TABLE C-2   Destination of U.S. High-Technology^a Exports (in billions of dollars)

Destination	1980	Percent	1985	Percent
CoCom less Canada	21.3	39	26.7	39
Canada	5.5	10	8.1	12
PRC	<1.0	<1	1.7	2
Bloc	<1.0	<1	<1.0	<1
All other countries	27.0	49	30.9	46
TOTAL	54.7	100	68.4	100

^{a}DoC-3 definition; see the note in Chapter 3.

SOURCE: U.S. Department of Commerce.

Between 30 percent and 40 percent of U.S. parent companies' exports are to foreign affiliates for their use in manufacturing facilities, incorporation in finished products, or resale in their original form.* It may be supposed that U.S. export controls would not affect this large intrafirm component of export trade; but this assumption ignores the fact that affiliates' sales of controlled products are themselves subject to licensing and accompanying restrictions on reexporting. For multinational firms that market primarily through foreign affiliates, any adverse competitive effects of controls initially will show up abroad in affiliates' sales performance. Eventually, U.S. export trade will be affected; but the linkages back to U.S. corporate operations may be difficult to measure directly.

Destinations of Controlled Exports

The vast bulk of controlled U.S. trade is with Western countries, nearly one-half of it with other CoCom members. In the sample of IVL applications on which final action was taken in the first week of June 1986, Eastern bloc applications accounted for 3 percent of the total number, the PRC for 6.5 percent, CoCom countries for 46.2 percent, and other Western countries for 44.3 percent. The value of license applications in the sample by destination shows roughly the same distribution. And both distributions are similar to the breakdown of all U.S. high-technology exports by destination, excluding Canada for which validated licenses are not required. (See Tables C-2 and C-3.) High-technology trade with China

---

*Shares of exports to affiliated and unaffiliated parties vary widely among high-technology industries affected by controls. Intrafirm trade exceeds exports from the United States to independent firms in computing/office equipment, electronic components, and instruments. In machinery, communications equipment, and transportation equipment the pattern is reversed.

TABLE C-3   Distribution of Sample of Processed IVL Applications by Destination

Destination	Total Applications	Percentage of Sample	Average Value ($000)	Percentage of Value
Bloc	48	3.0	128.10	<1.0
PRC	105	6.5	1,830.20[a]	2.9
15 Western countries[b]	296	18.3	319.00	9.9
Other Western countries	421	26.0	410.70	19.6
CoCom less Canada	747	46.2	602.30	66.5

[a]Exaggerated by inclusion in the sample of a very large aircraft sale.
[b]Non-CoCom countries subject to a presidential directive authorizing Defense Department review of certain applications.

SOURCE: Quick, Finan analysis of Commerce Department export license data.

expanded at a rapid rate between 1980 and 1985, but the level remains relatively small. U.S. high-technology trade with bloc countries has been insignificant in recent years.

Product Composition of Affected Exports

COMPOSITION BY INDUSTRY CATEGORY

Notwithstanding the large volume of trade and broad range of products affected, export licensing is concentrated in a relatively few industrial categories that account for a large share of U.S. exports of manufactures—electronic components and computers, aircraft and aircraft engines and parts, instrumentation, and manufacturing and communications equipment.

Table C-4 shows the 10 largest U.S. Control List categories, ranked by value, of approved applications for manufactured goods in FY1985. These 10 categories alone accounted for 92 percent of the value of all approved IVLs. Ranking Control List categories by the number of applications shows a similar high degree of concentration; six of the largest categories by value also appear on this list. (See Table C-5.)

Use of distribution licenses shows a similar pattern.* The items for which survey respondents had authority to export under their licenses fell into 65 U.S. Control List categories. But by far the largest number of

---

*An exception is the absence from the distribution license sample of aircraft, aircraft engine, and related equipment producers who account for nearly one-quarter of the value of approved IVLs as well as a large number of IVL applications.

TABLE C-4   Approved Individual License Applications for
Manufactures to All Countries in FY1985 (ranked by dollar value)

Rank	ECCN	No. of Approvals	Value ($ billions)	Percent of Total Value	Category
1.	1565	42,110	26.1	52.1	Electronic computing equipment
2.	1460	536	7.8	15.6	Nonmilitary aircraft/ helicopters/engines
3.	4460	1,100	3.8	7.6	Nonmilitary aircraft/helicopters and engines/equipment
4.	1564	12,137	3.6	7.3	Electronic assemblies and integrated circuits
5.	1091	513	1.1	2.3	Numerical control equipment
6.	1572	2,205	1.1	2.2	Recording/reproducing equipment
7.	1355	2,631	1.0	2.0	Electronic device manufacturing equipment
8.	1519	1,505	0.6	1.2	Single/multichannel transmission equipment
9.	6399	3,917	0.5	1.0	General industrial equipment
10.	1485	920	0.5	1.0	Compasses/gyroscopes/ accelerometers
TOTAL		67,574	46.1	92.3	

SOURCE: Quick, Finan analysis of Department of Commerce export license data.

licenses—67 of 116—included or were limited to electronic computing equipment (ECCN 1565), followed by electronic assemblies and integrated circuits (ECCN 1564—41 licenses), electronic device manufacturing equipment (ECCN 1355—16 licenses), single- and multichannel transmission equipment (ECCN 1519), electronic testing and measuring equipment (ECCN 1529), and recording and reproducing equipment (ECCN 1572).

It should be noted that in some cases there is little correspondence between U.S. Control List categories and the more familiar Standard Industrial Classifications under which most economic data are collected and reported. For control purposes, for example, a great many products qualify as computing equipment (ECCN 1565) solely because they contain microprocessors. In FY1985 the Commerce Department approved a total of $26.1 billion of IVL applications alone under ECCN 1565; but according to trade data the United States exported only $15 billion of computers in calendar year 1985.

COMPOSITION BY LEVEL OF MILITARY SENSITIVITY

The distribution of licensed exports by level of military sensitivity shows a heavy concentration at the lower end of the spectrum. In the

TABLE C-5   Approved Individual License Applications for Manufactures
to All Countries in FY1985 (ranked by number of approvals)

Rank	ECCN	No. of Approvals	Percent of Total	Category
1.[a]	1565	42,110	48	Electronic computing equipment
2.[a]	1564	12,137	14	Electronic assemblies
3.[a]	6399	3,917	5	General industrial equipment
4.	1529	3,325	4	Measuring/ testing equipment
5.[a]	1355	2,631	3	Electronic device manufacturing equipment
6.	1537	2,350	3	Microwave equipment
7.[a]	1572	2,205	3	Recording/ reproduction equipment
8.	4529	2,089	2	Equipment, test, computerized electric
9.	6299	1,615	2	Equipment, electrical power-generating
10.[a]	1519	1,505	2	Transmission equipment
TOTAL		73,884	86	

[a]Also appears on the list of 10 largest categories by value.

SOURCE: Quick, Finan analysis of Commerce Department export license data.

sample of processed IVL applications categorized by Commerce Department examiners, slightly more than one-third of the cases fell within AEN limits;* slightly more than one-third fell between the AEN limit and the PRC green zone limit; 20 percent were above the green zone but still eligible for shipment under a distribution license; and 13 percent were ineligible for a distribution license. When actual exports under distribution licenses are taken into account, it is apparent that only a small proportion of licensed goods is considered extremely sensitive in that individual shipments must be reviewed and approved to all countries.

Firms Affected by Export Controls

Just as controls heavily affect only a few industries, the licensing system applies to a relatively small subset of U.S. based manufacturers. In FY1985, approximately 250 firms filed 50 or more individual license

---

*Roughly one-half of these AEN-level cases, 17 percent of the total sample, involved exports to CoCom member countries for which validated license requirements were dropped in December 1985. It is unclear why many firms were continuing to submit applications 6 months after the adoption of the general license G-COM. The Commerce Department usually processes applications that need not have been submitted.

applications, with their total (approximately 33,000) constituting about one-fourth of all IVL applications received by the Department of Commerce. The top 164 firms accounted for about half of the total value of IVL applications. Survey data in combination with Commerce Department data suggest that between 2,000 and 3,000 U.S.-based firms are applying for licenses each year.

Among the 170 respondents to the Quick, Finan survey, 70 percent were small companies (under $50 million in annual domestic sales), 12 percent were medium-sized ($50 million to $250 million), and 18 percent were large companies (over $250 million). The average small firm reported that 68 percent of its 1985 exports were under validated licenses, the average medium-sized firm, 47 percent, and the average large firm, 56 percent.

The distribution license is generally regarded as the preserve of large multinational firms, but the Merrill survey revealed great diversity in the size of licensees. Respondents included 44 small companies (less than $25 million annual domestic sales), 39 medium-sized companies ($25 million to $250 million), and 23 large companies (more than $250 million). Nevertheless, the average value of 1985 distribution license-covered exports by firm size was $2 million, $25 million, and $100 million, respectively. Thus, it is the case that large companies, although in the minority, account for most of the exports and an even higher percentage of other foreign sales under distribution licenses. According to the findings of Quick, Finan, exporters that rely entirely on individual validated licenses are almost exclusively small firms.

The number of foreign enterprises—U.S. affiliates, distributors, and unrelated firms—that have some involvement with the U.S. control system is much larger than the number of U.S.-based exporters that seek and use licenses. In April 1985, before the implementation of new Commerce Department regulations that resulted in the removal of a large number of foreign consignees, more than 20,000 consignees were qualified on U.S. distribution licenses, although many were listed on two or more licenses. In addition, several thousand other foreign businesses are affected by the terms of individual validated licenses.

ADMINISTRATION OF NATIONAL SECURITY
EXPORT CONTROLS

The U.S. government's handling of export license applications affects business operations in several ways. A long-standing concern of the business community, Congress, and licensing agencies has been the time it takes to process licenses. License review delays, especially unpredictable delays, may impose additional carrying and transportation costs, erode customer confidence in the reliability of U.S. suppliers, and in extreme cases result in contract penalties or lost sales. Licensing actions short of outright denial, such as the return of applications with requests for additional information or the approval of licenses with conditions on the configuration or use of the product, may have similar consequences. Delays and uncertainty—and their associated costs—are more troublesome for small companies than for large ones.

This section examines export control administration from both government and private sector perspectives and mainly with respect to individual validated licenses and reexport authorizations. According to respondents to the Merrill survey, the processing of distribution license applications and amendments (e.g., to add foreign consignees or extend their approved sales territories) often entails delays and uncertainty. Nevertheless, a distribution license can substitute for tens, hundreds, and even thousands of individual licenses. Distribution license holders prize its flexibility and believe that they could not be competitive without it. As experienced users of IVLs, many distribution license holders associate those licenses with difficulties in responding to consumers, high administrative costs, and a high risk of losing business to foreign competitors.

This section also examines other issues of administrative efficiency and corporate behavior. First, to what extent does the licensing system, in practice rather than by design, treat firms of various sizes differently? That is, does the system discriminate against small firms? Second, does the government's handling of export licenses reflect differences in the military importance of various products and in the risk of diversion associated with various country destinations of U.S. exports? In other words, does the system discriminate among transactions in ways that serve the purpose of export controls? Third, to what extent do foreign companies comply with U.S. reexport controls? That is, is this unique, controversial feature of the U.S. system an effective means of control?

License Processing Times

OVERALL DISTRIBUTION

As reported by the Commerce Department, the average processing times for various types of cases and destinations for most of the first quarter of 1986 are shown in Table C-6. For the department the processing time extends from the day receipt of a license application is recorded to the day of license issuance or other final action. The overall average processing time according to this definition is 27 days; but the distribution is very skewed. While 74 percent of cases are completed in less than 25 days, approximately 5 percent of cases extend beyond 100 days.

TABLE C-6   Profile of Commerce Department Processing Times[a] for Individual Licenses from January 5, 1986, to April 5, 1986

Average	Destination Countries					
	All Free World	Cocom	15 Western[b]	Total Bloc	PRC	
All Cases	21	14	36	75	64	27
Nonreferred Cases	16	13	24	29	18	16
Referred Cases	49	31	57	132	156	73
Other Agency Processing Times						
State	30	64	18	40	331	31
Defense	6	48	5	31	34	8
Energy	8	3	12	28	71	9
CoCom	0	0	0	114	66	68
CIA	41	41	0	40	59	44
SNEC[c]	126	0	106	0	0	126
Other	0	7	6	41	63	16
All Agency Average	9	7	6	41	63	16

[a]Average number of days from recorded entry into the system through license issuance.

[b]Non-CoCom countries subject to the presidential directive authorizing Defense Department review of certain applications because of perceived diversion risk.

[c]Subgroup on Nuclear Export Coordination.

SOURCE: Department of Commerce export license data.

From the perspective of the firm applying for a license, the processing time extends from the mailing or delivery of an application to receipt of a notice of action. This is a better measure of the system's performance because it governs the timing of transactions and shipments. For the cases approved in April 1986, the average total processing time was 54 days, twice as long as the Commerce Department processing time. One-third of all cases took more than 30 days. Figure C-1 compares the distribution of cases completed in April 1986 according to the two definitions of processing time, and Figure C-2 shows the same comparison on a cumulative basis.* Under the Commerce Department definition, 80 percent of the cases are completed in less than 30 days, whereas only one-half of the cases are disposed of in that period under the total processing time definition.

---

*In both figures, cases returned without action (RWAd) are included in the total processing time distributions but not in the Commerce processing time distributions. This extends the right-hand tails of the total processing time distributions but presents a more accurate picture because at the time the sample was taken, RWAs were occurring in about one out of six license cases.

237

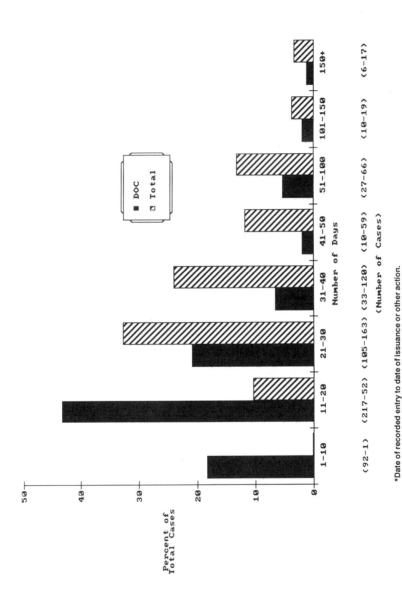

FIGURE C-1 Distributions of DoC* versus total† processing times for individual licenses approved in April 1986.

238

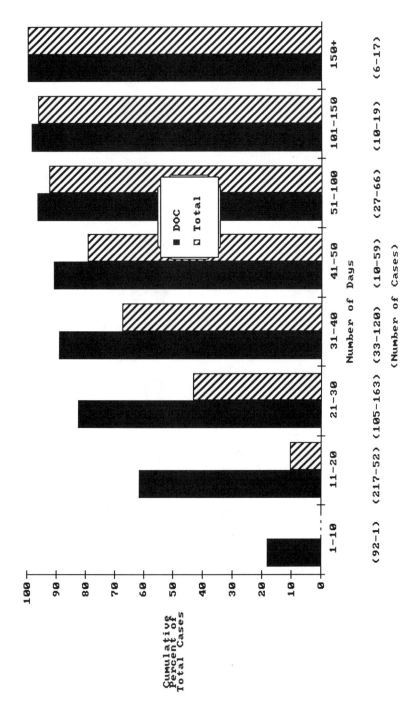

SOURCE: Quick, Finan analysis of Commerce Department export license data.

FIGURE C-2 Cumulative comparison of DoC versus total processing times for individual licenses approved in April 1986.

By Destination

If the sample of April 1986 approvals is divided between West-West and West-East (including PRC) transactions, two very different distributions of total processing time result. More than one-half of West-East cases take more than 50 days to process, but only 15 percent of West-West cases take that long. (See Figure C-3.)

Processing times vary not only between West and East but also among Free World destinations and between China and the Eastern bloc in ways that are consistent with U.S. government assessments of the risk of diversion to Soviet military uses or to undesirable PRC uses. Average processing times by the Commerce Department definition were lowest for CoCom cases (14 days), more than double that time (36 days) for the 15 non-CoCom Western countries covered by the President's directive authorizing Defense Department review, almost twice as long again for China cases (64 days),* and highest for bloc cases (75 days). (See Table C-6.)

By Level of Military Sensitivity

Although processing times vary with the diversion risk associated with different country group destinations, they do not vary significantly with the military sensitivity of the items proposed for export. A summary of average processing times by the Commerce Department definition for each combination of destination and level of sensitivity is presented in Table C-7.

By Firm Size

It was hypothesized that small firms experience longer processing times than large firms because they have fewer resources to devote to coping with the licensing system. Under the Commerce Department definition the distribution of average processing times does not support the hypothesis; but a significant difference emerges when total processing times are examined and if destination is also taken into account. On average, small firm applications take 14 percent longer to process. In West-West trade the small firm average is 46 days and the large firm average is 35 days. Almost one-half of large company West-East licenses are approved within

---

*The analysis of processing times was undertaken at a time of transition in licensing procedures for China cases. Among other changes, CoCom agreed to raise the levels of technology requiring CoCom review and approval. Presumably, these changes have reduced average processing times for licenses to the PRC.

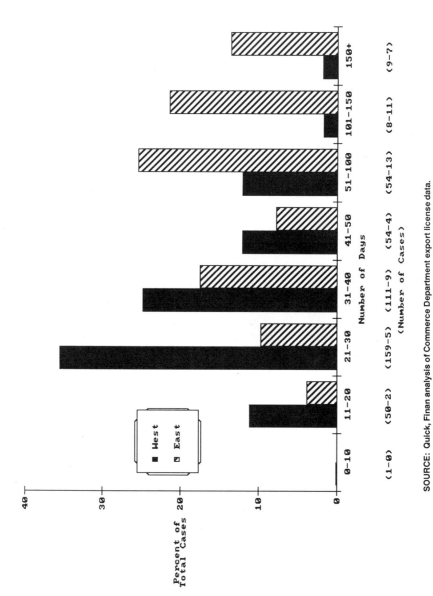

SOURCE: Quick, Finan analysis of Commerce Department export license data.

FIGURE C-3   Distributions of total processing times for individual licenses approved in April 1986: West versus East.

TABLE C-7　Average Commerce Department Processing Times (in days) by Level of Military Sensitivity and Destination

Destination	Multilateral Control				Unilateral Control	
	AEN	PRC	DL	>DL	DL	>DL
Bloc[a]	46	103	[b]	[b]	[b]	[b]
	(27)[c]	(9)				
PRC	23	81	144	119	[b]	[b]
	(39)	(41)	(8)	(11)		
15 Western	39	41	36	43	31.9	[b]
countries	(89)	(110)	(43)	(36)	(10)	
Other Western	27	35	33	31	35	[b]
countries	(158)	(129)	(59)	(38)	(21)	
CoCom	19	26	26	23	21.7	[b]
	(270)[d]	(196)	(133)	(87)	(38)	

[a]No licenses in the sample were to USSR destinations.
[b]Insufficient sample size.
[c]( ) = number of cases.
[d]These cases need not have been filed because the items were eligible for general license G-COM as of December 1985.

SOURCE: Quick, Finan analysis of sample of individual cases completed in the first week of June 1986.

40 days versus only 13 percent of small company applications. (See Table C-8.)*

License Actions

The Commerce Department denies very few license applications—between 1 and 2 percent. This is not a significant measure of the restrictiveness of the system because companies generally avoid submitting applications that are likely to be rejected or that will require inordinate time and effort to get approved. Moreover, companies occasionally withdraw applications (i.e., request an RWA) to modify them or to avoid an adverse decision.

More commonly, RWAs occur when the Commerce Department requests additional information, suspects errors on the application, or

---

*In the sample a number of extremely protracted Soviet bloc cases submitted by large firms raised their average processing time well above that for small firms. The share of cases completed within 40 days is more representative of companies' experience. The possibility that the firm size effect is a function of differences in the product composition of small and large firm exports was examined at least with respect to major U.S. Control List categories. The results suggest that line of business does not explain differences in processing time.

TABLE C-8   Total Processing Time for IVL Applications of Large Versus Small Firms[a] by Destination

Average total processing times		West-West	West-East[b]
All firms	53 days		
Large firms	49 days		
Small firms	56 days		
Large firms		West-West	West-East[b]
Average processing time (days)		35	145
Percent <40 days		75	46
Percent >40 days		25	54
Percentage of Total		88	12
Small firms			
Average processing time (days)		46	96
Percent <40 days		70	13
Percent >40 days		30	87
Percentage of Total		91	9

[a]Size classification based on number of domestic employees: large firms, >1,000; small firms, <1,000.
[b]Includes China.

SOURCE: Quick, Finan analysis of sample from Commerce Department export license data.

suggests modification of the proposed transaction.* Prior to a recent change in the department's handling of RWAs, one of about every six IVL applications was returned for one or more reasons. This rate is somewhat misleading because some cases are RWAd a number of times. Nevertheless, the frequency is sufficiently high to represent a significant share of the licensing load and a significant source of uncertainty for exporters.

LICENSE DENIALS

Table C-9 summarizes adverse licensing actions for different combinations of destination and level of military sensitivity. It shows that no AEN-level items were denied. Although the denial rate was higher for extremely sensitive items requiring an individual license regardless of destination than for items eligible for export under a distribution license, only a handful of cases in each category were rejected. Three were to countries covered by the presidential directive and one each to bloc, PRC,

---

*The consultants did not examine cases in detail to determine either what proportion of RWAs are on applicants' versus licensing officials' initiative or the reasons in either case.

and CoCom destinations. In the Quick, Finan survey, small companies reported a slightly higher denial rate than large companies. (See Table C-10.)

LICENSE APPLICATIONS RETURNED WITHOUT ACTION

In the sample of RWAs drawn from the Commerce Department data bank, the small firm share was not significantly larger than the small firm share of licenses filed. But small company survey respondents reported an RWA rate more than double that of large and medium-sized firms as well as a higher rate of license approvals with conditions. (See Table C-10.) In the sample of licenses categorized by destination and level of military sensitivity, RWAs were most frequent for CoCom cases. No AEN-level case was RWAd. (See Table C-9.)

Reexports

Reexports are often authorized in advance in connection with IVL applications for exports from the United States or in qualifying a foreign consignee to resell U.S.-origin goods under a distribution license. Resellers and users of U.S. components may also seek a separate individual reexport authorization from the Department of Commerce. It is possible

TABLE C-9 Distribution of Adverse Actions on IVL Applications by Destination and Level of Sensitivity

Destination	Multilateral Control				Unilateral Control	
	AEN	PRC	DL	>DL	DL	>DL
Bloc						
Denied	0	0	0	1	0	0
RWAd	0	0	0	0	0	0
PRC						
Denied	0	0	0	1	0	0
RWAd	0	3	0	2	0	0
15 Western countries						
Denied	0	1	1	0	0	1
RWAd	0	1	2	2	0	0
Other Western countries						
Denied	0	0	0	0	0	0
RWAd	0	0	4	2	0	0
CoCom						
Denied	0	1	0	0	0	0
RWAd	0	9	5	2	1	1

SOURCE: Quick, Finan analysis of sample from Commerce Department license files.

only to approximate the value of reexports under the first two authorities and only for U.S. affiliates. Depending on firm size, between 15 percent (in the case of small companies) and 82 percent (in the case of large companies) of distribution licenses are used for the reexport authority accorded foreign consignees. Sales by foreign affiliates under distribution licenses in 1985 were on the order of $22 billion.

Requests for individual reexport authorizations totalled approximately $6.4 billion and constituted about 10 percent of the Commerce Department licensing load in 1985. Analysis of the sample of these applications (summarized in Tables C-11 and C-12) not only shows their country origin and destination of the reexports but also gives some indication of foreign companies' compliance with this unique, controversial feature of the U.S. control system. The overwhelming majority (about 90 percent by value) of reexport applications are from U.S.-headquartered companies and their foreign affiliates. Unrelated foreign firms initiate only 10 percent of applications. The disparity is greatest in the case of applications from CoCom member countries, which are 80 percent of the total number. Between 87 percent and 98 percent of the submissions originating in three major CoCom countries were traced to U.S. affiliates. (See Table C-12.)

TABLE C-10   Action on Individual Validated Licenses and Processing Times by Size of Exporter[a]

	Average	Large	Medium	Small
1. Action on License Applications				
–Percent approved	91	93	92	88
–Percent approved with modification	6	3	7	8
–Percent denied	1	<1	<1	2
–Percent RWAd	7	4	5	11
2. Average processing time (in days)				
–Free World				
Average	45	38	40	48
Longest 5%[b]	97	46	68	119
–Communist countries	136	132	174	132
–China	119	107	136	127

[a]Respondents grouped as follows: large firms, exports greater than $250 million; medium-sized firms, exports between $25 to $250 million; small firms, exports under $25 million.

[b]These cases were the 5 percent of total applications that took more than the reported number of days to process.

SOURCE: Quick, Finan survey of U.S.-based companies.

TABLE C-11   Profile of Actions on Reexport Applications

Year	Approved	Denied	RWAd	Cancelled	Total	Value ($ bil)
FY83	7,041	111	688	8	7,848	2.5
FY84	9,699	148	1,575	8	11,430	3.6
FY85	12,055	164	1,858	11	14,088	7.4

Reexport Applications in FY1985 by Destination

	Denied	% Total	RWAd	% Total
To CoCom	11	0.08	366	2.60
To non-CoCom*a*	156	1.11	1,512	10.73

Reexport Applications in FY1985 by Source and Destination

From	To	Denied	% Total	RWAd	% Total
CoCom	CoCom	8	0.06	271	1.92
Non-CoCom	CoCom	3	0.02	95	0.67
CoCom	Non-CoCom	61	0.43	576	4.09
Non-CoCom	Non-CoCom	95	0.67	936	6.64

*a*Includes bloc destinations.

SOURCE: Department of Commerce export license data.

Because U.S. parent companies' shipments to their foreign affiliates are less than one-half of their exports, it is reasonable to conclude that non-U.S. firms based in other CoCom countries frequently ignore or are unaware of U.S. reexport authorization requirements. This is not surprising in view of the allies' hostility to U.S. extraterritorial controls. A few non-CoCom European governments have agreed to require their exporters to show evidence of compliance with the rules of the country of origin when reselling foreign-controlled goods or components.

EFFECTS OF CONTROLS ON BUSINESS

Administrative Costs

The Quick, Finan and Merrill surveys requested detailed information on the administrative costs firms incur in complying with national security export controls, taking into account all personnel time, overhead, and expenses devoted to preparing and filing applications, training corporate personnel in required procedures, hiring outside consultants and legal assistance, and recordkeeping, reporting, and auditing. The accuracy of the responses depends on how such expenses are allocated in corporate accounts. In most companies, export administration is not a budget line item.

TABLE C-12   Distribution of a Sample of Reexport Applications by Source

Percent of applications from CoCom countries	81
Percent of applications from non-CoCom countries	19
Percent of value from CoCom countries	93.3
Percent of value from non-CoCom countries	6.7
Percent of value from U.S. firms/affiliates	89.1
Percent of value from foreign firms/affiliates	10.9
Percent of firms exporting to CoCom countries	41.2
Percent of firms exporting to non-CoCom countries	58.7

Reexport Applications from Selected Countries[a] by National Ownership of Originating Firms

CoCom Countries	Percent U.S. firms	Percent foreign firms
A	98.2	1.6
B	91.5	8.5
C	86.6	13.4
Non-CoCom Countries[b]		
D	66.8	33.2
E	61.3	38.7
F	18.3	81.7

[a]Names of countries are not identified at the request of the Department of Commerce.
[b]Countries with which the United States has bilateral control arrangements.

SOURCE: Quick, Finan analysis of sample from Commerce Department export license data.

With these caveats, direct compliance costs do not appear to be a significant burden for most exporters. Based on the data obtained from the 170 respondents to the Quick, Finan survey, it is estimated that U.S. firms are currently spending approximately $500 million on export administration. A small share of this amount is for outside service providers.

Current expenditures nevertheless represent a sharp increase over pre-1985 expenditures, largely as a result of May 1985 regulations requiring distribution license holders and their foreign consignees to ensure against the diversion of controlled items to the Soviet bloc by establishing internal control and recordkeeping systems subject to onsite inspection by agents of the license holder and the U.S. government. Respondents to the Merrill survey reported that distribution license compliance costs increased more than five times, to approximately $100 million, as a consequence of the change in regulations.* Currently, average

---

*In the late 1970s the Commerce Department all but ceased to audit ongoing activities under distribution licenses and to enforce the conditions on their use. This may have encouraged a minimal compliance effort on the part of license holders.

expenditures are $21,000 by small companies, $76,000 by medium-sized companies, and $649,000 by large companies, although within each group there is extremely wide variation. Although it might be assumed that installing an internal control program is more expensive than maintaining it, that is not an assumption shared by many license holders. Three-fourths of the respondents expect their 1986-1987 compliance costs to be higher than current expenditures. The 107 license holders in the sample employ 747 people, 20 percent or more of whose time is devoted to distribution license compliance. Sixty percent of these employees are foreign based.

Perceived Competitive Effects

Overwhelmingly, survey respondents are of the view that U.S. national security export controls have a negative effect on their ability to compete in international markets. This is perceived to be a function of: (1) the greater complexity, coverage, and stringency of U.S. controls relative to those of other industrialized and newly industrializing countries; and (2) the increasing availability outside the United States of competitive products and services subject to fewer or no restrictions. More than one-half of respondents reported that they have lost Free World as well as bloc sales primarily as a consequence of controls. Forty percent have had existing customers express a preference for or an intention to shift to non-U.S. sources of supply to avoid entanglement in U.S. controls. One-fourth indicated that the system is causing an erosion of the international distribution and marketing networks of U.S. companies with a consequent loss of business. A majority of the respondents expects these problems to become more severe in the next few years.

Two unrelated recent changes in the Export Administration Regulations, imposing new controls or relaxing existing controls, permit tests of these claims and partial estimates of actual competitive costs.

The Case of Analytic Instruments

Normally, it is extremely difficult to quantify the relationship between changes in export regulations and changes in export sales. The case of analytic instruments, however, provides a unique opportunity to isolate the effects of discrete regulatory changes on a particular category of exports.

As far back as 1979, there was industry concern about U.S. unilateral export controls on products that, although not militarily sensitive themselves, contained embedded microprocessors with potential military applications. In April 1984 the Commerce Department announced decontrol of roughly half of the categories of unilaterally controlled instruments. Following completion of the multilateral review of the CoCom International List late in 1984, however, the department issued new regulations that had the effect of reinstituting validated license requirements for most of the same instruments.*

To test the effects of these changes on instruments trade, ECCN 4529B was cross-referenced to commodity 711 (excluding 711.8001) on Schedule E, U.S. Exports, and export data were obtained for the period 1978 through 1985. The analysis was limited to exports to CoCom countries, excluding Canada, for which validated licenses are not required. Exchange rates, level of foreign industrial production, and changes in price levels were accounted for along with two terms to capture the effects of changes in the regulations.†

The results indicate that the regulatory changes had a statistically significant effect on exports. When controls were relaxed early in 1984, U.S. analytic instrument exports increased (by the third quarter of the

---

*Until 1984, analytic instruments containing microprocessors were covered by ECCN 4529B (the letter indicating a unilateral U.S. control). Recontrol resulted from changes in the International List specifications for computing equipment, changes that were subsequently incorporated in ECCN 1565A on the U.S. Control List. Many industry observers believe that implementation of the CoCom agreement has not been uniform, but no thorough effort has been made to determine which products are being controlled multilaterally versus unilaterally.

†The following equation was specified:

$$RAI = a + b_1*IP + b_2*XR + b_3*D_1 + b_4*D_2$$

The variables of the regression are defined to be:

RAI = value of real U.S. exports of analytic instruments to CoCom (less Canada)
 IP = weighted, aggregated industrial production indexes for CoCom countries (excluding the United States and Canada)
 XR = four-quarter moving average of weighted exchange rates for CoCom countries (excluding the United States and Canada)
 D_1 = time dummy for 1984.2 to 1985.1 (represents loosening of export controls) values: 84.2 = .25, 84.3 = 1.0, 84.4 = .5, 85.1 = .25
 D_2 = time dummy for 1985.2 to 1985.3 (represents tightening of export controls) values: 85.2 = .5, 85.3 = 1.0

where:

coefficient	(t-statistic)
a = -20.80	$(-1.41)a$
b_1 = 0.92	$(-12.01)b$
b_2 = -0.27	$(6.39)b$
b_3 = 3.34	$(1.33)a$
b_4 = -4.93	$(-1.82)b$

$\overline{R}$ = 0.87
F = 42.20
Time period = 1978.2 to 1985.3
*a*Significant at the 0.10 level.
*b*Significant at the 0.05 level.

year) roughly 7 percent over what they would have been without the change. When the relaxation was reversed late in 1984, exports (by the third quarter of 1985) were 12 percent below what they would have been if licensing requirements had not been reimposed.

These fluctuations in trade reflect only the short-run observable effects probably attributable to export controls. In the long term the regulatory changes may erode demand for U.S. products. Also not reflected in the analysis are the effects these restrictions may have had on foreign transactions in similar instrumentation produced abroad with U.S. technology or containing U.S. components.

The Case of Foreign Consignees Under Distribution Licenses

Under the Export Administration Regulations (section 373.3), as revised in May 1985, foreign consignees under U.S. distribution licenses must for the first time also establish internal control programs. The required features vary with the nature of consignees' activities (e.g., end use or reselling) but in general parallel those of the license holders' internal controls—screening transactions against the U.S. Table of Denial Orders, a diversion risk profile, and criteria of "sensitive" nuclear uses; training personnel; and maintaining records subject to audit by the license holder and the U.S. government. The combination of increased financial costs, foreign sensitivities to the extraterritorial application of U.S. law, and, in the case of firms located in other CoCom countries, the duplication of effort entailed in complying with domestic as well as U.S. controls raises a concern that the new requirements discourage companies from doing business with U.S. suppliers.

Surveyed in May 1986, only 1 month after the regulations became fully effective, U.S. license holders responding (accounting for about 18 percent of the total number of licenses) reported the loss or removal of 32 percent of all their consignees—1,175 out of 3,686 in the sample—in the 12 months since the regulations were issued. Business changes unrelated to the regulations, inactive sales, and product decontrol actions were reported to account for one-half of the drop-outs for which respondents gave explanations; but the expense of compliance and consignees' refusal to comply accounted for 40 percent of the cases. (See Table C-13.)

As expected, among the drop-outs, independent foreign firms far outnumbered affiliates of U.S. license holders—by ratios of 11 to 1 among small firms, 17 to 1 among medium-sized firms, and 16 to 1 among large companies. Furthermore, almost all of the independent former foreign consignees were engaged in either reselling U.S. products in the form received or in selling foreign-made products with attached or incorporated U.S. components.

TABLE C-13   Reasons for Loss or Removal of Foreign Consignees from Distribution Licenses from April 1985 to May 1986

	No. of Firms Citing	No. of Consignees
1. Directly related to new regulations		
Expense/burden of compliance given volume of business	10	202
Consignees declined to assume responsibility	8	27
Consignees refused to comply	10	21
License holder could not rely on consignees to comply	1	1
Country no longer eligible	2	—
Consignees failed to certify	2	2
Consignees switched to non- U.S. sources	1	—
2. Indirectly related to regulations		
Consignees not active customers	25	138
Lack of business	13	52
Consolidation of licenses	5	20
Included in affiliate reexport territory	2	43
3. Other reasons		
Business change without regard to regulatory changes	13	144
Products decontrolled (now GDEST)	2	3

SOURCE: Merrill survey of distribution license holders.

More often than not, business is continuing with former consignees under different licensing arrangements. To simplify compliance, some license holders have consolidated consignees under fewer licenses. Others are using an affiliated consignee to serve independent former consignees, although without the reexport authority the latter previously enjoyed. Finally, as a direct consequence of the regulatory changes, 65 percent of respondents expect to apply for 67 percent more individual licenses and reexport authorizations than they used in 1985.

Despite these adjustments, which in most cases entail additional administrative costs and uncertainty, 28 licensees (25 percent of respondents) reported that the loss of 164 consignees has meant an immediate loss, albeit small, of business for the foreseeable future. They estimated this loss, over a 3-year period, at $78.6 million, confirming that these consignees, although active customers, were low-volume ones. Extrapolating to all license holders, the total loss is in the range of $450 million.

Most license holders consider this an acceptable price to pay to retain their distribution licenses. Nevertheless, the favorable benefit-cost margin has narrowed considerably for smaller companies that are apprehensive about being held accountable for the conduct of foreign customers with whom they have little leverage. Moreover, companies of all sizes reported that it is becoming more difficult to recruit new consignees; some consignees have reduced their orders even though remaining on a license; and in general the United States may be imposing too many restrictions to retain and expand its foreign customer base.

These concerns are reinforced by perceptions of widespread foreign availability of products eligible for distribution licenses. Reporting on 114 distribution licenses, respondents claimed in 91 cases that comparable products are available from non-U.S. sources. Major CoCom partners (Japan, Germany, France) have bulk export authorizations for West-West trade, but only the French license has restrictions and procedures comparable to those of the U.S. distribution license.

CONCLUSIONS

Coverage of the Licensing System

National security export controls reach a major portion of U.S. international business activity. In 1985 two-fifths of all U.S. exports of manufactured goods, excluding military equipment, received some form of prior government screening and approval to prevent Soviet acquisition of items of military value. In addition, controls applied to a large share of U.S. affiliates' international sales and to foreign companies' resales of U.S.-origin products and original sales of foreign products incorporating U.S. components or technology.

With the exception of pharmaceuticals and many chemicals, export controls affect most of the high-technology sector, in which U.S. producers have long enjoyed a strong comparative advantage but are now vulnerable to foreign competition. The $62 billion in 1985 exports under national security controls compares to $68.5 billion in total high-technology exports. It is estimated that the United States registered a deficit of $2 to $3 billion in high-technology goods in 1986, the first such deficit since the category was identified. Only 7 years ago, high-technology exports exceeded imports by $27 billion.

Ninety-six percent of licensed exports are to Western countries; roughly half go to the NATO allies and Japan. According to U.S. government and CoCom criteria, many controlled items are of less than critical military value. One-third of licensed transactions involve products that under CoCom rules may be sold to the Soviet Union without multilateral review and approval. Two-thirds involve products that may be sold to the People's Republic of China without CoCom concurrence.

Administration of Controls

Efforts to improve the efficiency of the U.S. control system have focused primarily on reducing the average time individual license applications are under review by one or more agencies of the U.S. government. This objective does not address several problematic characteristics of license processing that emerge from analysis of survey and government data:

- The formal license review process occupies as little as one-half of the average time from submission of a license application to receipt of an export authorization or notification of other action.
- A small but not insignificant number of cases extend beyond 100 days—or nearly four times the average processing time.
- Small firms experience longer processing times and more uncertainty about licensing outcomes than do large firms.
- Processing times, at least for applications to destinations other than the Eastern bloc, do not vary consistently with the degree of military sensitivity associated with different levels of technology, as judged by the United States and its CoCom partners.

The treatment of cases involving the least sensitive (i.e., AEN) technology suggests that the controls at this level may be largely a paper exercise for license applications to the Eastern bloc as well as for those to Western countries. A sample of processed applications contained no AEN cases that were either denied or returned without action. On the other hand, for reasons that are unclear but merit further investigation, exporters continued to submit applications for AEN-level items to CoCom countries several months after they became eligible for a general license and no longer needed approval. It is doubtful, too, that the requirement that foreign companies seek U.S. approval to reexport certain U.S.-origin products and incorporated components is an effective or enforceable instrument of control, at least within CoCom.

Cost of Controls

The amount of trade affected by export controls is so large that even a marginal negative competitive effect is likely to have significant economic consequences. Additional high-technology exports of $3 billion would be sufficient to convert the current U.S. deficit in that category into a trade surplus. Simply by virtue of the geographical distribution of U.S. exports, the costs of export controls fall primarily on West-West rather than on West-East trade.

The aggregate economic costs of controls are exceedingly hard to determine. But for one category of products—analytic instruments—from which validated licensing requirements were first removed but on which they were subsequently reimposed, it has been possible to estimate the short-run trade effects of regulatory actions, independent of changes in exchange rates, production, and prices. Decontrol had a positive effect on U.S. exports to CoCom countries other than Canada of about 7 percent; recontrol reduced exports to those countries by about 12 percent.

Similarly, the recent imposition of new accounting and auditing requirements on foreign customers that receive controlled goods under U.S. distribution licenses has already caused some erosion of the distribution networks of U.S. exporters and a small loss of business.

D

Estimate of Direct Economic Costs Associated with U.S. National Security Controls

WILLIAM F. FINAN
Quick, Finan & Associates

The following is a report submitted to the Panel on the Impact of National Security Controls on International Technology Transfer of the Committee on Science, Engineering, and Public Policy of the National Academy complex. The principal investigator was Dr. William F. Finan of Quick, Finan & Associates, Suite 340, 1020 19th Street, N.W., Washington, DC 20036. The material in this study is a follow-on to the Quick, Finan report "Analysis of the Effects of U.S. National Security Controls on U.S. Headquartered Industrial Firms," which was submitted to the panel on August 15, 1986. This report draws heavily on the data and analyses presented in that earlier submission, which hereafter will be cited as "Analysis of the Effects of Export Controls" (either vol. I or vol. II).

INTRODUCTION

The purpose of this report is to estimate the aggregate economic cost imposed by U.S. national security export controls on U.S. firms and on the U.S. economy. It is based on the best information available regarding U.S. export controls and the scope of economic activity covered by those controls. Much of the information used for this estimate was developed to support the efforts of the above-named panel to understand the operation and effects of the U.S. export licensing system. (Obviously, additional information would have permitted the development of a more refined estimate covering all elements of the system.) For several reasons, the

254

cost estimate is believed to have a downward bias: (1) a conscious effort was made to err toward the conservative side and therefore keep the estimate at the lower end of the possible range; (2) as discussed later, only a portion of the possible economic costs was tabulated; and (3) the estimate attempts to capture only short-run costs and does not reflect longer-term costs. These issues will be discussed in more detail in the report.

The competitive position of U.S. firms in international markets is a function of many factors, only one of which is U.S. export controls. The effects of controls on competitiveness cannot be completely isolated from the effects of other factors such as price (including exchange rates), product quality, and before-and-after sales assistance and service. Although some of these other factors—exchange rates, for example—cut across all export sectors, the effects of export controls vary by industry sector. Our earlier report indicated that a limited set of U.S. industries incur the greatest economic cost. The categories we identified as bearing most of the competitive costs associated with U.S. export controls include communications equipment, aircraft and parts, computers/office equipment, scientific instruments, electronic components, and machine tools. These industry categories accounted for about 70 percent of the total U.S. high-technology exports in 1985 and in the same year about 30 percent of total U.S. foreign sales of manufactured products (which includes U.S. exports and products manufactured abroad by U.S. firms). It is estimated that these categories account for about 85 percent of U.S. licensed exports of manufactured goods.

In principal, as we discussed in our earlier report, U.S. export controls would, under ideal circumstances, have very little if any relative[1] competitive effect on U.S. firms. This would be the case if U.S. controls and procedures were identical to those of other countries that subscribe to the multilateral international coordinating committee (CoCom). But in fact U.S. controls and procedures differ; the differences arise from the greater reach of U.S. controls, the greater stringency with which foreign sales are regulated, the extraterritorial application of U.S. controls, and the greater complexity of U.S. procedures. When combined, these differences mean that U.S. firms bear competitive as well as administrative costs in complying with U.S. export controls.

Estimating in full the international competitive effects of U.S. export controls is difficult because the ways in which those effects manifest themselves are numerous and diffused. For example, measurable competitive effects vary depending on country of destination and type of control; that is, the export control system creates a large number of possible economic effects for the different combinations of destination, type of license, and type of economic cost being evaluated.

TABLE D-1   Export Control Economic Cost Analysis

Factors Covered	Examples of Factors Not Covered
1. Direct administrative compliance cost 2. Lost sales for U.S. manufacturing operations in 1985, both for West-West and for West-East trade 3. Lost employment (due to lost export sales—item 2 above) 4. Direct research and development (R&D) impact (due to overall lost foreign sales) 5. Lost profits (due to overall lost foreign sales) 6. Lost revenues due to denial of licenses	1. Indirect administrative costs 2. • Lost sales for nonmanufactures • Sales of products manufactured by a foreign firm incorporating components or technology of U.S. origin • Sales lost due to U.S. nuclear or foreign policy controls (see Figure D-3) 3. Indirect R&D impact (for example, technical data restraints, controls on foreign scientists in U.S. industrial labs, etc.) 4. Indirect employment consequences due to items 1, 2, or 3 5. Uncertainties created by variability of license processing 6. Discouragement effect for small businesses in West-West trade due to complexity of license procedures (i.e., they forego attempting to export) 7. Long-term influence of U.S. controls on U.S.-foreign customer relations (qualitative evidence is that U.S. firms in some cases are the least preferred of suppliers if all else is equal or nearly equal) 8. Warehousing and other costs incurred when available products must await a license

Table D-1 summarizes the type of economic costs for which estimates were developed as part of preparing an overall economic cost estimate for the U.S. export control process. The costs included in the overall cost estimate tend to be fairly direct and short term in nature. The table also lists a number of economic costs that are not covered in the overall cost estimate. The general reasons for excluding from the aggregate calculation of costs the items listed in column 2 of the table were as follows: (1) lack of data, (2) lack of a defined analytical procedure to frame the estimation procedure, or (3) a judgment that the effects were likely to be second-order in nature. To repeat, the cost estimate we present covers only a subset of the potential economic costs—namely, short-term, direct revenue losses and associated employment loss.

The remainder of this report is divided into three sections and an annex. In the first section the coverage of U.S. export controls is reviewed in terms of value of foreign sales for 1985. Foreign sales include sales by U.S. affiliates abroad as well as direct U.S. exports to unaffiliated purchasers.

The next section examines how security benefits related to export controls vary with the level of criticality—a measure of the degree of military importance[2] of the technology or item being exported. The security benefits from controls are assumed to be greatest for exports of high-criticality items. We also indicate how competitive costs may be related to the level of criticality of a particular technology or product. The competitive costs of U.S. export controls are shown to be mostly concentrated in the low- and medium-criticality technologies[3] in goods shipped to countries that participate in a system of controls on exports to Warsaw Pact nations. When the distribution of benefits is combined with the distribution of competitive costs, the conclusion emerges that the economic costs of U.S. export controls are greatest for exports of items of low and medium levels of criticality, while U.S. controls on these items contribute least to avoiding diversion.

Finally, the third section summarizes the estimates for the aggregate economic costs as identified in the preceding table. These estimates relate primarily to lost direct export revenues, even though the foreign affiliates of U.S. firms also experience additional lost revenues beyond those estimated.[4] The report concludes with an annex explaining the method of calculation of the economic cost estimates.

SCOPE OF U.S. FOREIGN SALES COVERED BY VALIDATED LICENSING

The scope of U.S. economic activity covered by U.S. export controls can be best understood through the use of a simple framework. (Only trade in manufactured products is examined.) Looking first just at U.S. exports, total U.S. export trade of manufactured products can be divided into two categories as shown in Figure D-1: trade covered by export controls (requiring a validated license) and trade that is not covered (self-licensed).[5] The horizontal lines of Figure D-1 divide total export trade by category of destination. The three regional groupings identified are those of most relevance to the issue of licensed trade: the Eastern bloc countries and the People's Republic of China (PRC), the non-CoCom "Western" nations, and the CoCom countries.

But the possible scope of economic activity influenced by the U.S. licensing system is broader than just U.S. exports; it also covers some of the sales of U.S. foreign affiliates (see Figure D-2). The economic cost analysis presented in this paper is based on this broader definition where it is appropriate for use in calculating a cost for the U.S. economy. It should be noted, however, that even this broader definition does not indicate the full scope of possible economic activity influenced by the U.S. licensing system because U.S. controls also reach some of the sales

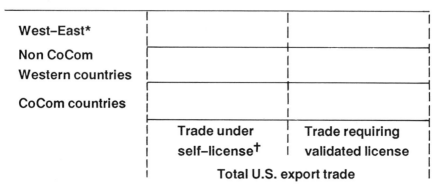

*West–East refers to trade with bloc countries and the PRC.
†For example, the general destination license (GDEST).

FIGURE D-1   Schematic of coverage of the U.S. export control system

of non-U.S. firms. The sales of foreign-owned enterprises including unaffiliated distributors, sales operations, foreign manufacturers, and so on also can be affected in certain circumstances.[6] This report attempts to estimate only those economic impacts directly related to U.S. enterprises; it does not reach into this last area (i.e., sales of foreign-owned enterprises) because of the limitations of available information (and not because of a belief that the effects on foreign operations are inconsequential). An estimated $80 billion of U.S. foreign sales were covered by U.S. export controls in 1985—a value that is at the low end of the range as explained in the annex entitled "Calculation of Economic Costs." It is likely that broadening the scope to include foreign firms would increase severalfold the figure for the economic activity influenced by U.S. controls.

Returning, then, to U.S. foreign sales as the basis for measurement, the activity needs to be allocated among the various destinations and license types. But for purposes of evaluating the economic effect of U.S. export controls, the basic framework outlined in Figures D-1 and D-2 is too simple. Further subdivisions by destination and type of license are necessary because the economic effects vary across these subcategories. Moving to Figure D-3, trade under validated licensing is divided into major categories according to type of export control (i.e., national security, foreign policy, nuclear/other). The economic cost estimate developed in this report covers only those costs associated with self-licensed trade and with national security controls (the shaded areas of Figure D-3).[7]

The geographic divisions have been further broken down. The Eastern-bloc category is divided into the People's Republic of China and all other bloc countries, including the Soviet Union. This differentiation is needed because of the more liberal licensing policy for trade to the PRC relative to that for the Soviet Union and the other bloc countries. Similarly, Canada is separated from other CoCom countries because the United States does not require validated licensing of most exports for use or consumption in Canada, although changes in U.S. reexport license procedures could have a direct effect on U.S.-Canadian trade. Finally, 15 Western countries are treated differently in the license review process than are other non-CoCom Western destinations (following a presidential directive authorizing Defense Department review of certain applications from these countries). This necessitates establishing a separate category for these nations.

The segment of trade covered by national security controls also must be split into subcategories to reflect the fact that the types of validated licenses used for national security purposes have differential effects on business activity. This breakdown, however, is kept somewhat simplified by showing only two validated license categories: bulk licenses (principally the distribution license) and individual validated licenses (IVLs).

In our earlier report to the panel, the total value of U.S. foreign sales to Western destinations under some form of validated license was estimated

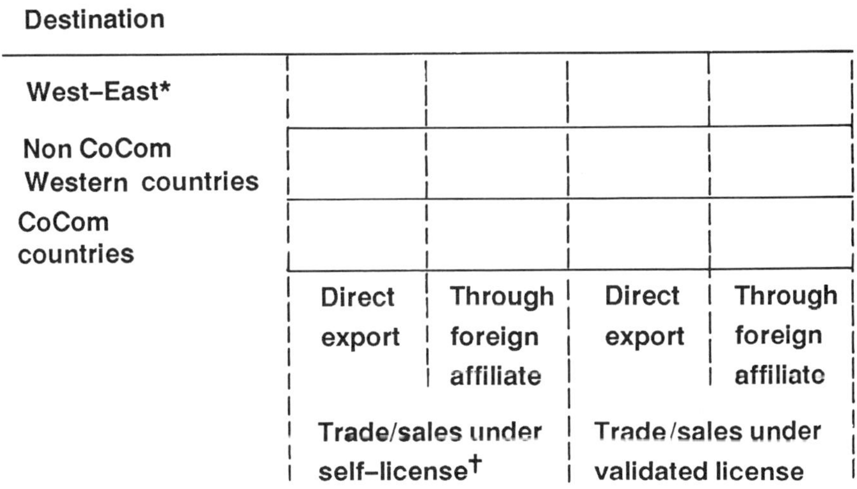

Destination

West–East*				
Non CoCom Western countries				
CoCom countries				
	Direct export	Through foreign affiliate	Direct export	Through foreign affiliate
	Trade/sales under self–license†		Trade/sales under validated license	

*West–East refers to trade with bloc countries and the PRC.

†For example, the general destination license (GDEST).

FIGURE D-2 Expanded scope of U.S. economic activity covered by U.S. export control system.

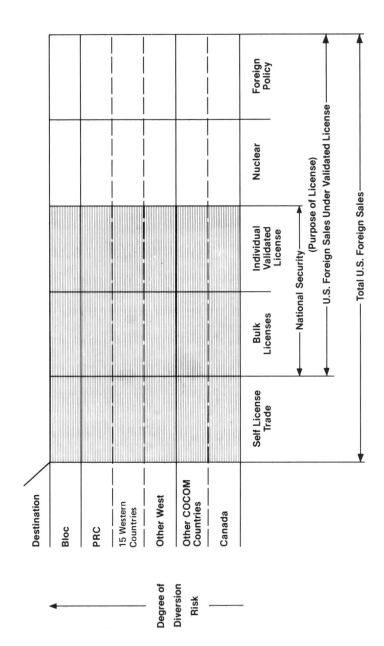

■ = Covered by economic impact estimate

FIGURE D-3   Scope of U.S.-foreign sales covered by economic impact estimate.

to be $78 billion in 1985. An additional $2 to $3 billion is estimated to have been shipped to the bloc (including the USSR) and the PRC under license. Figure D-4 shows the estimated allocation of licensed foreign sales of U.S. firms by level of criticality and destination for 1985. Total Canadian foreign sales related to the U.S. export license system are shown only for reference. An estimated 97 percent of U.S. validated license sales are made to Western destinations. Or, looked at in terms of level of military criticality, an estimated 94 percent of licensed trade falls below the high-criticality threshold (i.e., the items are eligible for shipment under a distribution license).

RELATIONSHIP OF BENEFITS AND COSTS TO LEVEL OF CRITICALITY

This section examines the relationship between several key factors that ultimately influence the distribution of costs and benefits associated with U.S. export controls. Figure D-5 illustrates how the value of costs and benefits varies with the degree or level of military criticality of an item. This figure summarizes a crucial point regarding the likely distribution of competitive costs and security benefits: As the level of "military" criticality increases, competitive costs fall,[8] while the security benefits of controls increase. To explain this conclusion, several essential concepts useful to characterizing the export control process must first be defined. We start by examining the relationship of security benefits from controls to the level of military criticality.

Export controls are intended to enhance Western security by denying, or at least delaying, the transfer of militarily useful products and technology to the Soviet Union and other proscribed destinations. The security benefits of export controls for a particular technology or product vary directly with the potential damage to national security that a loss of that technology or product would cause; that is, the higher the degree of military usefulness of a particular product or technology, the greater the security benefit of denying its transfer to proscribed destinations. *Criticality* is the term used to reflect the degree of military usefulness, which in turn is reflected in the degree of classification by CoCom and U.S. authorities. Therefore, a higher degree of criticality indicates a greater need for control because of the greater extent of national security risk.

Diversion risk (from the U.S. perspective) is defined to be a function of the quality of controls in the destination country and the degree of access to non-U.S. sources of comparable products or technology.[9] Higher diversion risk is associated with the absence of adequate controls in a destination country. U.S. unilateral control measures can reduce the diversion risk of an export to such a country only to the extent that a

262

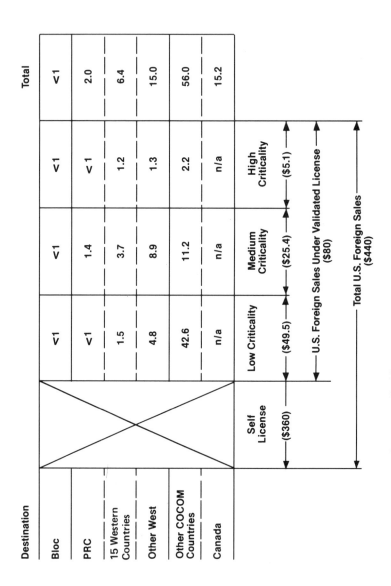

Destination	Self License ($360)	Low Criticality ($49.5)	Medium Criticality ($25.4)	High Criticality ($5.1)	Total
Bloc		<1	<1	<1	<1
PRC		<1	1.4	<1	2.0
15 Western Countries		1.5	3.7	1.2	6.4
Other West		4.8	8.9	1.3	15.0
Other COCOM Countries		42.6	11.2	2.2	56.0
Canada		n/a	n/a	n/a	15.2

U.S. Foreign Sales Under Validated License ($80)

Total U.S. Foreign Sales ($440)

n/a = not applicable

Foreign Sales = Direct Exports + Foreign Affiliate Sales

FIGURE D-4   Estimated distribution of licensed U.S. foreign sales by level of criticality and destination, 1985 ($ billions).

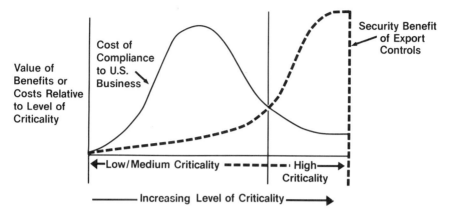

FIGURE D-5 Distribution of benefits and costs of export controls relative to level of criticality.

comparable product is not available to the destination country without U.S. export controls. Thus, either adequate indigenous export controls or greater U.S. controllability is associated with a lower degree of diversion risk. It also can be postulated that, as the level of criticality increases, the degree of foreign access to an equivalent non-U.S. technology or product tends to decline.[10] This implies that U.S. controllability increases with the level of criticality.

Given the relationships between controllability and other factors, we conclude that as the level of criticality rises the security benefits associated with U.S. export controls increase. To conclude, security benefits are not uniformly distributed across all levels of criticality but rather are concentrated in the region of highly critical technology and/or products.

The relationship between the economic costs associated with export control compliance and level of criticality can now be examined. As established from a sample of license applications, a substantial proportion of the items covered by the export licensing system are low-criticality items—that is, comparatively low-technology items.[11] Any technology edge one might expect a U.S. firm to have relative to its foreign competitors is less likely to exist for this low-end category. In addition, as non-U.S. sources for these items increase, the more likely it becomes that U.S. export controls will drive foreign customers away from U.S. sources. The result is that the cost borne by U.S. firms of lost sales associated with export control compliance is greatest for those items with the lowest degree of military criticality.

A qualitative assessment (based on interviews and analysis) performed in the earlier study indicates how the extent of the economic impact of controls varies across the different destinations and levels of technology.

TABLE **D-2** Qualitative Assessment of the Degree of Economic Impact by Level of Criticality and by Destination

Criticality	Degree of Impact	Destination	Degree of Impact
Low	2.8	Bloc	1.0
Medium	4.4	PRC	1.6
High	1.0	15 Western countries	3.8
		Other Western nations	3.9
		CoCom countries	3.1

NOTE: The table excludes self-license and Canadian trade categories.

(Figure D-6 illustrates these variations; the darker the shading, the greater the degree of economic impact.) Western destination, low- and medium-criticality items are the most affected.[12] Table D-2 summarizes the qualitative assessment by weighting the impact estimates, using data shown in Figure D-4, for each combination of destination and level of criticality. The purpose of the table is to summarize where the economic costs associated with U.S. controls are estimated to be the greatest. The numbers simply indicate relative orders of magnitude. Weights from Figure D-4 were applied to the qualitative scale shown in Figure D-6 and averaged, either for columns (i.e., by level of criticality) or for rows (i.e., by destination). On a scale of 0 to 5, 0 indicates no effect and 5 indicates the greatest effect. This qualitative assessment suggests that economic costs are greatest for West-West trade on low- and medium-technology products.

ESTIMATE OF ECONOMIC COSTS ASSOCIATED WITH U.S. EXPORT CONTROLS

A reasonable estimate of the direct, short-run economic costs to the U.S. economy associated with U.S. export controls was on the order of $9.3 billon in 1985. This is a very conservative estimate because it does not cover all aspects of economic costs and it only applies to a subset of the potential scope of business activity influenced by U.S. export controls. (Table D-3 details the major components of this figure.) Associated just with lost U.S. exports was a reduction in U.S. employment of 188,000 jobs. If we were to calculate the overall impact on the aggregate U.S. economy of the value of lost export sales and the reduced R&D effort, the associated loss for the U.S. 1985 GNP would be $17.1 billion.[13]

In evaluating the economic cost estimates presented in Table D-3, it is useful to keep in mind both the framework developed earlier in this report (see the section entitled "Scope of U.S. Foreign Sales Covered By Validated

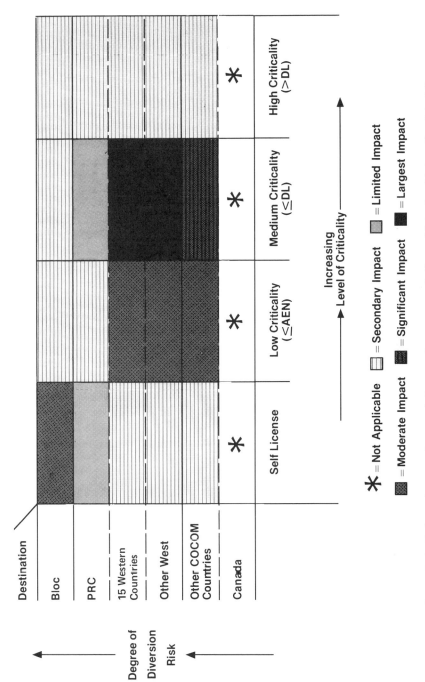

FIGURE D-6 Estimated extent of economic impact of export controls (beyond intentional international denial).

TABLE **D-3**   Components of the Estimated Economic Impact of Export Controls in 1985 (in billions of dollars)

Component	Impact
Administrative cost to firms	0.5
Lost West-West export sales	5.9
Lost West-East export sales	1.4
Reduced research and development spending	0.5
Value of licenses denied	0.5
Lost profits on export and foreign sales	0.5
TOTAL	9.3

NOTE: Employment loss = 188,000 jobs.

Licensing") and the qualitative assessment presented in Figure D-6, because, even though only a single overall cost estimate is presented, the costs of export controls vary considerably across the different combinations of level of criticality and destination. The assumptions and process used to prepare the cost calculations are covered in detail in the annex that follows.

ANNEX

CALCULATION OF ECONOMIC COSTS

A. ADMINISTRATIVE COSTS $0.5 BILLION

This estimate was developed from a survey of U.S. firms that utilize validated licenses. (See "Analysis of the Effects of Export Controls," vol. II, for a discussion of the survey.) Administrative costs were narrowly defined to be those directly associated with ongoing export control administration and compliance. The estimate excludes any special costs due to exceptional license problems—for example, the involvement of a company's chief executive officer to assist in obtaining a license.

B-1.   REVENUE LOSS FOR WEST-WEST EXPORTS $5.9 BILLION

As discussed in the body of this report, it is important when estimating economic impact to distinguish by type of license, level of criticality, and destination. The estimate is built around determining the effects on U.S. export trade under IVLs to CoCom destinations other than Canada. Unless otherwise specified, U.S. export trade is only U.S. direct exports and excludes the value of U.S. foreign sales. (The value of U.S. direct exports is included in the value of U.S. foreign sales.) The analysis builds on an econometrically developed estimate of the effect of controls on one industrial category—analytic instruments. This estimate then formed the basis to extrapolate the likely impact across all segments of licensed U.S. manufactured exports.

We chose this approach for several reasons. First, the estimate is based on empirical rather than anecdotal evidence. It is the only estimate we are aware of that has been developed from actual trade data. It is useful to note that the size of the effects is consistent with the general anecdotal evidence, conclusions of knowledgeable experts interviewed in the course of preparing this report, and information developed in a survey of U.S. firms prepared for the panel. A second reason for using the analytic instruments estimate is that there is no clear reason to believe that the analytic instruments case is extreme or unique. It must be recognized that the effects of U.S. export controls—that is, lower overall U.S. foreign sales—are built into the level of current U.S. exports. Therefore, it is difficult to extract from general U.S. trade data and other data currently available to the panel measures of the extent of the impact of controls. The analytic instruments case, on the other hand, permitted us to make an empirical appraisal of the degree to which the unilateral elements of the U.S. export control process influence the level of U.S. exports in the affected sectors. (The reader should keep in mind that it is only the degree of "unilateralness" of the U.S. system that affects U.S. firms' competitiveness.) As indicated in the introduction to this report, we believe further data would permit a more accurate assessment. Therefore, the estimate is developed to indicate a reasonable order of magnitude. Obviously, further efforts could refine it and allow a greater degree of precision. But it should be recognized that the limits of available data were reached in preparing this estimate.

Tables A-1 and A-2 present data from a sample[14] of 1,600 IVLs, which permit calculation of the distribution of U.S. IVLs by value and number for the level of criticality and destination. The distribution of trade under bulk licenses (predominantly the distribution license) was assumed to follow the same distribution with respect to level of criticality. This assumption results in 34 percent of the value of bulk license trade being classified as medium criticality (i.e., above AEN but within the distribution license level),[15] and the balance as low criticality (i.e., below the AEN level). (Because many firms using bulk licenses reported they do not take the trouble to reclassify their low technology items below the AEN level—out of the licensing system, this assumption probably overstates the average level of technology supplied under bulk licenses.)

Using the distribution of trade by destination for each level of technology (see Table A-2), the 1985 foreign sales for each level of criticality (see Figure D-4) were distributed across the different destinations. Table A-3 shows the base trade data on U.S. foreign sales by destination. The foreign sales data were taken from a U.S. Department of Commerce 1982

TABLE A-1   Distribution of License Sample By Destination and Level of Technology [in thousands of dollars and (number of licenses)]

Destination	Level of Criticality			
	AEN	≤PRC	≤DL	>DL
Bloc	1,540	810	384[a]	3,744
	(28)	(9)	(3)	(8)
PRC	4,641	10,320	275	4,667[b]
	(39)	(43)	(10)	(13)
15 Western countries	11,430	11,440	16,200	28,140
	(90)	(110)	(54)	(42)
Other Western nations	35,091	35,100	31,504	31,150
	(159)	(130)	(82)	(50)
CoCom countries	314,720	62,088	21,971	51,490
	(280)	(199)	(173)	(95)
TOTAL	367,422	119,758[c]	70,334[c]	119,191
PERCENTAGE OF TOTAL VALUE	54.3	17.7	10.4	17.6

[a]Used overall average.
[b]Used non->DL average.
[c]Medium category is the sum of ≤PRC and ≤DL columns.

SOURCE: Based on the sample of individual validated licenses. See Appendix E, "Analysis of the Effects of Export Controls," vol. II.

benchmark survey on U.S. foreign operations. The allocations presented in these tables, especially for the 15-Western-countries and other-Western-nations destination categories, could only be estimated because published Department of Commerce data were not disaggregated sufficiently by individual country destination to permit an exact allocation. However, it is believed that the relative magnitudes are reasonable.

TABLE A-2   Column Proportions for the Distribution of Licenses by Destination for Level of Technology

Destination	AEN	≤PRC	≤DL	>DL
Bloc	0.4	0.7	0.5	3.1
PRC	1.3	8.6	0.4	3.9
15 Western countries	3.1	9.6	23.0	23.6
Other Western nations	9.6	29.3	44.8	26.1
CoCom countries	85.7	51.8	31.2	43.2
TOTAL[a]	100.0	100.0	100.0	100.0

[a]Due to rounding, totals may not equal exactly 100.0 percent.

SOURCE: Table A-1.

TABLE A-3   Estimated Distribution of U.S. Foreign Sales in 1982 (in billions of dollars)

Destination	Computing Equipment		Other Equipment		Electrical Equipment		Other Transportation Equipment		Instruments		TOTAL
	a^a	b^b	a	b	a	b	a	b	a	b	
Canada	2.5	0.1	1.3	0.6	3.5	0.9	1.0	1.4	1.1	0.2	12.6
Other CoCom countries	17.0	0.5	10.1	0.7	12.2	3.4	1.4	4.8	10.0	0.7	60.8
Other Western nations	1.7	0.5	0.1	1.9	9.6	5.6	0.1	5.3	1.3	1.0	27.1
15 Western countries	1.0	0.1	0.5	0.2	1.7	0.7	0.5	1.2	0.3	0.1	6.3
TOTAL	22.2	1.2	12.0	3.4	27.0	10.6	3.0	12.7	12.7	2.0	106.8

^{a} Sales by U.S. foreign affiliates.
^{b} Direct export sales to unaffiliated parties.

NOTE: For some geographic groupings and/or product groupings, Bureau of Economic Analysis (BEA) data were not available. Therefore, an estimate was made for these groups consistent with overall BEA data. The distribution is believed to be a reasonable representation of the pattern of U.S. foreign sales by destination for the major product categories associated with use of a U.S. validated license. The 1982 values were uniformly inflated by a factor of 1.21 to yield 1985 values. The factor accounts for inflation and real growth in the 1982-1985 time frame. The 1982 value was rounded to $107 billion, and the 1985 value was rounded to $130 billion.

SOURCE: Calculated from data in U.S. Department of Commerce, Bureau of Economic Analysis (BEA), *U.S. Direct Investment Abroad: 1982 Benchmark Survey Data* (Washington, D.C.: GPO, 1985); and a special BEA tabulation of 1982 export data using the benchmark survey data.

The estimated 1982 U.S. export value was $42.5 billion for five industrial categories whose export trade was covered by validated licensing (see Table A-4). This was adjusted to a 1985 value of $51 billion. (The 1982 value was inflated by a factor of 1.21 to yield the 1985 value. The factor accounts for inflation and real growth in the 1982-1985 time frame.)

Data developed from a survey of U.S. distribution license holders suggest that the five industrial categories represented about 84 percent of total U.S. licensed export trade in 1985, which is estimated to be about $62 billion.[16] The $11 billion difference is accounted for in trade under validated licensing spread across a large number of U.S. manufacturers' export categories. To prepare the cost estimate, this trade was assumed to

TABLE A-4   Estimated Allocation of U.S. Foreign Sales Between U.S.
Direct Exports and Foreign Affiliates in 1982[a] (in billions of dollars)

Destination	Total Foreign Sales[b]	Exports to Affiliates[c]	Exports to Nonaffiliates	Total Exports[d]
Canada	12.6	3.6	3.0	6.6
Other CoCom countries	60.8	4.5	10.6	15.1
Other Western nations	27.1	3.6	14.3	17.9
15 Western countries	6.3	0.6	2.3	2.9
TOTAL	106.8	12.3	30.2	42.5

[a]Adjusted to a 1985 basis, the total estimate increases from $42.5 billion to $51 billion.
[b]Total foreign sales figures include both exports to affiliates and exports to nonaffiliates.
[c]Exports to affiliates (column b) cannot be deducted from total foreign sales (column a) to estimate sales originating from foreign affiliates because U.S. content is measured at a different point in the process.
[d]Total exports = exports to affiliates + exports to nonaffiliates.

SOURCE: Estimated from data in Tables III.G.4 and III.G.9, U.S. Department of Commerce, Bureau of Economic Analysis, *U.S. Direct Investment Abroad: 1982 Benchmark Survey Data* (Washington, D.C.: GPO, 1985); and from the allocation developed above in Table A-1.

go to the four destination groups (Canada, other CoCom countries, other Western nations, and the 15 Western countries) in the same proportion as the five high-tech categories. This total value of $62 billion was divided between IVL-covered trade and bulk license trade (predominantly export trade under distribution licenses) and self-licensed trade (i.e., under general license GDEST). A 1985 IVL coverage of $36 billion was used; this figure includes trade with the PRC and bloc countries, which represented approximately 8 percent of the total or about $3 billion. A 1985 bulk license coverage of $26 billion for exports was used.[17] (See Table 9, "Analysis of the Effects of Export Controls," vol. I, for an estimate of service and project license coverage.)

The level of lost sales associated with U.S. exports in 1985 to Western destinations was estimated as follows. The fraction of U.S. exports under IVLs to nonbloc and PRC destinations (33/59) was applied to the total 1985 export trade for each major destination (15 Western countries, CoCom countries, and so forth) to get the 1985 value of IVL exports to each destination.

For the other-CoCom-countries category, a direct estimate of the degree of lost sales had been made for one segment of U.S. manufactured exports, analytic instruments. (See Appendix B.1, "Analysis of the Effects of Export Controls," vol. II.) The range of impact of U.S. controls on analytic instruments exports was from 7 to 12 percent. The analytic instruments case, in which U.S. interpretation of essentially multilateral controls was changed—first loosened and then tightened—allows a measurement of how differential U.S. licensing practices influence U.S. exports, even within a multilateral framework. The empirical result is believed to be consistent with qualitative appraisals covered in the first report to the panel. We prepared our estimate from this base because it is the first quantitative estimator that has been made for the economic impact of controls, even though it covers only a small portion of U.S. licensed trade. It should be treated as an order-of-magnitude estimate.

For the purposes of this analysis, a value of 10 percent was used as the measure of lost sales—the midrange of the analytic instruments estimates. This estimate of 10 percent for lost sales due to export controls was then applied to the entire category of other-CoCom-countries trade under IVLs. To obtain lost sales estimates for the other destination categories (15 Western countries and other Western nations), the 10 percent rate of lost sales was scaled relative to the other-CoCom-countries level using the qualitative factors contained in Table D-2. (For example, other-Western-nation destinations were assessed to be affected to a greater degree; the 10 percent estimator was scaled by 1.26, the differential relative to the other-CoCom-countries category.) The overall estimate for the value of lost U.S. export sales in 1985 under the IVL was $3.8 billion.

For the bulk license component of export trade, the same process was used. Bulk licenses were estimated to cover a particular fraction (26/59) of total U.S.-licensed exports. Relative to the rate of lost sales under IVLs, it was assumed that distribution license-covered trade was affected to only half the degree that IVL-covered trade was affected. This is a subjective assessment based on responses to a questionnaire that indicated that U.S. firms were losing some sales of bulk-licensed trade. (See "Analysis of the Effects of Export Controls," vol. I, pp. 54-56.) The overall amount of lost sales estimated for bulk-licensed exports was $1.5 billion.

Finally, the impact on self-licensed exports was subjectively estimated to be one-tenth the IVL rate. The total value of U.S. foreign self-licensed sales influenced by U.S. export controls was estimated to be $62 billion. These are sales for those categories of manufactures in which some foreign sales are under validated licenses. If all U.S. self-licensed foreign sales were covered, the figure would be six times greater. This impact arises indirectly, principally due to U.S. reexport requirements and overall U.S. license policy. Again, the degree of lost sales is believed to be consistent with the firm interviews. (See Section V, "Analysis of the Effects of Export Controls," vol. I, pp. 57-69.) This segment of export trade was estimated to have lost sales of $0.6 billion. (It should be noted that, while the rate of lost sales for the non-IVL categories is subjective, the base to which that rate is applied is calculated using data from the Department of Commerce and U.S. businesses.)

To summarize, the overall estimate for lost sales of U.S. exports to Western destinations was calculated to be $5.9 billion ($3.8 IVL, $1.5 bulk, $0.6 self-license). (Canadian trade was excluded from the calculations except in the self-license segment because U.S. reexport procedures cover even Canadian reexports.)

B-2. ASSOCIATED GNP LOSS $11.8 BILLION

A GNP multiplier of 2 was applied to the direct U.S. export loss to calculate the associated loss to the U.S. economy due to lower U.S. exports. This multiplier value was based on discussions with economists at several government and financial institutions who regularly calculate and apply U.S. GNP multipliers.

C-1. REVENUE LOSS FOR WEST-EAST EXPORTS[18] $1.4 BILLION

With respect to the bloc countries and the Soviet Union, the evidence developed in our earlier report suggests that, generally, U.S. firms have given up trying to trade with the bloc countries and the Soviet Union. Whereas other CoCom countries exported approximately $16 billion of manufactures to the bloc and the Soviet Union in 1985, U.S. exports were well under $1 billion. (These figures include both licensed and self-licensed trade.) Obviously, part of this large disparity is due simply to the advantages the European Community-based firms have as a result of long-standing business relationships and simple geography. Still, if U.S. controls and procedures were more closely harmonized with those of other CoCom countries, U.S. sales would be higher. In West-West trade, most of the economic impact associated with U.S. export controls fell on license-related foreign sales; for trade with the bloc, however, our qualitative assessment suggests that the self-licensed segment was the area for which the value of lost sales was more significant. (See Table D-2 and Table A-5 for the basis of this appraisal. Note that Table D-2 excludes self-licensed trade.) This appraisal should be kept in mind in evaluating the estimate of lost U.S. sales to the bloc. Self-licensed trade with the bloc is influenced because of U.S. licensing requirements on services and support (including training) and on spare parts, and because of general U.S. licensing policy, which makes the United States less preferred as a source of supply.

The value of European Community and Japanese manufactures trade to the bloc was about $16 billion in 1985. Of the total, we estimated that roughly 10 percent occurred under a validated license. (For the U.S.

TABLE A-5   Notes on Figure D-6 of the Extent of Economic Impact
Beyond Intentional Denial

Destination	Level of Criticality[a]			
Bloc	3(a)	1(b)	1(b)	1(b)
PRC	2(f)	1(c)	2(c)	1(j)
15 Western countries	1(f)	3(d)	5(e)	1(j)
Other Western nations	1(f)	3(d)	5(e)	1(j)
Other CoCom countries	1(f)	3(g)	4(h)	1(j)
Canada	1(f)	2(g)	3(i)	1(j)
	SL	LC	MC	HC

[a]CODES:

   0 = No effect.
   1 = Secondary impact.
   2 = Limited impact.
   3 = Moderate impact.
   4 = Significant impact.
   5 = Largest impact.

(a) Spare parts and training cause competitive problems; makes it difficult to support a basic level of trade.
(b) Limited volume of opportunity; reexport not an issue nor is rate of denial.
(c) Reexport not a problem.
(d) U.S. reexport authorization and intensive level of end user screens create problems.
(e) Heavy degree of U.S. screens on destination and problems with U.S. reexport authority.
(f) Spillover effect (i.e., U.S. controls on some items) creates broad disincentive to rely on U.S. source.
(g) If an end user wants to incorporate U.S.-licensed technology and components, more than minimal problems are created in relation to other CoCom-based sources of supply.
(h) Additional screens and reexport authority.
(i) Reexport authority; cannot reexport in this category without approval.
(j) Little opportunity in general for foreign purchaser to go elsewhere (i.e., the U.S. technology edge offsets the U.S. red tape disadvantage).

SL = Self-license.
LC = Low criticality.
MC = Medium criticality.
HC = High criticality.

firms, we estimated that nearly 20 percent of 1985 manufactures foreign sales was under license. We assumed that the other CoCom countries had only half the proportion of trade covered by license. Because this is a global average, however, it may understate the volume of trade under validated license to the bloc.) Using a 10 percent validated license figure suggests that roughly $14.4 billion of European Community and Japan manufactures trade with the bloc was self-licensed. We also assumed that total Western trade of manufactures to the bloc was the total market available; any lost U.S. sales are shifted to other Western sources. If U.S. firms could capture at least half the same share of that total market as they do of total world manufactures trade (roughly 20 percent), this would suggest that the amount of lost U.S. sales to the bloc countries because of export controls was about $1.4 billion in 1985.

Focusing just on the licensed segment, the estimate would be considerably less. Assuming that 10 percent of CoCom manufactures trade with the bloc is licensed and assuming that U.S. firms would have captured an additional 10 percent of the licensed trade, then the lost sales figure would be $0.1 billion. We used the estimate for the self-licensed segment because, as indicated earlier, the qualitative appraisal is that the economic impact falls mainly on the self-licensed segment.

C-2.   Associated GNP Loss $2.8 billion

The multiplier used for West-West export sales loss was also used here for West-East losses.

D-1.   R&D Direct Spending Loss $0.5 billion

We have included an estimate of lost R&D effort because the export licensing system tends to focus on the R&D-intensive sectors of the U.S. economy. The estimate simply takes the fraction of total lost foreign revenues that, on average, would be used to fund R&D. The R&D-to-sales ratio for the high-technology firms covered by the validated licensing system was estimated to be 9.2 percent[19] in 1983. This ratio was used to calculate the lost R&D input associated with lower U.S. exports and an additional component due to lower overall total U.S. foreign sales. The reduction in U.S. R&D spending was estimated to be about $0.48 billion. (This represents about a 1 to 2 percent reduction in the overall level of industrial R&D spending for the five high-technology sectors covered in our estimate.)

D-2.   Associated GNP Loss $1.5 billion

A multiplier of 3[20] was used to estimate the overall GNP loss associated with the reduction in R&D spending. This suggests that the overall loss to the U.S. economy from lower R&D spending was $1.5 billion.

E-1.   Value of Licenses Denied $0.5 billion

See Table 10, "Analysis of the Effects of Export Controls," vol. I. The figure represents the actual value of licenses denied in 1985.

E-2.   ASSOCIATED GNP LOSS $1.0 BILLION

F.   LOST PROFITS ON LOST EXPORTS $0.5 BILLION

Table III.D.8, "Income Statement of Affiliates, Industry of U.S. Parent by Account," from the BEA benchmark survey data (see Table A-3) shows net income for the five high-tech manufacturing affiliates to be about 6.2 percent of the value of sales. This is applied to the total value of lost export sales and foreign affiliate sales, assuming that the rate of profit in 1985 was the same and uniform for export sales and foreign affiliate sales.

G.   ANNUAL EMPLOYMENT LOSS   188,000

The direct export loss associated with U.S. export controls was $7.3 billion. The annual job loss of 188,340 was based on a value of 25,800 jobs lost per $1 billion of exports lost.[21]

NOTES

1. "Relative" in this context is defined with respect to firms headquartered in other countries that subscribe to the multilateral control system (CoCom).
2. Military importance is defined by the extent of control exerted by CoCom and the United States. Based on the definitions contained in CoCom and U.S. licensing concepts, we define four basic levels of military importance. In their ascending order, they are: (1) items eligible for national discretion in exporting to the Soviet bloc (administrative exception note or AEN); (2) items eligible for national discretion and permission for reexport to the People's Republic of China ($\leq$PRC); (3) items eligible for the distribution license ($\leq$DL); and (4) items not eligible for export using a distribution license ($>$DL). In the last category, some items are included for reasons other than national security.
3. These categories are developed from the nomenclature outlined earlier in note 2. Low-criticality items fall within CoCom national discretion (AEN) levels; medium criticality includes all items above the AEN level but below the distribution license level. High-criticality items are those not eligible for the distribution license.
4. The impact of U.S. controls on affiliate sales cannot be dismissed as inconsequential—for some U.S. multinationals, their foreign affiliates may be their only customers for U.S. exports.
5. Technically, all U.S. exports require a license. A large proportion of U.S. exports are shipped under a self-license; that is, the exporter is not required to submit a license application and receive specific prior authorization. Included in the self-license segment are exports made under the general destination license (GDEST); we also consider as self-licensed trade, for the purposes of this analysis, general licensed trade (shipped under the G-COM license).
6. This arises because the extent of the foreign firms' sales (including reexport) is affected by incorporating U.S. parts and components, and they, therefore, may avoid relying upon a U.S. source.
7. Practically speaking, this narrower definition of scope cannot always be maintained.

Not all the data developed in our first report to the panel could be categorized by type of export control (i.e., national security, foreign policy, nuclear nonproliferation, short-supply, and crime control). To keep this in perspective, however, in those cases in which we were able to identify licenses by national security versus other types of controls, 99 percent of the license cases were classified as national security. This indicates that the basic data overwhelmingly reflect national security controls. See Table E.3, Data Appendices, "Analysis of the Effects of U.S. Export Controls," vol. II. It should also be noted that most U.S. businesses, and especially foreign users of U.S.-controlled products, do not realize there is a distinction among the different types of controls. Management decisions are based on the need to obtain a license and not on the underlying government rationale for requiring the license.

8. Administrative compliance costs probably increase. But, although the administrative cost per transaction is high, the total cost, which includes competitive costs, is low in relation to low-level technology items since the number of transactions is only about 15 percent of total licensed transactions. See "Analysis of the Effects of Export Controls," vol. I, pp. 57-69, for a discussion of the relationship between compliance and administrative costs and level of military criticality and destination. Firms that were interviewed indicated that compliance and administrative costs increased with the level of military criticality and with diversion risk.

9. Diversion risk could also be defined as a function of military usefulness; that is, the risk would be directly related to criticality. But here we use a different definition by defining diversion risk as a function of destination country characteristics.

10. The notion is that the higher the technical performance of the item or the greater the degree of sophistication of the technology, the more likely it is that the United States is the principal source of the technology. The reader should note that we are not claiming the United States has a monopoly on high-criticality technology. Rather, we are saying that on balance the United States is more likely to have the dominant position in this category (i.e., high-criticality items) than in the less critical categories.

11. See "Analysis of the Effects of Export Controls," vol. I, pp. 40-44.

12. The extent of the economic impact (beyond intentional denial) is a function both of the volume of trade in a particular category, the screens applied to end users, and other factors such as the necessity for U.S. reexport control authority, which may result in the avoidance of U.S. products by foreign (Western) firms. Table A-5 in the annex annotates Figure D-6 with the simplified evaluations that led to the conclusions on the degree of impact for each level of technology and destination.

13. This estimate is the multiplier impact of the lost export revenues and lower R&D effort on the overall U.S. economy. Multiplier refers to the change in overall U.S. GNP associated with the decrease in U.S. exports or reduction in R&D spending. In economic parlance, it is the change in aggregate spending associated with a change in external or autonomous spending (in this case, a reduction in exports or R&D). See, for example, pp. 65-70 in Rudiger Dornbush and Stanley Fischer, *Macroeconomics* (New York: McGraw-Hill, 1978), for further discussion.

14. See Appendix A, "Analysis of the Effects of Export Controls," vol. II, for a discussion of the sample. The numbers simply indicate relative orders of magnitude. Weights from Figure D-4 were applied to the qualitative scale shown in Figure D-6 and averaged, either for columns (i.e., by level of criticality) or for rows (i.e., by destination). On a scale of 0-5, 0 indicates no effect and 5 equals the largest effect.

15. There cannot be any high-criticality bulk license trade because high-criticality items are defined as items not eligible for the distribution license.

16. See Stephen Merrill, "International Business Under the Distribution License," prepared for the panel.

17. This includes $22 billion for U.S. distribution license trade coverage and $4 billion for trade under other types of bulk licenses. The estimated coverage of $42 to $56 billion for bulk licenses presented in the earlier report to the panel refers to both U.S. exports *and* foreign sales.

18. We do not include PRC trade in the scope of West-East exports. No explicit estimate is made with respect to the U.S.-PRC trade.

19. Calculated for high-technology manufacturing industries, except chemicals and allied products, from data in Appendix Tables 4-5 and 4-7, *Science Indicators: The 1985 Report* (National Science Board).

20. This multiplier was taken from M. Baily and R. Lawrence, "The Need for a Permanent Tax Credit for Industrial Research and Development" (The Coalition for the Advancement of Industrial Technology, February 1985), pp. 61-63.

21. Source: Lester A. Davis, "Contribution of Exports to U.S. Employment," in *United States Trade Performance in 1985 and Outlook,* pp. 92-94.

E

Glossary

Administrative exception note (AEN) A note appended to certain CoCom International List categories describing commodities that can be approved for sale to CoCom-proscribed destinations solely at national discretion.

Automatic licensing procedure As mandated by the Export Administration Amendments Act of 1985, a requirement that individual validated license applications for most exports to CoCom nations must be approved automatically by Export Administration 15 working days after filing unless the applicant is notified that more time (not to exceed 15 additional working days) is required. At the end of the 15- (or 30-) working-day period, the export is deemed to be licensed, even if no document or communication to that effect has been sent or received.

Bilateral In the context of this report, referring to two-sided negotiations or agreements between two nations regarding export controls.

CoCom (Coordinating Committee on Multilateral Export Controls) An informal organization that cooperatively restricts strategic exports to controlled countries. It consists of 16 member nations: Belgium, Canada, Denmark, France, the Federal Republic of Germany, Greece, Italy, Japan, Luxembourg, the Netherlands, Norway, Portugal, Spain, Turkey, the United Kingdom, and the United States.

Commodity Any article, material, or supply except technical data.

278

Community of common controls A proposed cooperative arrangement for trade in controlled commodities among Free World nations that share an expressed willingness to adhere to common or equivalent national security export controls. Under such an arrangement, licenses would be required (from the cooperating nation shipping a controlled commodity) only for the export of controlled commodities to nations not a party to the arrangement.

Consignee In the context of this report, the recipient of a shipment of commodities or technical data subject to national security export controls.

Continuous review The process within CoCom by which one-fourth of the entries on the International List are reviewed each year on an ongoing basis and particular entries may be reviewed within any one-year period at the request of a member nation. Changes to list entries are published annually by member nations.

Country groups Seven groups of foreign countries, established by the Commerce Department for export control purposes and designated by the symbols Q, S, T, V, W, Y, and Z (see Figure 4-3 on pp. 84–85). Canada is not included in any country group and is referred to by name in the Export Administration Regulations.

Customs-free (bonded) zones Storage and transfer sites in various nations within which commodities in transit are not, for administrative and legal purposes, considered to be imports and therefore are not subject to inspection.

Distribution license A special 2-year license, without dollar value or quantity limits, authorizing the export of eligible commodities to approved consignees in specified countries. Distribution license consignees must be foreign distributors or users of the licensed commodity in Free World countries.

Diversion Shipment of militarily significant dual use products and technology to unapproved end users, either directly, through the export of controlled products without a license (i.e., smuggling), or indirectly, through transshipment using a complex chain of increasingly untraceable reexports.

Dual use In the context of this report, describes technology or products that have both military and commercial applications.

Embargo A legal prohibition on commerce.

End use The purpose or application for which controlled commodities or technical data will be used by a consignee.

End-user check   An investigation by officials of the Department of Commerce or Department of State to confirm that a consignee is reputable and is engaged in the business claimed in statements to licensing authorities.

End-use statement   A formal declaration by a consignee of the specific purpose or application for which controlled commodities or technical data will be used.

Espionage   Covert efforts to obtain illicitly—by theft, bribery, or blackmail—protected information or technology that is classified or of relevance to military systems.

Exception request   An application by a CoCom member, in support of an application by a domestic firm, seeking the approval of all member nations to permit the export of a commodity subject to CoCom controls to a proscribed destination.

Extraterritoriality   In the context of this report, the assertion by the U.S. government that its export control regulations govern trade in U.S.-controlled commodities and technical data of U.S. origin outside the territorial boundaries of the United States.

Farewell   The French intelligence community codename for a high-level Soviet official who provided France with extensive information on the scope, organization, and successes of covert Soviet technology acquisition activities in the West.

Favorable consideration   A category of items on the CoCom International List that, by agreement among the members, will be considered favorably for export to proscribed destinations, on a case-by-case basis, provided the proposed transactions meet certain conditions specified in accompanying notes.

Foreign availability   According to the Export Administration Act of 1979, a state existing when a non-CoCom-origin item of comparable quality is available to adversaries in quantities sufficient to satisfy their military needs. Foreign availability may apply to items that CoCom-proscribed nations manufacture domestically or buy freely from uncontrolled sources.

Foreign national   Any person who is not a citizen of the United States and who has not been lawfully admitted for permanent residence in the United States under the Immigration and Naturalization Act.

Free World   In the context of this report, nations not subject to the CoCom strategic trade embargo.

General embargo   Restrictions maintained through CoCom to prevent exports of certain munitions, nuclear, and dual use items to proscribed destinations. Exceptions to the embargo are granted only for specific transactions on a case-by-case basis and must be approved unanimously.

General license   An export license established by the U.S. Department of Commerce for which no application is required and for which no document is granted or issued. General licenses are available for use by all persons or organizations, except those listed in and prohibited by the provisions of the Export Administration Regulations Supplement No. 1 to Part 388; the licenses permit exports within the above provisions as prescribed in the regulations. These general licenses are not applicable to exports under the licensing jurisdiction of agencies other than the Department of Commerce.

Globalization   The spread of business activities to numerous and diverse countries around the world.

Goods in transit   Goods that are being transported from a vendor's point of origin to the premises of a foreign consignee.

Import certificate/delivery verification (IC/DV) procedure   A procedure sometimes used by the United States, other CoCom countries, Austria, and Hong Kong to monitor the movement of exports of militarily strategic commodities. When the IC/DV procedure is required by an exporting country for a specific transaction, an importer certifies to the government of the importing country that he will be importing specific commodities and will not reexport them except in accordance with the export control regulations of that country (i.e., the importing country). The government of the importing country, in turn, certifies to the exporting country that such representations have been made prior to the transaction. After the commodities have been shipped, the importer's government certifies that the controlled items have been received by the designated consignee.

Individual validated license (IVL)   Written approval by the U.S. Department of Commerce granting permission, which is valid for 2 years, for the export of a specified quantity of products or technical data to a single recipient. Individual validated licenses also are required, under certain circumstances, as authorization for reexport of U.S.-origin commodities to new destinations abroad.

International List   The CoCom list of dual use commodities and technical data that are subject to validated licensing requirements when proposed for export from CoCom countries to other nations.

Keystone equipment   Sophisticated devices essential to the successful operation/completion of manufacturing processes. (Some examples include process control equipment and specialized machine tools.)

Letter of assurance　A written statement from the foreign recipient of restricted technical data under restriction that the data will not be made available to proscribed nations.

Merchant (firms)　Firms that sell their products on the open market, as opposed to producing only for internal consumption.

Militarily Critical Technologies List (MCTL)　A document originally mandated by Congress listing technologies that the Department of Defense considers to have current or future utility in military systems. It briefly describes arrays of design and manufacturing know-how; keystone manufacturing, inspection, and test equipment; and goods accompanied by sophisticated operation, application, and maintenance know-how. Military justification for each entry is included in the classified version of the list.

Multilateral　As used in this report, referring to agreements or negotiations among three or more nations to reach common accord on national security export controls and procedures.

National discretion　A level of CoCom control under which some items on the International List, as indicated in administrative exception notes, may be licensed for sale to proscribed nations by one member country without the approval of the others.

National interest exception　A determination by the U.S. Secretary of Commerce, in accordance with Section 12(c) of the Export Administration Act of 1979, permitting the confidential disclosure of information obtained by the Commerce Department for consideration of or concerning export license applications.

National security export controls　Procedures designed to regulate the transfer of technology from one country to another in such a way as to protect militarily important technologies from acquisition by potential adversaries (see the Export Administration Act of 1979, as amended).

Nexus　Connection or linkage.

President's Export Council　A group established by executive order in 1973 and reconstituted in 1979 to provide a forum on current and emerging problems and issues in U.S. foreign commerce. Its members include primarily leaders in business, industry, and agriculture and members of Congress.

Proscribed countries　In terms of national security export controls, Albania, Bulgaria, Cuba, Czechoslovakia, Estonia, the German Democratic Republic, Hungary, Kampuchea, Laos, Latvia, Lithuania, the Mongolian People's Republic, North Korea, the People's Republic of China, Poland, Rumania, the USSR, and Vietnam.

Reexport The exportation of commodities or technical data from one foreign destination to another at any time after initial export from the country of origin.

Reverse engineering Reproduction of a unique product based solely on examination and analysis of a sample of the product.

Secrecy orders An order issued, at the request of a defense agency, by the Patent and Trademark Office of the Department of Commerce, which prohibits or limits the use of an innovation described in a patent application and the dissemination of related, underlying technical information.

Shipper's export declaration (SED) Any declaration required under regulations of the Department of Commerce and other U.S. government departments or agencies in connection with exports.

Strategic goods and technologies Items designed especially or used principally for development, production, or utilization of arms, ammunition, or military systems; items incorporating unique technological know-how, the acquisition of which might give significant direct assistance to the development and production of arms, ammunition, or military systems; and items in which proscribed nations have a deficiency that hinders this development and production and that they are not likely to overcome within a reasonable period.

Sunset provision In the context of this report, a clause mandating the periodic review and automatic termination of a CoCom export restriction unless its continued inclusion on the International List has been rejustified and agreed upon.

Table of Denial Orders (TDO) A list included in the Export Administration Regulations of specific individuals or organizations that have been denied export privileges, in whole or in part. Orders are published in full in the *Federal Register*.

Technical data Information of any kind that can be used or adapted for use in the design, production, manufacture, utilization, or reconstruction of articles or materials. The data may take a tangible form, such as a model, prototype, blueprint, or an operating manual (the tangible form may be stored on recording media); or they may take an intangible form such as technical know-how. Software is considered technical data.

Technological commodity Mass-produced items that are marketed, distributed, and/or warehoused in large quantities for use by distributors and customers around the world. Most items that can be purchased from retail outlets on a cash-and-carry basis are also technological commodities. Examples of commodities currently subject to national security export controls are some personal computers and related peripheral devices, floppy discs, and microchips.

Technology transfer   In the context of this report, the acquisition by one country from another of products, technology, or know-how that directly or indirectly enables a qualitative or quantitative upgrading of deployed military systems or the development of effective countermeasures to military systems deployed by others.

Third countries   Free World nations that are not members of CoCom.

Transshipment   The transfer, by a series of separately documented shipments, of controlled products through one or more countries en route to a final destination that may be a proscribed country. Initially, the final destination—and in later transactions, the country of origin—are concealed to avoid export or reexport prohibitions.

Unilateral   In the context of this report, referring to actions relating to national security export controls that are taken by only one nation.

U.S. Control List   The list of commodities under the export control jurisdiction of the Commerce Department's Export Administration.

U.S. Munitions List   A list of defense articles and services, which was developed by the Department of Defense and is now maintained by the State Department with the advice of DoD. The International Traffic in Arms Regulations pertain only to items on the list and to directly related technical data, the export and reexport of which must be approved in advance by the State Department.

Validated license   Written approval issued by the governments of various nations granting limited permission to export controlled commodities or technical data, either on a single- or a multiple-transaction basis. In the case of the United States, validated licenses also are required, under certain circumstances, for reexport of U.S.-origin commodities to new destinations abroad.

F

List of Acronyms

AEA Atomic Energy Act of 1954, as amended
AECA Arms Export Control Act of 1976
AEN administrative exception notes
CoCom Coordinating Committee for Multilateral Export Controls
COL comprehensive operations license
COSEPUP Committee on Science, Engineering, and Public Policy, a joint committee of the National Academy of Sciences, the National Academy of Engineering, and the Institute of Medicine
DCS destination control statement
DoC Department of Commerce
DoD Department of Defense
DTSA Defense Technology Security Administration
EAA Export Administration Act of 1979, as amended
EAAA Export Administration Act Amendments of 1985
EAR Export Administration Regulations
ECCN export commodity control number
EEC European Economic Community
ESA European Space Agency
FY fiscal year
G-CEU general license-certified end user
G-COM general license-certain shipments to CoCom countries
G-DEST general license-shipments of commodities to destinations not requiring a validated license

G-FTZ   general license-exports of petroleum commodities from U.S. foreign trade zones and from Guam

G-NNR   general license-shipments of certain nonnaval reserve petroleum commodities

GKNT   State Committee for Science and Technology (USSR)

GLR   general license-return or replacement of certain commodities

GLV   general license-shipments of limited value

GNP   gross national product

GRU   Chief Directorate of Military Intelligence (USSR)

GTDA   general license-technical data available to all destinations

GTDR   general license-technical data restricted

GTE   general license-temporary exports

IC/DV   import certificate/delivery verification

ITAR   International Traffic in Arms Regulations

IVL   individual validated license

KGB   Committee for State Security (USSR)

MCTL   Militarily Critical Technologies List

MOU   memorandum of understanding

MIMOS   Malaysian Institute of Microelectronic Systems

MITI   Ministry of International Trade and Industry (Japan)

NASA   National Aeronautics and Space Administration

NATO   North Atlantic Treaty Organization

NIC   newly industrializing country

NMR   nuclear magnetic resonance

NSA   National Security Agency

NSC   National Security Council

NSDD   national security decision directive

NSF   National Science Foundation

OEL   Office of Export Licensing (Commerce Department)

OFA   Office of Foreign Availability (Commerce Department)

ONI   Office of Naval Intelligence (Navy)

OMC   Office of Munitions Control (State Department)

OSTP   Office of Science and Technology Policy (White House)

PEC   President's Export Council

PRC   People's Republic of China

PTO   Patent and Trademark Office (Commerce Department)

R&D   research and development

RWA   returned without action

SDI   Strategic Defense Initiative

SED   shipper's export declaration

SIG-FP   Senior Interagency Group on Foreign Policy

SIG-IEP   Senior Interagency Group on International Economic Policy

SIG-TST   Senior Interagency Group on the Transfer of Strategic Technology

SIG-TT   Senior Interagency Group on Technology Transfer (same as SIG-TST)

TDO   Table of Denial Orders

USSR   Union of Soviet Socialist Republics

VPK   Military-Industrial Commission (USSR)

G

List of Briefers, Contributors, and Liaison Representatives

BRIEFERS

WAYNE A. ABERNATHY, Economist, Committee on Banking, Housing and Urban Affairs, United States Senate

MAYNARD C. ANDERSON, Director, Security Plans and Programs, Department of Defense

WILLIAM T. ARCHEY, Acting Assistant Secretary for Trade Administration, Department of Commerce

HUGH BALAAM, Central Intelligence Agency

MONTY BALTAS, Office of Technology and Policy Analysis, Export Administration, Department of Commerce

RICHARD BARTH, Director, Office of Foreign Availability, Export Administration, Department of Commerce

DAVID C. BENNETT, U.S. Mission to the North Atlantic Treaty Organization, Brussels, Belgium

SUMNER BENSON, Deputy Director, Technology Cooperation and Security, Office of the Under Secretary of Defense for Policy, Department of Defense

ELI W. BIZIC, Economic Counselor, United States Embassy, Vienna, Austria

EDWARD J. BLACK, Vice President and General Counsel, Computer and Communications Industry Association

JOHN BOIDOCK, Director, Office of Export Administration, Department of Commerce

RUSS BOWEN, Central Intelligence Agency

HENRY BROWN, International Technical Director, Society for the Advancement of Materials and Process Engineering

STEPHEN D. BRYEN, Deputy Under Secretary of Defense for Trade Security Policy; Director, Defense Technology Security Administration, Department of Defense

ART BURROWS, Vice President for Washington Operations, AVCO Lycoming-Textron

MICHAEL CALINGAERT, Minister for Economic Affairs, United States Embassy, London, England

RICHARD CARLISLE, National Aeronautics and Space Administration

RAY CHASE, Director of Regulatory Affairs, Johnson and Johnson Ultrasound, Inc.

FERDINAND N. CIRILLO, Jr., Chief, Technology Transfer Assessment Center, Central Intelligence Agency

RICHARD W. CLARKE, Vice President, MTS Systems Corporation

MICHAEL CLEVERLY, Strategic Trade Officer, United States Embassy, London, England

JOHN B. COPELAND, Director, Export Administration, Motorola, Inc.

BRIAN CUNNINGHAM, General Counsel, Genentech, Inc.

ANSTRUTHER DAVIDSON, Acting Director, Office of Export Enforcement, Department of Commerce

JAMES DEARLOVE, Defense Intelligence Agency

BO DENYSYK, Vice President, International Affairs, Global USA

JOSEPH A. De ROSE, IBM Corporation

ROBERT DEUTSCH, Economic Officer, United States Embassy, Paris, France

ROGER DIEHL, Federal Bureau of Investigation

ARTHUR T. DOWNEY, Attorney, Sutherland, Asbell, and Brennan

GUY DuBOIS, Deputy Chief, Technology Transfer Assessment Center, Central Intelligence Agency

DOUG DWYER, President, Marconi Electronics, Inc.

LYN EDINGER, Senior Commercial Officer, Foreign Commercial Service, U.S. Consulate General, Hong Kong

KEITH FENNELL, Office of Intelligence Liaison, Department of Commerce

HARLOW FREITAG, Technology Transfer Committee, Institute for Electrical and Electronic Engineering

GLENN W. FRY, Investigator, Permanent Subcommittee on Investigations, Committee on Governmental Affairs, United States Senate

ROBERT GALLAGHER, Deputy Director, Office of Intelligence Liaison, Department of Commerce

ROBERT GELLMAN, Counsel, Subcommittee on Government Information, Justice, and Agriculture, Committee on Government Operations, U.S. House of Representatives

ROGER L. GROSSEL, Manager, Export Administration, Hewlett-Packard Company

LEE HAPPEL, Vice President for International Marketing, Landis Tool Co.

JOHN HARDT, Associate Director, Congressional Research Service, Library of Congress

EZRA D. HEITOWIT, Staff Director, Subcommittee on Science, Research, and Technology, U.S. House of Representatives

GEORGE HOLLIDAY, Economics Division, Congressional Research Service, Library of Congress

JOSEPH B. HOUSTON, Society for Photo-optical Instrumentation Engineering

L. E. JENNEKE, Chairman and Chief Executive Officer, Landis Tool Co.

JOHN KISER, Consultant, Kiser Research, Inc.

DONALD KLOSS, Export Sales Service Manager, Reliance Electric Co.

JOHN KONFALA, Defense Technology Security Administration, Department of Defense

BEN LEON, Institute for Electrical and Electronic Engineering

JOHN LEWIS, Federal Bureau of Investigation

TALBOT LINDSTROM, Deputy Director, Defense Technology Security Administration, Department of Defense

RAPHAEL LOPEZ, United States Customs Service

HAROLD P. LUKS, Arnold and Porter

LaMARR MALLONEE, Central Intelligence Agency

STANLEY J. MARCUSS, Milbank, Tweed, Hadley & McCloy

MICHAEL B. MARKS, Senior Policy Advisor to the Under Secretary for Security Assistance, Science, and Technology, Department of State

BOYD McKELVAIN, Manager of Technology Affairs, the General Electric Company

NICHOLAS MIHNOVETS, Defense Technology Security Administration, Department of Defense

R. BOOTH MITCHEM, Economic Officer, United States Embassy, Bonn, Federal Republic of Germany

GEORGE MUIR, Deputy Executive Secretary, Technology Transfer Intelligence Committee, Central Intelligence Agency

PATRICK MULLOY, Minority Staff Counsel, Committee on Banking, Housing, and Urban Affairs, United States Senate

DOUGLAS NORTON, National Aeronautics and Space Administration

ROBERT NYSMITH, Associate Administrator for the Office of Management, National Aeronautics and Space Administration

K. LEON ORCHARD, Ortech Industries, Inc.

PHILLIP PARKER, Federal Bureau of Investigation

RICHARD A. POPKIN, Confidential Assistant to the Assistant Secretary for Trade Administration, Department of Commerce

ROBERT PRICE, Acting Deputy Assistant Secretary for International Trade Controls, Bureau of Economic and Business Affairs, Department of State

DONALD J. QUINN, Executive Secretary, Technology Transfer Intelligence Committee, Central Intelligence Agency

PETER RAIMONDI, Defense Intelligence Agency

CAROL ROVNER, Electronic Industries Association

GEORGE SCHEMBER, Central Intelligence Agency

DAVID SCHLECHTY, Director, Country Policy Branch, Export Administration, Department of Commerce

WILLIAM SCHNEIDER, Jr., Under Secretary of State for Security Assistance, Science, and Technology, Department of State

JAMES SCHOFIELD, Vice President for Government Relations, Magnavox, Inc.

GLENN E. SCHWEITZER, Director, Advisory Committee on the U.S.S.R. and Eastern Europe, National Academy of Sciences

MICHAEL SEKORA, Defense Intelligence Agency

RICHARD SEPPA, Director, Office of Export Licensing, Export Administration, Department of Commerce

MARGARET SHEILDS, Central Intelligence Agency

RICHARD SHEPARD, Central Intelligence Agency

DENIS F. SIMON, Professor, Sloan School of Management, Massachusetts Institute of Technology

FRANCIS SOBIESZCZYK, Chief, Research Program Office, Office of the Under Secretary of Defense for Research and Engineering, Department of Defense

GERALD SULLIVAN, Assistant Deputy Under Secretary of Defense for Acquisition, Technology Cooperation/ Planning, Department of Defense

TOM SUTTLE, Institute for Electrical and Electronic Engineering

MICHAEL SWEIK, Central Intelligence Agency

JOSEPH J. TAFE, Chief, Export Control Enforcement Unit, Department of Justice

WILLIAM TAYLOR, Vice President, Ricoh Corporation

ELVIA THOMPSON, Defense Technology Security Administration, Department of Defense

ROBERT TURNER, Defense Technology Security Administration, Department of Defense

ROGER URBANSKI, Director, Strategic Investigations Division, U.S. Customs Service

THOMAS WAJDA, Science Attaché, U.S. Mission to the Organization
  for Economic Cooperation and Development, Paris, France
GARY WAUGH, United States Customs Service
TOLI WELIHOZKIY, Office of Foreign Availability, Export
  Administration, Department of Commerce
VAN A. WENTE, Chief, Scientific and Technical Information Branch,
  National Aeronautics and Space Administration
ROBIN WHITE, Economics Section, U.S. Embassy, Tokyo, Japan
SAMUEL WYMAN, Office of Science and Technology Policy, Executive
  Office of the President
ANTHONY YEN, President, Yen Enterprises Inc.
LEO YOUNG, Director, Research and Laboratory Management, Office
  of the Under Secretary of Defense for Research and Engineering,
  Department of Defense

CONTRIBUTORS

ROBERT E. ADAMS, Consultant
LOUIS AMEEN, Scientific Counselor, Embassy of Sweden,
  Washington, D.C.
LUC ARNOULD, Scientific Counselor, Embassy of Belgium,
  Washington, D.C.
F. BRETT BERLIN, Vice President, Government Relations, Cray
  Research, Inc.
DON BONKER, Member, U.S. House of Representatives (D-Wash.)
DONALD BOOTH, Economic Officer, United States Embassy, Brussels,
  Belgium
GORDON BOOZER, Mobilization Concepts Center, National Defense
  University
JEROME BOSKEN, Scientific Attaché, U.S. Embassy, Seoul, Korea
LEWIS BRANSCOMB, Vice President/Chief Scientist, IBM Corporation
J. FRED BUCY, former President, Texas Instruments
MICHAEL CALINGAERT, Minister for Economic Affairs, United States
  Embassy, London, England
MICHAEL CLEVERLY, Strategic Trade Officer, United States
  Embassy, London, England
ANTHONY R. COX, Counselor, Science and Technology, British
  Embassy, Washington, D.C.
JEAN-CLAUDE DERIAN, Scientific Counselor, Embassy of France,
  Washington, D.C.

ROBERT DEUTSCH, Economic Officer, United States Embassy, Paris, France

ROBERT DRISCOLL, U.S.-Asian Center for Technology Exchange

LYN EDINGER, Senior Commercial Officer, Foreign Commercial Service, U.S. Consulate General, Hong Kong

LYNDON EDWARDS, Department of Trade and Industry, London, England

CHARLES FERGUSON, Consultant, Massachusetts Institute of Technology

WILLIAM F. FINAN, Consultant, Quick, Finan, and Associates

MARK van FLEET, International Division, U.S. Chamber of Commerce

HANS FORSBERG, Ingenjorsventenskapsakademien, Stockholm, Sweden

DONALD J. GOLDSTEIN, Consultant, System Planning Corporation

MARTHA HARRIS, International Security and Commerce Programs, Office of Technology Assessment

RYOZO HAYASHI, Ministry of International Trade and Industry, Government of Japan

ROBERT HERZSTEIN, Attorney, Arnold and Porter

ARTHUR HO, First Secretary, Hong Kong Government Office, British Embassy, Washington, D.C.

ROBERT C. HOLLAND, President, Committee for Economic Development

JAE HEE HONG, Scientific Attaché, Embassy of Korea, Washington, D.C.

BRUCE HYMAN, Foreign Commercial Service, U.S. Embassy, Singapore

KANAME IKEDA, Counselor, Embassy of Japan, Washington, D.C.

BERND UWE JAHN, Scientific and Technological Affairs, Embassy of the Federal Republic of Germany, Washington, D.C.

ZULKAFRI ABDUL KARIM, Vice Consul, Commercial Section, Consulate General of Malaysia, New York

MME. A. de KERDREL, Direction de la Coopération Scientifique et Technique, Ministère des Relations Extérieures, Paris, France

FRANÇOIS LAFONTAINE, Counselor, Science and Technology, Delegation of the Commission of European Communities, Washington, D.C.

BERNARD LAUWAERT, Director, CoCom Division, Brussels, Belgium

STEFAN LEADER, Consultant, Eagle Research Group, Inc.

PETER J. LENNON, Commission of the European Communities, Brussels, Belgium

WILLIAM LEWIS, McKinsey & Lewis

HAROLD P. LUKS, Consultant, Arnold and Porter

ROMELLE S. MILLION, Verbatim Reporter, Million Reporting

R. BOOTH MITCHEM, Economic Officer, United States Embassy, Bonn, Federal Republic of Germany

HENRY R. NAU, Consultant, Professor of Political Science and International Affairs, George Washington University

BRUNO NEVE, Embassy of Belgium, Washington, D.C.

JACK H. NUNN, Senior Fellow, Mobilization Concepts Center, National Defense University

LIONEL H. OLMER, Attorney, Paul, Weiss, Rifkind, Wharton, and Garrison

JACK L. OSBORN, Vice President, Asia/Pacific, TRW Overseas, Inc.

MARTIN E. PACKARD, Assistant to the Board Chairman, Varian Associates

RICHARD N. PERLE, Assistant Secretary of Defense for International Security Affairs, Department of Defense

WILLIAM J. PERRY, Managing Partner, H&G Technology Partners

ANNE PINKNEY, Economic Counselor, United States Embassy, Stockholm, Sweden

CHRISTIAN PROSL, Economic Counselor, Austrian Embassy, Washington, D.C.

LEE YOKE QWANG, Economics Counselor, Embassy of Singapore, Washington, D.C.

WILLIAM RASTETTER, Director, Corporate Ventures, Genentech, Inc.

HAROLD RELYEA, Congressional Research Service, Library of Congress

BRIAN RINK, Economic Section, U.S. Embassy, Tokyo, Japan

ANNEMIEKE J. M. ROOBEEK, Amsterdam, The Netherlands

WILLIAM A. ROOT, Consultant

KAREN SANDBERG, Consultant, Quick, Finan, and Associates

DENIS F. SIMON, Consultant, Sloan School of Management, Massachusetts Institute of Technology

EUGENE B. SKOLNIKOFF, Director, Center for International Studies, Massachusetts Institute of Technology

HEDY E. SLADOVICH, Research Assistant

SOLVEIG B. SPIELMANN, Consultant, International Business Counselors, Inc.

CARL-OLAF TERNRYD, Ingenjorsventenskapsakademien, Stockholm, Sweden

MARK TOKOLA, U.S. Mission to the European Communities, Brussels, Belgium

THOMAS WAJDA, Science Attaché, U.S. Mission to the Organization for Economic Cooperation and Development, Paris, France

CORMAC P. WALSH, Consultant, Eagle Research Group, Inc.
ROBIN WHITE, Economics Section, U.S. Embassy, Tokyo, Japan
ROBERT I. WIDDER, Consultant, Eagle Research Group, Inc.
JAMES WOJTASIEWICZ, U.S. Embassy, Kuala Lumpur, Malaysia
TAIZO YOKOYAMA, Commercial Section, Embassy of Japan, Washington, D.C.

LIAISON REPRESENTATIVES

SUMNER BENSON, Senior Assistant to the Director, International Security Policy, Department of Defense
JOSEPH BORDOGNA, Dean, School of Engineering and Applied Science, University of Pennsylvania
JON L. BOYES, International President, Armed Forces Communication and Electronics Association
STEPHEN D. BRYEN, Deputy Under Secretary of Defense for Trade Security Policy, Department of Defense
ALAN T. CRANE, Project Director, Congress of the United States, Office of Technology Assessment
MICHAEL D. CRISP, Executive Assistant to the Director of the Office of Energy Research, Department of Energy
JOSEPH DeROSE, Program Director of Public Affairs, IBM Corporation
HARLOW FREITAG, Technology Transfer Committee, Institute of Electrical and Electronics Engineers
MARTHA C. HARRIS, Senior Analyst, Office of Technology Assessment
CHARLES HERZ, General Counsel, National Science Foundation
JOHN M. LOGSDON, Director, Graduate Program in Science, Technology, and Public Policy, George Washington University
OLES LOMACKY, International Programs and Technology, Office of the Under Secretary of Defense for Research and Engineering, Department of Defense
MICHAEL B. MARKS, Senior Policy Advisor to the Under Secretary for Security Assistance, Science, and Technology, Department of State
DONALD M. MATTOX, Sandia National Laboratories, American Vacuum Society
WILLIAM A. MAXWELL, Director of International Issues, Computer and Business Equipment Manufacturers Association
JOHN P. McTAGUE, Acting Director, Office of Science and Technology Policy, Executive Office of the President
WILLIAM K. NEWMAN, Project Director for Export Controls, National Security and International Affairs Division, General Accounting Office

ROBERT NYSMITH, Associate Administrator for the Office of
  Management, National Aeronautics and Space Administration
ROBERT L. PARK, Director, Office of Public Affairs, American
  Physical Society
MARY PAYROW-OLIA, Instructor of Political Science, U.S. Air Force
  Academy, National Defense University
RICHARD A. POPKIN, Confidential Assistant to the Assistant Secretary
  for Trade Administration, Department of Commerce
DONALD J. QUINN, Executive Secretary, Technology Transfer
  Intelligence Committee, Office of the Director of Central Intelligence,
  Central Intelligence Agency
HAROLD RELYEA, American Association for the Advancement of
  Science
DONALD J. RHEEM II, Special Assistant to the Secretary, Department
  of Health and Human Services
ROBERT R. SHANNON, President, Optical Society of America
JOEL SNOW, Science and Technology Affairs Staff, Office of Energy
  Research, Department of Energy
A. F. SPILHAUS, Jr., Executive Director, American Geophysical Union
JOSEPH J. TAFE, Chief, Export Control Enforcement Unit, Department
  of Justice
DALE R. TAHTINEN, Deputy Assistant Secretary for Trade Control,
  Department of State
GARY WALL, Director, Strategic Investigations Division, U.S.
  Customs Service
DONALD G. WEINERT, Executive Director, National Society of
  Professional Engineers
VAN A. WENTE, Chief, Scientific and Technical Information Branch,
  National Aeronautics and Space Administration
DAVID WILSON, American Association of Universities

H

Bibliography

WEST-EAST TECHNOLOGY TRANSFER

Overview

National Research Council, Board on International Scientific Exchanges, Commission on International Relations. *Review of the U.S./USSR Agreement on Cooperation in the Fields of Science and Technology*. Washington, D.C., May 1977. Evaluates the effectiveness of the Academy-managed exchange agreement with the Soviet Union and makes specific recommendations regarding the terms of and arrangements for its continuation.

Parrott, Bruce, ed. *Trade, Technology and Soviet-American Relations*. Bloomington: Indiana University Press, 1985. Contains essays that deal with trends in West-East trade and technology transfer since the high point of detente in the mid-1970s.

U.S. Congress, Joint Economic Committee. *Issues in East-West Commercial Relations*. Compendium of Papers, 95th Cong., 2d Sess., January 12, 1979.

U.S. Congress, Joint Economic Committee. *East-West Technology Transfer: A Congressional Dialog with the Reagan Administration*. 98th Cong., 2d Sess., December 19, 1984. A response from the Reagan administration to a set of questions from the Joint Economic Committee on a wide range of East-West (i.e., West-East) technology trade issues.

U.S. Congress, Senate, Committee on Banking, Housing, and Urban Affairs, Subcommittee on International Finance and Monetary Policy. *Hearing on East-West Trade and Technology Transfer*. 97th Cong., 2d Sess., April 14, 1982. Includes a written response to questions by Senators Garn, Heinz, and Armstrong.

U.S. Congress, Senate, Committee on Governmental Affairs, Permanent Subcommittee on Investigations. *Hearing on the Transfer of Technology to the Soviet Bloc*. 96th Cong., 2d Sess., February 20, 1980.

U.S. Congress, Senate, Committee on Governmental Affairs, Subcommittee on Investigations. *Hearings on the Transfer of United States High Technology to the Soviet Union and Soviet Bloc Nations*. 97th Cong., 2d Sess., May 4, 5, 6, 11, and 12, 1982. Includes testimony by Fred Asselin, staff investigator of the Permanent Subcommittee on Investigations; testimony by Adm. Bobby R. Inman, deputy director of the Central Intelligence Agency; and numerous relevant exhibits.

Wienert, Helgard, and John Slater. *East-West Technology Transfer: The Trade and Economic Aspects*. Paris: Organization for Economic Cooperation and Development, 1986. This study analyzes the main factors that determine East-West (i.e., West-East) trade in technology and technology-based products and the capacity of the Eastern countries for assimilating Western technology. It also presents the elements required to assess the advantages and disadvantages of West-East trade as a whole to the OECD countries.

Zaleski, Eugene, and Helgard Wienert. *Technology Transfer Between East and West*. Paris: Organization for Economic Cooperation and Development, 1980. Topics include: historical perspectives on West-East trade, statistical analyses, forms of technology transfer, Eastern and Western policies regarding technology transfer, the influence of transfers on Eastern economies, the effect of economic factors on transfers, and the effect of transfers on Western economies.

Aspects of the Soviet Economy and Military

U.S. Congress, Joint Economic Committee. *Selected Papers on the Soviet Economy in the 1980s: Problems and Prospects, Parts 1 and 2*. 97th Cong., 2d Sess., December 31, 1982.

U.S. Congress, Office of Technology Assessment. *Technology and Soviet Energy Availability*. OTA-ISC-153. Washington, D.C.: GPO, 1981. Examines the problems and opportunities that confront the USSR in its five primary energy industries—oil, gas, coal, nuclear, and electric power. It discusses plausible prospects for these industries in the next 10 years; identifies the equipment and technology most important to the USSR in these areas; evaluates the extent to which the United States is the sole or preferred supplier of such items; and analyzes the implications for both the entire Soviet bloc and the Western alliance of either providing or withholding Western equipment and technology.

U.S. Department of Defense. *Soviet Military Power*. Washington, D.C.: GPO, 1986. Comprehensive and detailed assessment of the Soviet bloc's military strength. Includes comparisons of the military strength of NATO versus the Warsaw Pact.

Soviet Acquisition Efforts

Melvern, Linda, Nick Anning, and David Hebditch. *Techno-Bandits*. New York: Houghton-Mifflin, 1984. Explores how the Soviets illicitly are acquiring high-technology products and capabilities from the United States.

Perle, Richard N. "Raiding the Free World's Technology." *Aerospace* (Spring 1982). Contends that the USSR has taken advantage of U.S. loose export controls and—legally or otherwise—acquired vital goods and equipment.

Perle, Richard N. "The Soviet Connection." *Defense 82* (February 1982). Adapted from congressional testimony of November 12, 1981, this article provides a limited (i.e., unclassified) statement of the Defense Department's concerns about Soviet access to U.S. science and technology.

U.S. Central Intelligence Agency. "Soviet Acquisition of Western Technology." April 1982. Describes the Soviet program to acquire U.S. and Western technology, the acquisition mechanisms used, the spectrum of Western technology that has contributed to Soviet military capability, and the problems of restricting the transfer of Western technological information.

U.S. Central Intelligence Agency, Technology Transfer Intelligence Committee. "Soviet Acquisition of Militarily Significant Western Technology: An Update." September 1985. Describes the Soviet program to acquire U.S. and Western technology, provides details on the structure of Soviet acquisition programs, and provides examples of Soviet requirements and successes.

U.S. Congress, Senate, Committee on Governmental Affairs, Permanent Subcommittee on Investigations. *Report on the Transfer of United States High Technology to the Soviet Union and Soviet Bloc Nations*. 97th Cong., 2d Sess., November 15, 1982. Includes examples of how the Soviets obtain American technology and congressional staff recommendations on commerce and national security agencies.

Wolton, Thierry. *Le KGB en France*. Paris: Grasset & Fasquelle, 1986. Describes the Soviet intelligence operation in France including the "Farewell affair," the story of the high-level Soviet employee who passed to the French government hundreds of critical, classified Soviet documents detailing the intensive Soviet technology acquisition effort.

The Soviet Ability to Absorb Western Technology

Agres, Ted. "Concerted Soviet Efforts Siphon Western Technology." *Industrial Research and Development* (June 1982). Examines a report published by the CIA, which warns of a Soviet effort to acquire Western technology of military significance through legal and illegal means.

Borstein, Morris. *East-West Technology Transfer: The Transfer of Western Technology to the USSR*. Paris: Organization for Economic Cooperation and Development, 1985. Investigates the Soviet interest in Western technology and how they acquire it, and assesses the impact of this transfer on the Soviet economy in general and on Soviet foreign trade in particular.

Taubes, Gary, and Glenn Garelik. "Soviet Science: How Good Is It?" *Discover* (August 1986). Examines the efficacy, efficiency, history, and practices of the scientific establishment in the Soviet Union.

Technology Transfer East to West

Kiser, John W. III. *Commercial Technology Transfer from Eastern Europe to the United States and Western Europe*. Report prepared for the U.S. Department of State. Washington, D.C.: Kiser Research, 1980. Considers commercial technology transfer from four East European countries—Czechoslovakia, Hungary, the German Democratic Republic, and Poland—to the United States and selected Western European countries. The report focuses on benefits derived by the United States from such transfers, principally from buying licenses.

Kiser, John W. III. "Tapping Eastern Bloc Technology." *Harvard Business Review* (March-April 1982). Assesses whether the United States should reconsider its view of Soviet bloc nations as technologically backward and investigate new processes and products from these markets.

CONTROLLING TECHNOLOGY TRANSFER

Assessing the Need for National Security Export Controls

Brown, Harold. *Thinking About National Security, Defense and Foreign Policy in a Dangerous World*. Boulder, Colo.: Westview Press, 1983. Examines the needs of U.S. national defense in light of foreign policy objectives and domestic policy constraints.

Carey, William D. "Science and the National Security." *Science* (November 6, 1981). Comments on the perceived concerns of military officials toward technology transfer.

President's Blue Ribbon Commission on Defense Management. *Quest for Excellence: Final Report to the President* (June 1986). Report of the Packard commission analyzing the U.S. Defense Department's management and organizational procedures. Includes recommendations aimed at revitalizing national security planning and budgeting, military organization and command, acquisition organization and procedures, and government-industry accountability.

Schneider, William, Jr. Remarks by the under secretary of state for security assistance, science, and technology before the World Business Council, Washington, D.C., March 22, 1983. The under secretary discusses the national security implications of export policy and states that the Reagan administration's trade policy toward the Soviet Union and the Warsaw Pact "cannot be divorced from our broad political security objectives vis-à-vis these countries. Our economic policies must support our key objectives of deterring Soviet adventurism, redressing the military balance between the West and the Warsaw Pact, and strengthening the Western Alliance."

Skolnikoff, Eugene B. "Technology Transfer to Other Countries: Life-Threatening or Unimportant?" Massachusetts Institute of Technology, April 22, 1982. Examines the overall question of technology transfers to other countries and assesses the costs and benefits of more stringent control measures.

U.S. Congress, Senate, Committee on Banking, Subcommittee on International Finance and Monetary Policy. *Hearing on Export Controls for National Security Purposes*. 97th Cong., 2d Sess., April 14, 1982. Testimony of Lawrence Brady (Commerce), Fred C. Ikle (DoD), Ernest B. Johnston (State), and Edward J. O'Malley (FBI).

Weinberger, Caspar W. "Technology Transfers to the Soviet Union." *The Wall Street Journal* (January 12, 1982). Support for and explanation of administration views on the need for export controls.

What to Control

Barnard, Richard. "Pentagon Mulls New Technology Secrets List." *Defense Week* (October 17, 1983). Reports on a multiagency task force on the control of information and documents relating to "militarily significant technologies." The task force favors the creation of an entirely new category of information to be routinely restricted by the Pentagon.

Brady, Lawrence J. "Taking Back the Rope: Technology Transfer and U.S. Security." Statement before the Association of Former Intelligence Officers, March 29, 1982.

Buchan, David. *Western Security and Economic Strategy Towards the East*. Adelphi Papers no. 192. London: International Institute for Strategic Studies, 1984. Discusses the importance of Western technology to Soviet economic and military power, the array of export controls maintained by CoCom, the consequences of trading with the East, and the case for differentiation between the Soviet Union and the nations in Eastern Europe.

Channon, Stanley L. *Status and Recommendations for Export Control of Composite Materials Technology*. IDA Paper P-1592. 2 vols. Institute for Defense Analysis, Science and Technology Division, September 1981. This report presents the results of a 27-month study of U.S. and foreign technology relating to organic matrix materials and a critical review of the relevant U.S. export control regulations. The advantages and disadvantages of export control and the effects of these controls on industrial innovation, academic research, and international technical communications are discussed. Suggested methods for handling proprietary information, emerging technology, and the involvement of foreign nationals in advanced composite materials technology are presented.

Eagle Research Group, Inc. "Report of the United States Munitions List Study." ERG 81-123F1. Prepared for the Office of Munitions Control, U.S. Department of State, April 14, 1981. This study was conducted to provide an analytical input into the final report to be submitted to Congress on the Militarily Critical Technologies List (MCTL), as required by the International Security and Development Cooperation Act of 1980.

Goodman, S. E. Memorandum on U.S. computer export control policies in relation to value conflicts and policy choice. Reviews U.S. export controls for computer products and know-how and examines the policy choices.

Gustafson, Thane. *Selling the Russians the Rope? Soviet Technology Policy and U.S. Export Controls.* Santa Monica, Calif.: The Rand Corporation, April 1981. Examines the objectives and assumptions of U.S. high-technology export control policy and describes the main developments in Soviet technology policy over the last 10 years, analyzing the reasons for Soviet technology lag and the implications for U.S. policy.

Gustafson, Thane. "U.S. Export Controls and Soviet Technology." *Technology Review* (February-March 1982). Examines whether the critical technologies approach can improve the export control system.

U.S. Department of Defense, Office of the Under Secretary of Defense for Research and Advanced Engineering. "The Militarily Critical Technologies List." October 1984. Catalog of technologies with important military applications.

U.S. Department of Defense, Office of the Director of Defense Research and Engineering. *An Analysis of Export Control of U.S. Technology—A DOD Perspective.* (Report of the Defense Science Board Task Force on Export of U.S. Technology.) Washington, D.C.: GPO, 1976. This is the so-called Bucy report, which examines a number of critical technologies, their impact on U.S. strategic requirements, the mechanisms through which information about them is transferred, and the current effectiveness of export controls and the CoCom agreement. "The principal findings of the Task Force are: design and manufacturing know-how are the key elements for control of strategic technology; this know-how is most effectively transferred when there is intent to do so, and the donor organization takes active steps in that direction; and high velocity, i.e., rapidly changing technologies, are the ones for which export controls are most effective in slowing the flow of technology."

U.S. General Accounting Office. *Export Controls: Need to Clarify Policy and Simplify Administration.* ID-79-16. Washington, D.C.: GPO, 1979. This report examines the decision-making apparatus for determining which technologies or products must be controlled and the effectiveness of the export control system. It also assesses both domestic and multilateral export control policies and includes an analysis of CoCom control procedures.

Control of Unclassified Information

Gould, Stephen D. "Secrecy: Its Role in National Scientific and Technical Information Policy." *Library Trends* (Summer 1986). Reviews federal policy for controlling scientific and technical information—particularly unclassified information—and presents commentary on such controls.

Greenstein, Ruth. "National Security Controls on Scientific Information." (Unpublished paper, 1982.) Analyzes the use of export controls to restrict free exchange of scientific information, particularly information only indirectly related to controlled hardware. Addresses the question of whether an export control system can be designed that meets national security objectives while maintaining a vital scientific base.

Nelkin, Dorothy. *Science as Intellectual Property: Who Controls Scientific Research?* New York: Macmillan Publishing Co., 1984. Discusses issues involving the ownership and control of scientific information.

Olson, Theodore B. Memorandum from the Office of the Assistant Attorney General on the constitutionality of the proposed revision of the technical data provisions of the International Traffic in Arms Regulations directed to William B. Robinson, Office of Munitions Control, U.S. Department of State, July 1, 1981.

Balancing Information Control With Open Communication

Center for Science and Technology Policy, Graduate School of Business Administration, New York University. *Current Issues in Export Controls of Technology* (November 1981). (Background information and summary of discussion.) Considers several issues involving the use of export controls to restrict the flow of technology. Presents the results of faculty discussions as to the most critical questions and impacts on the university/industrial research program.

Corson, Dale. "What Price Security?" *Physics Today* (February 1983). Evaluates the trade-offs among the dangers to national security that arise from technology transfers and the threats to the openness of scientific communication that are caused by too much secrecy.

Gould, Stephen B., ed. "Commentaries: Scientific Freedom and National Security." *Transaction/Social Science and Modern Society* (July-August 1986). Includes presentations made at the 1985 annual meeting of the American Association for the Advancement of Science: Langenberg, Donald N., "Secret Knowledge and Open Inquiry"; Benson, Sumner, "Overcoming Complacency"; Herring, Jan P., "Defining the Basics"; McKelvain, Boyd J., "Determining Military Criticality"; and Wallerstein, Mitchel B., "Nurturing a Dynamic System."

National Academy of Sciences. *Scientific Communication and National Security*. Washington, D.C.: National Academy Press, 1982.

Vol. I partial contents: current knowledge about unwanted technology transfer and its military significance; universities and scientific communication; the current control system; and general conclusions—balancing the costs and benefits of control.

Vol. II appendixes include: Wallerstein, Mitchel B., "The Historical Context of National Security Concerns About Science and Technology"; and Wallerstein, Mitchel B., "The Role of Foreign Nationals Studying or Working in U.S. Universities or Other Sectors."

Working papers of the Panel on Scientific Communication and National Security (available from the National Academy Press, 2101 Constitution Avenue, N.W., Washington, DC 20418): Alexander, Arthur J., "Soviet Science and Weapons Acquisition"; Kiser, John W. III, "East-West Technology Transfer"; Wallerstein, Mitchel B., "The Office of Strategic Information (OSI), U.S. Department of Commerce, 1954-1957"; Wallerstein, Mitchel B., "The Coordinating Committee for National Export Controls (CoCom)," with annex by John P. Hardt and Kate S. Tomlinson.

Relyea, Harold C., ed. *Striking a Balance: National Security and Scientific Freedom*. Washington, D.C.: American Association for the Advancement of Science, 1985. Papers presented during the 1982 AAAS annual meeting: Cheh, Mary M., "Government Control of Private Ideas"; Unger, Stephen H., "National Security and the Free Flow of Technical Information"; Denning, Peter J., "A Scientist's View of Government Control Over Scientific Communication"; Inman, Bobby R., "National Security and Technical Information"; Green, Harold P., "Information Control Under the Atomic Energy Act"; McCloskey, Paul N., Jr., "The Progressive Case and the Need to Amend the Atomic Energy Act"; Schwartz, Daniel C., "Scientific Freedom and National Security: A Case Study of Cryptography"; Relyea, Harold C., "Shrouding the Endless Frontier—Scientific Communication and National Security: The Search for Balance."

U.S. Congress, House of Representatives, Committee on Science and Technology, Subcommittee on Science, Research, and Technology and the Subcommittee on Investigations and Oversight. *Hearing on Scientific Communications and National Security.* 98th Cong., 2d Sess., May 24, 1984. Includes testimony by Dr. Paul E. Gray, president of the Massachusetts Institute of Technology; Dr. Roland Schmitt, senior vice president for corporate research and development, General Electric Company; and Dr. Edith W. Martin, deputy under secretary of defense for research and engineering.

U.S. TRADE ENVIRONMENT

U.S. Trade Performance

Cooper, Richard N. "Growing American Interdependence: An Overview." Paper prepared for a conference at the Federal Reserve Bank of St. Louis, October 1985. Investigates the increasing degree to which the United States is involved in the international economy and explores the consequences of this openness.

Finan, William F., et al. "The U.S. Trade Position in High Technology: 1980-1986." Report prepared for the Joint Economic Committee of the U.S. Congress, October 1986. Explores recent trends in American high-technology trade using data on a group of industries the Commerce Department defines as "high tech" on the basis of their heavy reliance on research and development expenditures. These industries include, among others, computers, scientific instruments, aircraft, and specialty chemicals, all of which maintained a strong international trade position until recent years.

National Research Council, Panel on Advanced Technology Competition and the Industrialized Allies. *International Competition in Advanced Technology: Decisions for America.* Washington, D.C.: National Academy Press, 1983. Describes the nature of technology in the context of international competition and recommends fundamental guidelines for national action. Focuses on relations among the major industrialized nations—Canada, the Federal Republic of Germany, France, Japan, the United Kingdom, and the United States.

Olmer, Lionel H. *U.S. Manufacturing at a Crossroads—Surviving and Prospering in a More Competitive Global Economy.* Washington, D.C.: U.S. Department of Commerce, International Trade Administration, 1985. Assesses the potential for erosion of the U.S. domestic manufacturing base.

U.S. Department of Commerce, International Trade Administration. *An Assessment of U.S. Competitiveness in High-Technology Industries.* February 1983. Describes the role of high technology in the U.S. economy, examines the international competition confronting U.S. industry, and explores policy options for reinvigorating U.S. industry.

U.S. Department of Commerce, International Trade Administration. *1985 U.S. Industrial Outlook: Prospects for Over 350 Manufacturing and Service Industries.* January 1985. Gives a detailed description of the performance of many of the industries that make up the U.S. industrial base.

U.S. Department of Commerce, International Trade Administration, Office of Trade and Investment Analysis. *The Rising Trading Power of the East Asian NICs.* (Prepared by Victoria L. Hatter.) October 1985. Examines the growth of four newly industrializing countries—South Korea, Taiwan, Hong Kong, and Singapore—in their new role as major manufactures traders. The report also discusses their major markets and suppliers and their most important export commodities.

U.S. Department of Commerce, International Trade Administration. *U.S. High Technology Trade and Competitiveness* (February 1985). (Prepared by Victoria L. Hatter.) Explores the performance of the United States and other major suppliers in terms of exports of high-technology manufactured goods from 1965-1982. Provides an overview of U.S. trade and competitiveness in high-technology goods.

U.S. Department of Commerce, International Trade Administration. *United States Trade—Performance in 1984 and Outlook*. Investigates the major causes and implications of U.S. trade performance in the context of an international economic environment.

Balancing National Security and Economic Vitality

Bonker, Don. "Protecting Economic Interests." *Issues in Science and Technology* (Fall 1986). Argues that U.S. export control policy has gone awry and that instead of wasting resources trying to control too many products, many of which have no strategic value, the administration should focus controls on advanced goods that can truly enhance the military capability of U.S. adversaries.

Business-Higher Education Forum. *Export Controls: The Need to Balance National Objectives*. Washington, D.C., 1986. Attempts to establish a framework for analyzing the myriad issues involved in the debate over export controls and for achieving the necessary balance between competing interests. The document sets out general principles that should guide policymaking and specific recommendations for improving the control system.

Freedenberg, Paul. "U.S. Export Controls: Issues for High Technology Industries." *National Journal* (December 18, 1982). "The debate over the renewal of the Export Administration Act is certain to be a major legislative battle. Many of the critical questions of trade and foreign policy, and national security which have proven to be so difficult to solve over the past few years will be highlighted in the Act renewal."

Hart, Gary W. (U.S. Senator, D-Colo.) "High Technology Trade Act of 1982." *Congressional Record* S. 2356 (Senate, April 1, 1982). Description of a proposed bill that offers a different view of how the United States can maintain its technological edge.

Mally, Gerhard. "Technology Transfer Controls." *Atlantic Community Quarterly* (Fall 1982). Examines U.S. export controls on dual use technologies to Warsaw Pact countries and Communist countries of East Asia.

Merrill, Stephen A. "Technological Change and Technological Transfer Policy." Paper prepared for the CSIS Quadrangular Forum Task Forces Meeting in Stowe, Vermont, July 1986. Explores the consensus within the Western Alliance for maintaining national security export controls and examines the changing environment in which the export control system must operate in order to evaluate near- and long-term adjustments to U.S. policy.

Merrill, Stephen A., ed. *Securing Technological Advantage: Balancing Export Controls and Innovation*. Washington, D.C.: Center for Strategic and International Studies, Georgetown University, 1985. Examines the current U.S. export control policy in terms of balancing national security interests with the desire to maintain domestic innovation. Recommends steps to alleviate current conflicts.

Packard, Martin E. "A Businessman's View of the Effect of Export Licensing on Technology Transfer to the USSR." 1981. Examines the many sources of technological information and the effectiveness of various control measures. Considers the costs and benefits of export licensing.

Seeger, Murray. "Tightening Up the High-Tech Trade." *Fortune* (December 28, 1981). "If the Reagan Administration decides to act alone in preventing high-tech know-how from reaching the Soviets, the effort could easily backfire. The best of America's Western competitors might sell Moscow all it is willing to pay for, while U.S. companies would be frozen out of the market."

U.S. Congress, House of Representatives, Committee on Armed Services, Technology Transfer Panel. *Hearings on Technology Transfer*. 98th Cong., 1st Sess., June 9, 21, and 23, and

July 13-14, 1983. Includes statements by Lionel Olmer, under secretary for international trade, Department of Commerce; Richard Perle, assistant secretary for international security policy, Department of Defense; and various representatives of industry.

U.S. Congress, House of Representatives, Committee on Foreign Affairs, Subcommittee on International Economic Policy and Trade. *Overview of U.S. International Competitiveness* (hearings). 97th Cong., 2d Sess., March, June, and August 1982. Includes statements by W. Stephan Piper, coordinator of aerospace trade policy, Office of the U.S. Trade Representative; Richard Kuba, international marketing director of the National Machine Tool Builders' Association; and Victor Ragosine, government affairs consultant, Ampex Corporation, representing the American Electronics Association.

U.S. Congress, House of Representatives, Committee on Science and Technology, Subcommittee on Science, Research, and Technology and Subcommittee on Investigations and Oversight. *Hearing on the Impact of National Security Considerations on Science and Technology.* 97th Cong., 2d Sess., March 29, 1982. Includes testimony by Admiral Bobby Inman, deputy director of the Central Intelligence Agency; Lawrence J. Brady, assistant secretary of commerce, International Trade Administration; and Dr. Frank Press, president of the National Academy of Sciences.

U.S. Congress, Senate, Committee on Small Business. *Hearing on Obstacles to Exporting Faced by Small Businesses.* 98th Cong., 1st Sess., February 11, 1983. Includes statements by John M. Fluke, chairman and chief executive officer, John Fluke Manufacturing Co.; and Max Gellert, president of ELDEC Corporation.

Wallich, Paul. "Technology Transfer at Issue: The Industry Viewpoint." *IEEE Spectrum* (May 1982). Identifies the nature of the commercial technology export problem and the position of the private sector.

THE U.S. EXPORT CONTROL SYSTEM

Overview

Berman, Harold J., and John R. Garson. "United States Export Controls—Past, Present, and Future." *Columbia Law Review* (May 1967). A comprehensive review of the legal aspects of U.S. export controls; also contains general background material.

Ellicott, John L. "Trends in Export Regulation." *Business Lawyer* (February 1983). "The United States exercises controls over exports under a number of statutes with a potentially broad reach. This article outlines the principal relevant statutes, considers national security export controls directed to the Soviet Union and its allies, and examines export controls imposed for foreign policy reasons. The article comments briefly on enforcement and concludes by discussing foreign responses to U.S. controls, particularly their extraterritorial applications."

Relyea, Harold C. *National Security Controls and Scientific Information.* Congressional Issue Brief No. IB82083, updated August 18, 1982. Succinct general policy background paper including bibliography.

Stoehr, Delia E. *Technology Transfer in 1984: U.S. Export Control of Dual Use High Technology.* Washington, D.C.: Naval War College, Center for Advanced Research, June 1984. A status report of the U.S. program for export control of dual use high-technology products. Reviews the perspectives of the government and industry, and of the academic and foreign players involved in the development of U.S. policy.

U.S. Congress, Office of Technology Assessment. *Technology and East-West Trade.* Washington, D.C.: GPO, November 1979. Identifies the economic, political, and military costs and benefits that accrue to the United States in its trade with the Soviet Union, the

Eastern bloc, and the People's Republic of China. Also includes comparative discussion of the trade policies adhered to by the principal Western allies of the United States: West Germany, France, the United Kingdom, and Japan.

U.S. Department of Commerce, International Trade Administration. "Overview of the Export Administration Program." October 1981. Provides a short summary of the legislative history, administrative organization, and enforcement procedures relating to the Export Administration Regulations. Also deals with interagency consultation and cooperation.

U.S. Department of Commerce, Office of Export Administration. *Export Administration Annual Report FY1984.* November 1985. Gives overview of the export control system and describes the activities undertaken by the International Trade Administration during fiscal year 1984.

Legislation

Executive Office of the President. "National Security Information." Executive Order No. 12356. *Federal Register* 47 (April 6, 1982):14877-14880.

U.S. Congress, Office of Technology Assessment. *Technology and East-West Trade: An Update.* Washington, D.C.: GPO, 1983. Summarizes the major provisions of the 1979 Export Administration Act, highlighting those provisions that have led to problems of interpretation or execution; recounts major provisions in U.S. export control policy toward the Soviet Union since 1979; and discusses the impacts and implications of those events—for the domestic economy, for U.S. political relations with the NATO allies and with the Soviet Union, and for U.S. national security. The report concludes with a discussion of the policy alternatives open to Congress in 1983.

U.S. Congress, Senate, Committee on Banking, Housing, and Urban Affairs. *Hearing on the Export Administration Act: Oversight on the Commerce Department's Fulfillment of its Responsibilities under the Export Administration Act.* 98th Cong., 2d Sess., February 3, 1983. Statements by Senators Garn, Proxmire, Heinz, Hawkins, and Mattingly and discussions with Senators Cohen and Nunn.

U.S. Congress, Senate, Committee on Governmental Affairs, Subcommittee on Investigations. *Hearings on the Transfer of Technology.* 98th Cong., 2d Sess., April 1984. Includes testimony by William Root, former chief, U.S. negotiating team to CoCom; Dr. Richard DeLauer, under secretary of defense for research and engineering, Department of Defense; and William T. Archey, acting assistant secretary for trade administration.

U.S. Congress, Senate, Committee on Banking, Housing, and Urban Affairs, Subcommittee on International Finance and Monetary Policy. *Hearing on International Affairs Functions of the Treasury and the Export Administration Act.* 97th Cong., 1st Sess., April 30, 1981. Includes testimony by Frank Conahan, director, International Division, GAO; and Dr. Oles Lomacky, director for technology trade, Office of the Secretary of Defense.

U.S. Congress, Senate, Committee on Banking, Housing, and Urban Affairs, Subcommittee on International Finance and Monetary Policy. *Hearings on Reauthorization of the Export Administration Act.* 98th Cong., 1st Sess., March 2 and 16 and April 14, 1983. Includes testimony by Lionel Olmer, under secretary of commerce for international trade; Richard N. Perle, assistant secretary of defense for international security; and William Schneider, under secretary of state for security assistance.

U.S. Congress, Senate, Committee on Finance, Subcommittee on International Trade. *Hearing on the Export Administration Act of 1983* (first session on S.979). 98th Cong., 1st Sess., August 4, 1983. Includes testimony by Lionel Olmer, under secretary of commerce for international trade; James Mack, public affairs director of the National Machine Tool Builders Association; and various senators.

Effectiveness of Licensing and Enforcement Practices

Conahan, Frank C. (director of the International Division, General Accounting Office). "The Administration of Export Controls under the Export Administration Act." (Statement before the Subcommittee on International Finance and Monetary Policy, Senate Committee on Banking, Housing, and Urban Affairs, April 30, 1981.) *Hearings on International Affairs Functions of the Treasury and the Export Administration Act.* 97th Cong., 1st Sess., 1982. Provides a critical analysis of the administration of export controls, including the constraints imposed by the necessity to seek compromise within CoCom and the inefficiencies of the bureaucratic review process.

Schlechty, David L. "Export Control Policy and Licensing Program of the Reagan Administration: New Focus—New Direction." *Federal Bar News & Journal* (January 1982). This paper presents a report on the administration's emerging West-East trade policy and its progress in implementing the 1979 Export Administration Act. It deals with the efforts over the past 12 months of improving the export control program.

U.S. Congress, Senate, Committee on Governmental Affairs, Permanent Subcommittee on Investigations. *Report on the Transfer of Technology.* 98th Cong., 2d Sess., October 5, 1984. Includes discussion of enforcement of the Export Administration Act and the dispute over organization of the Pentagon in export control processes.

U.S. Department of Defense, Office of the Under Secretary for Policy. "Assessing the Effect of Technology Transfer on U.S./Western Security: A Defense Perspective." February 1985. Presents results from the first in a series of annual assessments designed to estimate the impact on Western security of the international transfer of technology, goods, services, and munitions.

U.S. General Accounting Office. *Export Control Regulation Could Be Reduced Without Affecting National Security.* ID-82-14. Washington, D.C.: GPO, 1982. This report examines the process of review for export applications and considers ways in which the process could be streamlined without damaging U.S. national security. The report also discusses inefficiencies in the licensing review process and government efforts to curtail illegal export activity. "Industry is required to obtain export licenses for many more products than is necessary to protect national security. In fiscal year 1981, almost 65,000 export applications were processed but only 1 of every 17 was carefully examined by the Government. GAO found that: Almost half the export license applications received each year could be eliminated without affecting national security. There is a strong possibility for further reducing license requirements to close U.S. allies."

U.S. General Accounting Office. *Export Licensing: Commerce-Defense Review of Applications to Certain Free World Nations.* NSIAD-86-169. Washington, D.C.: GPO, 1986. This report examines export licensing at the Departments of Commerce and Defense under the terms of a January 1985 presidential directive to determine the nature and extent of differences resulting from the joint review. GAO reviewed how the Defense Department developed its recommendations and how the Commerce Department responded to these recommendations with licensing decisions. GAO found that Commerce approved about 65 percent of the license applications that Defense wanted to deny and denied about 1 percent of the licenses that Defense wanted to approve; Defense generally based its denial recommendations on general categories of concern rather than on specific adverse information related to individual license applications, whereas Commerce made licensing decisions principally based on the latter kind of information. According to GAO, the major issue dividing Commerce and Defense was the appropriateness of issuing export licenses when the foreign purchasers planned to resell the items to customers unknown to U.S. licensing authorities.

U.S. General Accounting Office. *Details of Certain Controversial Export Licensing Deci-*

sions Involving Soviet Bloc Countries. ID-83-46. Washington, D.C.: GPO, 1983. Provides short case studies on the considerations and actions attendant to each of eight controversial export licensing decisions. In seven of the eight cases, the military risk of exporting each product or technology was recognized, deliberated, and often lessened by some means before the export was approved. In one case, military risk was not recognized, and the government licensed the export of a product containing technology critical to antisubmarine warfare.

U.S. Extraterritorial Controls

Dekker, W. "The Technology Gap: Western Countries Growing Apart?" Speech delivered at the Atlantic Institute for International Affairs, Paris, December 5, 1985. Expresses the concerns of the European business community regarding recent trends in the extraterritorial application of U.S. export controls.

U.S. Congress, Senate, Committee on Governmental Affairs, Permanent Subcommittee on Investigations. *Hearing on the Transfer of Technology and the Dresser Industries Export Licensing Actions*. 95th Cong., 2d Sess., October 3, 1978. Includes testimony by J. Fred Bucy, chairman, Special Defense Science Task Board; and Dr. Ruth Davis, deputy under secretary for research and engineering.

INTERNATIONAL CONTROL OF TECHNOLOGY

Aeppel, Timothy. "The Evolutions of Multilateral Export Controls: A Critical Study of the COCOM Regime." *The Fletcher Forum* (Winter 1985). Describes the differing perspectives and national styles of the CoCom members and argues that they have reduced the effectiveness of CoCom. Explores ways to revitalize the effort.

Bertsch, Gary K. *East-West Strategic Trade, COCOM and the Atlantic Alliance*. Atlantic Papers no. 49. Paris: Atlantic Institute for International Affairs, 1983. The author notes that "the progression from control on strategic exports to the East, on which there was, and is, a substantial consensus within the [Atlantic] alliance, to controls as sanctions or penalties for Soviet political behavior, catalyzed debate within the Western Alliance on the many tough questions about East-West trade, technology transfer and export controls." This work traces the history of Western technology sales to the East and export controls, and it examines Western efforts to control the sales of strategic technology.

Bertsch, Gary K., et al. *East-West Technology Transfer and Export Controls*. Osteuropa-Wirtschaft, June 1981. "This paper examines (1) the nature (mechanisms, level, and impact) of West to East technology transfers, (2) the performance (responsiveness and effectiveness) of the multilateral coordinating committee (COCOM) in restricting the eastward flow of technology, and (3) competing Western rationales for restricting technology transfers." The paper concludes that while COCOM's survival in the short term may rest on its ability to deal with the exigencies of the moment, its long-term effectiveness depends on agreement on a coherent, realistic export control rationale. In the absence of such agreement, any new system is likely to display many of the shortcomings of the one it replaces.

Frost, Ellen L., and Angela E. Stent. "NATO's Troubles with East-West Trade." *International Security* 8 (Summer 1983):179-200. Argues that the NATO "alliance should thus move toward a two-track East-West trade policy, combining long-term predictability with short-term flexibility, so that the West can agree on continuity in the major security-related aspects of trade while reserving some instruments of commerce to respond to short-term political developments."

Relyea, Harold C. "Business, Trade Secrets, and Information Access Policy Developments in Other Countries: An Overview." *Administrative Law Review* (Spring 1982). Presents capsule descriptions of existing or emerging policy concerning the right of access to official information or records held by governments in Western Europe, Australia, New Zealand, Canada, and Scandinavia. Special consideration is given to the implications for business, commercial records, and trade data. A final section explores the issue of transborder data flows.

Sternheimer, Stephen. *East-West Technology Transfer: Japan and the Communist Bloc.* Beverly Hills: Sage Publications, 1980. Analyzes Japan's policy of exporting advanced technology to the Communist bloc in light of the U.S. determination to restrict the flow of such technology for strategic reasons.

Yergin, Angela Stent. *East-West Technology Transfer: European Perspectives.* Beverly Hills: Sage Publications, 1980. Assesses British, French, and West German policies to limit technology transfer to Communist countries, particularly in light of CoCom and U.S. policies.

Index

171-172
thrust of U.S. decision making, 5, 26-27,
173-177
see also U.S. export control policy

R

Reexport controls
countries affected by, 92
on defense articles and service, 80
de minimus requirements for, 189, 210
effectiveness, 158, 252
enforcement by CoCom countries, 108,
123, 139-141
initiation of, 73
lost sales due to, 11, 158, 271
opposition to, 9, 12, 16, 18, 99, 125,
144-147, 149, 154, 158, 186, 187, 192,
194, 195, 199, 210-211, 245
of other Western nations, 99
products affected by, 92
purpose of, 139, 145
recommendation on elimination of, 14,
25, 171
requirements for foreign compliance
with, 94-95
tolerance of, 196, 197, 199-200, 212
Reexports
CoCom country applications for, 244-246
diversion of technology through, 41, 45
U.S. licenses, 83, 92, 105, 107, 112, 117,
196, 243-246
volume of U.S. trade approved for, 117
Reverse engineering, efficacy of, 5, 47

S

Scientific measuring equipment, *see*
Analytic equipment
Secrecy orders, as national security export
controls, 91-92, 127-128, 162
Semiconductors
Malaysian exports of, 205, 218
technological lead in, 63
U.S. exports to Soviet Union, 75
Siberian pipeline embargo, 96, 102 *n.* 19,
137, 144, 187, 193, 195
Singapore
bilateral agreement between U.S. and,
212-213
diversions of technology through, 208,
209
export control by, 209, 217-218
technological capabilities, 204

views on U.S. export control system,
220
Smuggling, *see* Diversion
South Korea
diversion of technology by, 207-208
export control by, 100, 101, 212, 216
technological capabilities, 66, 203-204,
205
technology transfer between Japan and,
204
trade with PRC, 206
views on U.S. export control system,
211-212, 216, 219
Soviet military development
civilian scientists involved in, 50
contributions of Western technology to,
45-49
U.S. development compared with, 48
Soviet technology acquisition
administrative structure for, 42
channels, 4, 41-45
cost savings from, 46, 110
expenditures, 9, 106
funding and human resources for, 50
intelligence evidence on, 4-5, 40-42, 46
proportion of items subject to national
security controls, 42
recommended use of intelligence on, 177
reports of, 46; *see also* Farewell
documents
success of, 4, 9, 16-17, 154-155
through non-CoCom Free World
countries, 45, 52
U.S. concerns about, 52
see also Diversion; Espionage
Soviet Union
Pacific rim countries' perceptions about,
205-206
relaxation of U.S. controls on exports
to, 75
state of science and technology in, 49-51
and U.S. technological development
compared, 5-6, 47-49
U.S. trade loss with, 122-123
Space, technological leadership in, 64
Strategic Defense Initiative, information
sharing and coproduction, 146, 185,
198
Sweden
export control policies, 199-200
handling of goods in transit, 190, 199
views on U.S. export control system,
199-200, 202
Switzerland, compliance with reexport
requirements, 107